Neural Networks in Business Forecasting

G. Peter Zhang
Georgia State University, USA

D1701172

IRM Press
Publisher of innovative scholarly and professional
information technology titles in the cyberage

Hershey • London • Melbourne • Singapore

Acquisitions Editor:	Mehdi Khosrow-Pour
Senior Managing Editor:	Jan Travers
Managing Editor:	Amanda Appicello
Development Editor:	Michele Rossi
Copy Editor:	Bernard J. Kieklak, Jr.
Typesetter:	Jennifer Wetzel
Cover Design:	Michelle Waters
Printed at:	Integrated Book Technology

Published in the United States of America by
   IRM Press (an imprint of Idea Group Inc.)
   701 E. Chocolate Avenue, Suite 200
   Hershey PA 17033-1240
   Tel: 717-533-8845
   Fax: 717-533-8661
   E-mail: cust@idea-group.com
   Web site: http://www.irm-press.com

and in the United Kingdom by
   IRM Press (an imprint of Idea Group Inc.)
   3 Henrietta Street
   Covent Garden
   London WC2E 8LU
   Tel: 44 20 7240 0856
   Fax: 44 20 7379 3313
   Web site: http://www.eurospan.co.uk

Library of Congress Cataloging-in-Publication Data

Neural networks in business forecasting / G. Peter Zhang, editor.
     p. cm.
Includes bibliographical references and index.
   ISBN 1-59140-215-8 (s/c)
   1. Business forecasting--Mathematical models. 2. Neural networks
(Computer science)--Industrial applications. I. Zhang, G. Peter,
1963-   .
   HD30.27.N484 2004
   658.4'0355'0285632--dc22
                                                        2003017697

British Cataloguing in Publication Data
A Cataloguing in Publication record for this book is available from the British Library.

All work contributed to this book is new, previously-unpublished material. The views expressed in this book are those of the authors, but not necessarily of the publisher.

Neural Networks in Business Forecasting

Table of Contents

Preface

Forecasting forms the foundation for strategic, tactical, as well as operational decisions in many business organizations. Its role in successful planning in finance, marketing, production, personnel, and other functional areas is well established. Increasingly, businesses have recognized the importance of accurate forecasting in effective operations and enhanced competitiveness.

Artificial neural networks (ANNs) are a relatively recent and promising method for business forecasting. The success of ANN applications can be attributed to their unique features and powerful pattern recognition capability. Unlike most traditional model-based forecasting techniques, ANNs are data-driven, self-adaptive, and nonlinear methods that do not require specific assumptions on the underlying data generating process. These features are particularly appealing for practical forecasting situations where data are abundant or easily available, yet the theoretical model or the underlying relationship is not known. In addition, ANNs have universal functional approximation ability and are capable of capturing any type of complex relationship. Since the number of possible nonlinear relationships in business data is typically large, ANNs have the advantage in approximating them well.

ANNs have been successfully applied to a wide range of forecasting problems in almost all areas of business, industry, and science. For example, in financial applications, ANNs have been used for predicting bankruptcy or business failure, exchange rate, interest rate, futures price, stock return, trading volume, capital market index, initial public offering price, property value, and many others. In marketing, we have seen applications in forecasting long distance telephone usage, future orders, market share, market response, product and retail sales, and airline passenger volumes. Numerous forecasting applications in other areas such as accounting, management information system, and operations have also been reported in the literature.

This book aims to provide for researchers and practitioners with recent developments in business forecasting with neural networks. Three types of research papers are included in the book: (1) review articles that provide summaries and guidelines for neural network applications, (2) case studies that demonstrate successful applications, and (3) studies that address practical issues for improving ANN model building and implementation.

Chapter 1 by Zhang provides an overview of forecasting using artificial neural networks. It gives a brief introduction to the neural networks and discusses the advantages of using ANNs for forecasting. This chapter identifies a wide range of forecasting application areas from the literature and summarizes the general issues and implementation guidelines in neural network forecasting.

Chapter 2 by Parsons and Dixit reviews the literature of neural network applications for market response prediction and marketing effort planning. Several traditional market response models such as sales response models, market share models, and brand choice models are examined, followed by discussions of neural network applications in these settings.

Chapter 3 by Thawornwong and Enke provides a survey of the literature on neural network forecasting for stock returns. The authors examine various methodological issues of ANNs in stock return forecasting applications.

In Chapter 4, Walczak addresses the issue of how to best forecast emerging market indexes. Various neural network models utilizing different levels of global information are constructed to forecast the Singapore, Malaysian, and Mexican stock market indexes. This chapter demonstrates that, especially for emerging markets, inclusion of heterogeneous or global market information can improve neural network forecasting performance over similar homogeneous models that do not consider information from other markets.

Chapter 5 by West and Dellana demonstrates a successful application of time delayed neural networks in forecasting the level of biochemical oxygen demand (BOD), an important wastewater quality index. The proposed neural networks are tested against several benchmark linear models such as naïve, exponential smoothing, and ARIMA with intervention.

Chapter 6 by Law and Pine presents a case study of Hong Kong tourism demand forecasting. Income, relative price, population, exchange rate, hotel rate, and marketing expenses are chosen to be input variables to predict tourist arrivals to Hong Kong from five countries/regions.

In Chapter 7, Kiang, Fisher, Hu, and Chi describe the use of a self-organizing map (SOM) network to predict market segment membership in a telecommunication company. The model building procedure of the proposed extended SOM network is detailed and applied to a residential market data set from AT&T.

Chapter 8 by Lee, Booth, and Alam presents a comparative study between feedforward and SOM networks in bankruptcy prediction. In addition, the performance of these two types of neural networks is compared with that of logistic regression and discriminant analysis.

In Chapter 9, Hu, Shanker, and Hung present a detailed case study of consumer choice prediction. The focus is on how to design and develop neural networks that are parsimonious, yet able to provide accurate forecasts. A feature selection method is proposed and applied to predict consumer choice of various telecommunication modes.

Chapter 10 by Li, Pang, Yu, and Troutt reports on an application of recurrent neural networks (RNNs) to model and forecast short-term exchange rate movements. Time series of daily observations on four exchange rates are collected and used in the study. Forecasting results of RNNs are compared with those of moving average and exponential smoothing models.

Chapter 11 by Zhang demonstrates that by combining both linear and nonlinear models, time series forecasting accuracy can be significantly improved. The motivations of and the literature on forecasting combining are discussed. The proposed combining approach is used to forecast three monthly US industrial production data sets.

In Chapter 12, Kline investigates the issue of multi-step forecasting. The study focuses on two methods: the joint method that uses one single network with multiple output nodes to directly forecast all future points in a forecast horizon and the independent method that uses a dedicated network to forecast each future point in the horizon. Experimenting with 149 quarterly time series, the author concludes that the independent method is better used for a short forecasting horizon and the joint method is better for a relatively longer time horizon.

Chapter 13 by Morantz, Whalen, and Zhang proposes a weighted window approach for time series forecasting. With this approach, very old data including forecast errors will receive much less weights than very recent observations. The effectiveness of the proposed method is tested with seven economic time series.

Finally, in Chapter 14, Nargundkar and Priestley examine and compare several model building and evaluation methods for consumer risk prediction in the credit industry. Using a large data set on applicants for car loans in the US, they find that each modeling technique has its own merits and the best method to use often depends on the evaluation method and the cost of misclassification errors.

ACKNOWLEDGMENTS

Editing a refereed research book is a challenging job. This book would not have been possible without the effort and support of authors, reviewers, and the staff at Idea Group Publishing (IGP). Many book chapters underwent several rounds of review and revision. I would like to thank all authors for their contributions to the field of business forecasting with artificial neural networks and in particular to this book.

I am grateful to all reviewers involved in the review process. Many authors of chapters included in this book also served as referees of other chapters. I would acknowledge the work of the following reviewers: Victor Berardi, Kent State University; David Booth, Kent State University; David Enke, University of Missouri at Rolla; John Grznar, University of Illinois at Springfield; Craig Hill, Georgia State University; Michael Hu, Kent State University; Doug Kline, University of North Carolina at Wilmington; Rob Law, Hong Kong Polytechnic University; Kidong Lee, University of Incheon; Dat-Dao Nguyen, California State University at Northridge; Min Qi, Kent State University; Charlene Riggle, University of South Florida; Ram Sriram, Georgia State University; Marvin Troutt, Kent State University; Steven Walczak, University of Colorado at Denver; David West, East Carolina University; JingTao Yao, University of Regina.

The staff at IGP provided wonderful resources and assistance. Special thanks go to Mehdi Khosrow-Pour for inviting me to produce this book and Jan Travers for providing helpful information and answering questions to keep the book on schedule.

Finally, I would like to thank my department chair at Georgia State University, Dr. Richard Deane, for his encouragement and support throughout this project.

G. Peter Zhang
Georgia State University, USA
April 2003

Chapter I

Business Forecasting with Artificial Neural Networks: An Overview

G. Peter Zhang, Georgia State University, USA

ABSTRACT

Artificial neural networks have emerged as an important quantitative modeling tool for business forecasting. This chapter provides an overview of forecasting with neural networks. We provide a brief description of neural networks, their advantages over traditional forecasting models, and their applications for business forecasting. In addition, we address several important modeling issues for forecasting applications.

INTRODUCTION

The recent upsurge in research activities into artificial neural networks (ANNs) has proven that neural networks have powerful pattern classification and prediction capabilities. ANNs have been successfully used for a variety of tasks in many fields of business, industry, and science (Widrow et al., 1994). They have fast become a standard class of quantitative modeling tools for researchers and practitioners. Interest in neural networks is evident from the growth in the number of papers published in journals of diverse scientific disciplines. A search of several major databases can easily result in hundreds or even thousands of "neural networks" articles published in one year.

One of the major application areas of ANNs is forecasting. There is an increasing interest in forecasting using ANNs in recent years. Forecasting has a long history and the importance of this old subject is reflected by the diversity of its applications in different disciplines ranging from business to engineering. The ability to accurately predict the future is fundamental to many decision processes in planning, scheduling, purchasing, strategy formulation, policy making, and supply chain operations. As such, forecasting is an area where a lot of efforts have been invested in the past. Yet, it is still an important and active field of human activity at the present time and will continue to be in the future. A survey of research needs for forecasting has been provided by Armstrong (1988).

Forecasting has been dominated by linear methods for many decades. Linear methods are easy to develop and implement and they are also relatively simple to understand and interpret. However, linear models have serious limitation in that they are not able to capture any nonlinear relationships in the data. The approximation of linear models to complicated nonlinear relationships is not always satisfactory. In the early 1980s, Makridakis (1982) organized a large-scale forecasting competition (often called M-competition) where a majority of commonly used linear methods were tested with more than 1,000 real time series. The mixed results show that no single linear model is globally the best, which may be interpreted as the failure of linear modeling in accounting for a varying degree of nonlinearity that is common in real world problems.

ANNs provide a promising alternative tool for forecasters. The inherently nonlinear structure of neural networks is particularly useful for capturing the complex underlying relationship in many real world problems. Neural networks are perhaps more versatile methods for forecasting applications in that not only can they find nonlinear structures in a problem, they can also model linear processes. For example, the capability of neural networks in modeling linear time series has been studied and confirmed by a number of researchers (Hwang, 2001; Medeiros et al., 2001; Zhang, 2001).

In addition to the nonlinear modeling capability, ANNs also have several other features that make them valuable for forecasting tasks. First, ANNs are data-driven nonparametric methods that do not require many restrictive assumptions on the underlying process from which data are generated. As such, they are less susceptible to the model misspecification problem than parametric methods. This "learning from data or experience" feature of ANNs is highly desirable in various forecasting situations where data are usually easy to collect, but the underlying data-generating mechanism is not known or pre-specifiable. Second, neural networks have been mathematically shown to have the universal functional approximating capability in that they can accurately approximate many types of complex functional relationships. This is an important and powerful characteristic, as any forecasting model aims to accurately capture the functional relationship between the variable to be predicted and other relevant factors or variables. The combination of the above-mentioned characteristics makes ANNs a very general and flexible modeling tool for forecasting.

Research efforts on neural networks as forecasting models are considerable and applications of ANNs for forecasting have been reported in a large number of studies. Although some theoretical and empirical issues remain unsolved, the field of neural network forecasting has surely made significant progress during the last decade. It will not be surprising to see even greater advancement and success in the next decade.

ARTIFICIAL NEURAL NETWORKS

Artificial neural networks (ANNs) are computing models for information processing and pattern identification. They grow out of research interest in modeling biological neural systems, especially human brains. An ANN is a network of many simple computing units called neurons or cells, which are highly interconnected and organized in layers. Each neuron performs the simple task of information processing by converting received inputs into processed outputs. Through the linking arcs among these neurons, knowledge can be generated and stored regarding the strength of the relationship between different nodes. Although the ANN models used in all applications are much simpler than actual neural systems, they are able to perform a variety of tasks and achieve remarkable results.

Over the last several decades, many types of ANN models have been developed, each aimed at solving different problems. But by far the most widely and successfully used for forecasting has been the feedforward type neural network. Figure 1 shows the architecture of a three-layer feedforward neural network that consists of neurons (circles) organized in three layers: input layer, hidden layer, and output layer. The neurons in the input nodes correspond to

Figure 1: A Typical Feedforward Neural Network

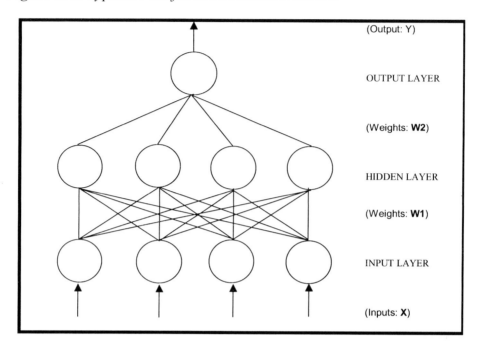

the independent or predictor variables (**x**) that are believed to be useful for forecasting the dependent variable (y) which corresponds to the output neuron. Neurons in the hidden layer are connected to both input and output neurons and are key to learning the pattern in the data and mapping the relationship from input variables to the output variable. With nonlinear transfer functions, hidden neurons can process complex information received from input neurons and then send processed information to the output layer for further processing to generate forecasts. In feedforward ANNs, the information flow is one directional from the input layer to the hidden layer then to the output layer without any feedback from the output layer.

In developing a feedforward neural network model for forecasting tasks, specifying its architecture in terms of the number of input, hidden, and output neurons is an important task. Most ANN applications use only one output neuron for both one-step-ahead and multi-step-ahead forecasting. However, as argued by Zhang et al. (1998), it may be beneficial to employ multiple output neurons for direct multi-step-ahead forecasting. The input neurons or variables are very important in any modeling endeavor and especially important for ANN modeling because the success of an ANN depends to a large extent on the patterns represented by the input variables. What and how many variables to use should be considered carefully. For a causal forecasting problem, we need to specify a set of appropriate predictor variables and use them as the input variables. On the other hand, for a time series forecasting problem, we need to identify a number of past lagged observations as the inputs. In either situation, knowledge of the forecasting problem as well as some experimentation based on neural networks may be necessary to determine the best number of input neurons. Finally, the number of hidden nodes is usually unknown before building an ANN model and must be chosen during the model-building process. This parameter is useful for approximating the nonlinear relationship between input and output variables.

Before a neural network can be used for forecasting, it must be trained. Neural network training refers to the estimation of connection weights. Although the estimation process is very similar to that in linear regression where we minimize the sum of squared errors (SSE), the ANN training process is more difficult and complicated due to the nature of nonlinear optimization involved. There are many training algorithms developed in the literature and the most influential one is the backpropagation algorithm by Werbos (1974) and Rumelhart et al. (1986). The basic idea of backpropagation training is to use a gradient-descent approach to adjust and determine weights such that an overall error function such as SSE can be minimized.

In addition to the most popular feedforward ANNs, many other types of neural networks can also be used for forecasting purposes. In particular, recurrent neural networks (Connor et al., 1994; Kuan et al., 1995; Kermanshahi, 1998; Vermaak & Botha, 1998; Parlos et al., 2000; Mandic & Chambers, 2001; Husken & Stagge, 2003) that explicitly account for the dynamic nonlinear pattern can be a good alternative to feedforward type ANNs for certain time series forecasting problems. In a recurrent ANN, there are cycles or feedback connections among neurons. Outputs from a recurrent network can be directly fed back to inputs, generating dynamic feedbacks on errors of past patterns. In this sense, recurrent ANNs can model richer dynamics than feedforward ANNs in the same way that linear autoregressive and moving average (ARMA) models have certain advantages over autoregressive (AR) models. However, much less attention has been paid to the research and applications of recurrent ANNs and the superiority of recurrent ANNs over feedforward ANNs has not been established. The practical difficulty of using recurrent neural networks may lie in the facts that (1) recurrent networks can assume many different architectures and it may be difficult to specify appropriate model structures to experiment with and (2) it is more difficult to train recurrent ANNs due to the unstable nature of training algorithms.

For an in-depth coverage of many aspects of ANNs, readers are referred to a number of excellent books including Smith (1993), Bishop (1995), and Ripley (1996). For ANNs for forecasting research and applications, readers may consult Azoff (1994), Weigend and Gershenfeld (1994), Gately (1996), Zhang et al. (1998), and Remus and O'Connor (2001).

FORECASTING APPLICATIONS OF NEURAL NETWORKS

The use of ANNs for forecasting has received great attention from many different fields. Given the fact that forecasting problems arise in so many different disciplines and the literature on forecasting with ANNs is scattered in so many diverse fields, it is difficult to cover all neural network forecasting applications. Table 1 provides a sample of recent business forecasting applications with ANNs reported in the literature from 1995 to 2003. For other forecasting applications of ANNs, readers are referred to several survey articles such as Dougherty (1995) for transportation modeling and forecasting, Wong and Selvi (1998) and Fadlalla and Lin (2001) for financial applications, Zhang et al. (1998) for general forecasting areas, Krycha and Wagner (1999) for management science applications, Vellido et al. (1999) and Wong et al. (2000) for business applications, Maier and Dandy (2000) for water resource forecasting, and Hippert et al. (2001) for short-term load forecasting.

As can be seen from Table 1, a wide range of business forecasting problems have been solved by neural networks. Some of these application areas include accounting (forecasting accounting earnings, earnings surprises; predicting bankruptcy and business failure), finance (forecasting stock market movement, indices, return, and risk; exchange rate; futures trading; commodity and option price; mutual fund assets and performance), marketing (forecasting consumer choice, market share, marketing category, and marketing trends), economics (forecasting business cycles, recessions, consumer expenditures, GDP growth, inflation, total industrial production, and US Treasury bond), production and operations (forecasting electricity demand, motorway traffic, inventory, new product development project success, IT project escalation, product demand or sales, and retail sales), international business (predicting joint venture performance, foreign exchange rate), real estate (forecasting residential construction demand, housing value), tourism and transportation (forecasting tourist, motorway traffic, and international airline passenger volume), and environmental related business (forecasting ozone level and concentration, air quality).

Table 1: A Sample of ANN Forecasting Application Areas

Problems	Studies
Accounting earnings, earnings surprises	Callen et al. (1996), Dhar and Chou (2001)
Business cycles and recessions	Qi (2001)
Business failure, bankruptcy, or financial health	Yang (1999), Zhang et al. (1999), Mckee and Greenstein (2000), Anandarajan et al. (2001), Atiya (2001)
Consumer expenditures	Church and Curram (1996)
Commodity price, option price	Kohzadi et al. (1996), Yao et al. (2000)
Consumer choice, marketing category, market development, market segments, market share, marketing trends	Agrawal and Schorling (1996), West et al. (1997), Aiken and Bsat (1999), Wang (1999), Jiang et al. (2000), Vellido et al. (1999)
Electricity demand	Elkateb et al. (1998), Darbellay and Slama (2000), Hippert et al. (2001)
Exchange rate	Zhang and Hu (1998), Leung et al. (2000a), Nag and Mitra (2002)
Futures trading	Kaastra and Boyd (1995), Ntungo and Boyd (1998)
GDP growth, inflation, industrial production	Tkacz (2001), Chen et al. (2001a), Tseng et al. (2001)
International airline passenger volume, tourist demand, travel demand	Nam and Schaefer (1995), de Carvalho et al. (1998), Law (2000)
Inventory control	Bansal and Vadhavkar (1998), Partovi and Anandarajan (2002)
Joint venture performance	Hu et al. (1999)
Mutual fund net asset, mutual fund performance	Chiang et al. (1996), Indro et al. (1999)
Ozone concentration and level, environmental prediction, air quality	Prybutok et al. (2000), Ruiz_Surez et al. (1995), Murtagh et al. (2000), Kolehmainen et al. (2001)
Product demand, product sales, retail sales	Ansuj et al. (1996), Luxhoj et al. (1996), Charytoniuk et al. (2000), Alon et al. (2001), Kuo (2001), Zhang and Qi (2002)
Project escalation, project success	Thieme et al. (2000), Zhang et al. (2003)
Residential construction demand, housing value	Hua (1996), Goh (1998), Nguyen and Cripps (2001)
Stock return, stock indices, stock trend, stock risk	Wang and Leu (1996), Wittkemper and Steiner (1996), Desai and Bharati (1998), Saad et al. (1998), Qi (1999), Leung et al. (2000b), Chen et al. (2003)
Traffic	Doughetry and Cobbett (1997), Kirby et al. (1997), Chen et al. (2001b), Dia (2001), Qiao et al. (2001)
US treasure bond	Cheng et al. (1996)

Some of the applications, such as bankruptcy prediction, are generally considered as classification, not forecasting problems. However, in many situations, not only do we want to predict the class membership, but more importantly we also need to know the likelihood or probability that a firm is going bankrupt. In this sense, we can treat this type of problem as a forecasting problem: forecasting the probability of failure in the future.

ISSUES IN ANN MODELING AND FORECASTING

Developing an ANN model for a particular forecasting application is not a trivial task. Although many good software packages exist to ease users' effort in building an ANN model, it is still critical for forecasters to understand many important issues surrounding the model building process. It is important to point out that building a successful neural network is a combination of art and science and software alone is not sufficient to solve all problems in the process. It is a pitfall to blindly throw data into a software package and then hope it will automatically give a satisfactory solution.

An important point in effectively using ANN forecasting is the understanding of the issue of learning and generalization inherent in all ANN forecasting applications. This issue of learning and generalization can be understood with the concepts of model bias and variance (Geman et al., 1992). Bias and variance are important statistical properties associated with any empirical model. Model bias measures the systematic error of a forecasting model in *learning* the underlying relations among variables or time series observations. Model variance, on the other hand, relates to the stability of models built on different data samples from the same process and therefore offers insights on *generalizability* of the prediction model.

A pre-specified or parametric model, which is less dependent on the data, may misrepresent the true functional relationship and, hence, cause a large bias. On the other hand, a flexible, data-driven model may be too dependent on the specific data set and, hence, have a large variance. Bias and variance are two conflicting terms that impact a model's usefulness. Although it is desirable to have both low bias and low variance, we may not be able to reduce both terms at the same time for a given data set because these goals are conflicting. A model that is less dependent on the data tends to have low variance but high bias if the pre-specified model is incorrect. On the other hand, a model that fits the data well tends to have low bias but high variance when applied to different data sets. Hence, a good predictive model should have an "appropriate" balance between model bias and model variance.

As a model-free approach to data analysis, neural networks tend to fit the training data well and thus have low bias. But the price to pay is the potential overfitting effect that causes high variance. Therefore, attention should be paid to address issues of overfitting and the balance of bias and variance in neural network model building.

The major decisions a neural network forecaster must make include data preparation, input variable selection, choice of network type and architecture, transfer function, and training algorithm, as well as model validation, evaluation and selection. Some of these can be solved during the model building process while others must be considered before actual modeling starts.

Neural networks are data-driven techniques. Therefore, data preparation is a critical step in building a successful neural network model. Without a good, adequate, and representative data set, it is impossible to develop a useful, predictive ANN model. Thus, the reliability of ANN models depends to a large extent on the quality of data.

There are several practical issues around the data requirement for an ANN model. The first is the size of the sample used to build a neural network. While there is no specific rule that can be followed for all situations, the advantage of having large samples should be clear because not only do neural networks have typically a large number of parameters to estimate, but also it is often necessary to split data into several portions to avoid overfitting, select model, and perform model evaluation and comparison. A larger sample provides a better chance for neural networks to adequately approximate the underlying data structure. Although large samples do not always give superior performance over small samples, forecasters should strive to get as large of a sample as they can. In time series forecasting problems, Box and Jenkins (1976) have suggested that at least 50 or, even better, 100 observations are necessary to build linear ARIMA models. Therefore, for nonlinear modeling, larger sample size should be more desirable. In fact, using the longest time series available for developing forecasting models is a time-tested principle in forecasting (Armstrong, 2001). Of course, if data in the sample are not homogeneous or the underlying data generating process in a time series changes over time, then a larger sample may even hurt performance of static neural networks as well as other traditional methods.

The second issue is data splitting. Typically for neural network applications, all available data are divided into an in-sample and an out-of-sample. The in-sample data are used for model fitting and selection, while the out-of-sample is used to evaluate the predictive ability of the model. The in-sample data sometimes are further split into a training sample and a validation sample. Because of the bias and variance issue, it is critical to test an ANN model with an independent out-of-sample which is not used in the neural network training and model selection phase. This division of data means that the true size of sample used in model building is smaller than the initial sample size. Although there is no consensus on how to split the data, the general practice is to allocate more data for model building and selection. That is, most studies in the literature use convenient ratio of splitting for in- and out-of- samples such as 70%:30%, 80%:20%, or 90%:10%. It is important to note that in data splitting, the issue is not about what proportion of data should be allocated in each sample. But, rather, it is about sufficient data points in each sample to ensure adequate learning, validation, and testing. Granger (1993) suggests that for nonlinear modeling at least 20% of the data should be held back for an out-of-sample evaluation. Hoptroff (1993) recommends that at least 10 data points should be in the test sample while Ashley (2003) suggests that a much larger out-of-sample size is necessary in order to achieve statistically significant improvement for forecasting problems.

Data preprocessing is another issue that is often recommended to highlight important relationships or to create more uniform data to facilitate ANN learning, meet algorithm requirements, and avoid computation problems. Azoff (1994) summarizes four methods typically used for input data normalization. They are: along channel normalization, across channel normalization, mixed channel normalization, and external normalization. However, the necessity and effect of data normalization on network learning and forecasting are still not universally agreed upon. For example, in modeling and forecasting seasonal time series, some researchers (Gorr, 1994) believe that data preprocessing is not necessary because the ANN is a universal approximator and is able to capture all of the underlying patterns well. Recent empirical studies (Nelson et al., 1999), however, find that pre-deseasonalization of the data is critical in improving forecasting performance. Zhang and Qi (2002) further demonstrate that for time series containing both trend and seasonal variations, preprocessing the data by both detrending and deseasonalization should be the most appropriate way to build neural networks for best forecasting performance.

Neural network design and architecture selection are important yet difficult tasks. Not only are there many ways to build an ANN model and a large number of choices to be made during the model building and selection process, but also numerous parameters and issues have to be estimated and experimented with before a satisfactory model may emerge. Adding to the difficulty is the lack of standards in the process. Numerous rules of thumb are available, but not all of them can be applied blindly to a new situation. In building an appropriate model for the forecasting task at hand, some experiments are usually necessary. Therefore, a good experiment design is needed. For discussions of many aspects of modeling issues, readers may consult Kaastra et al. (1996), Zhang et al. (1998), Coakley and Brown (1999), and Remus and O'Connor (2001).

As stated earlier, many types of ANN have been used for forecasting. However, the multilayer feedforward architecture is by far the best developed and most widely applied one for forecasting applications. Therefore, our discussion will be focused on this type of neural network, although it may be applied to other types of ANN.

A feedforward ANN is characterized by its architecture and determined by the number of layers, the number of nodes in each layer, the transfer or activation function used in each layer, as well as how the nodes in each layer are connected to nodes in adjacent layers. Although partial connections between nodes in adjacent layers and direct connections from input layer to output layer are possible, the most commonly used ANN is the so-called "fully connected" network in that each node at one layer is fully connected only to all of the nodes in the adjacent layers.

The size of the output layer is usually determined by the nature of the problem. For example, in most forecasting problems, one output node is naturally used for one-step-ahead forecasting, although one output node can also be employed for multi-step-ahead forecasting, in which case iterative forecasting mode must be used. That is, forecasts for more than two steps ahead in the time horizon must be based on earlier forecasts.

This may not be effective for multi-step forecasting as pointed out by Zhang et al. (1998), which is in line with Chatfield (2001) who discusses the potential benefits of using different forecasting models for different lead times. Therefore, for multi-step forecasting, one may either use multiple output nodes or develop multiple neural networks each for one particular step forecasting.

The number of input nodes is perhaps the most important parameter for designing an effective neural network forecaster. For causal forecasting problems, it corresponds to the number of independent or predictor variables that forecasters believe are important in predicting the dependent variable. For univariate time series forecasting problems, it is the number of past lagged observations. Determining an appropriate set of input variables is vital for neural networks to capture the essential underlying relationship that can be used for successful forecasting. How many and what variables to use in the input layer will directly affect the performance of neural network in both in-sample fitting and out-of-sample forecasting, resulting in the under-learning or overfitting phenomenon. Empirical results (Lennon et al., 2001; Zhang et al., 2001; Zhang, 2001) also suggest that the input layer is more important than the hidden layer in time series forecasting problems. Therefore, considerable attention should be given to determine the input variables, especially for time series forecasting.

Although there is substantial flexibility in choosing the number of hidden layers and the number of hidden nodes in each layer, most forecasting applications use only one hidden layer and a small number of hidden nodes. In practice, the number of hidden nodes is often determined by experimenting with a number of choices and then selected by the cross-validation approach or performance on the validation set. Although the number of hidden nodes is an important factor, a number of studies have found that forecasting performance of neural networks is not very sensitive to this parameter (Bakirtzis et al., 1996; Khotanzad et al., 1997; Zhang et al., 2001).

For forecasting applications, the most popular transfer function for hidden nodes is either logistic or hyperbolic and it is the linear or identity function for output nodes, although many other choices can be used. If the data, especially the output data, have been normalized into the range of [0, 1], then logistic function can be used for the output layer. In general, different choices of transfer function should not impact much on the performance of a neural network model.

Once a particular ANN architecture is of interest to the forecaster, it must be trained so that the parameters of the network can be estimated from the data. To be effective in performing this task, a good training algorithm is needed. Training a neural network can be treated as a nonlinear mathematical optimization problem and different solution approaches or algorithms can have quite different effects on the training result. As a result, training with different algorithms and repeating with multiple random initial weights can be helpful in getting a better solution to the neural network training problem. In addition to the popular basic backpropagation training algorithm, users should be aware of many other (sometimes more effective) algorithms. These include so-called second-order approaches, such as conjugate gradient descent, quasi-Newton, and Levenberg-Marquardt (Bishop, 1995).

ANN model selection is typically done with the basic cross-validation process. That is, the in-sample data is split into a training set and a validation set. The ANN parameters are estimated with the training sample, while the performance of the model is evaluated with the validation sample. The best model selected is the one that has the best performance on the validation sample. Of course, in choosing competing models, we must also apply the principle of parsimony. That is, a simpler model that has about the same performance as a more complex model should be preferred.

Model selection can also be done with all of the in-sample data. This can be achieved with several in-sample selection criteria that modify the total error function to include a penalty term that penalizes for the complexity of the model.

In-sample model selection approaches are typically based on some informa-tion-based criteria such as Akaike's information criterion (AIC) and Bayesian (BIC) or Schwarz information criterion (SIC). However, it is important to note the limitation of these criteria as empirically demonstrated by Swanson and White (1995) and Qi and Zhang (2001). Other in-sample approaches are based on pruning methods such as node and weight pruning (Reed, 1993), as well as constructive methods such as the upstart and cascade correlation approaches (Fahlman & Lebiere, 1990; Frean, 1990).

After the modeling process, the finally selected model must be evaluated using data not used in the model-building stage. In addition, as ANNs are often used as a nonlinear alternative to traditional statistical models, the performance of ANNs needs to be compared to that of statistical methods. As Adya and Collopy (1998) point out, "if such a comparison is not conducted, it is difficult to argue that the study has taught us much about the value of ANNs." They further propose three evaluation criteria to objectively evaluate the perfor-mance of an ANN: (1) comparing it to well-accepted (traditional) models; (2) using true out-of-samples; and (3) ensuring enough sample size in the out-of-sample (40 for classification problems and 75 for time series problems). It is important to note that the test sample served as out-of-sample should not in any way be used in the model-building process. If the cross-validation is used for model selection and experimentation, the performance on the validation sample should not be treated as the true performance of the model.

Although some of the above issues are unique to neural networks, some are general issues to any forecasting method. Therefore, good forecasting practice and principles should be followed. It is beneficial to consult Armstrong (2001), which provides a good source of information on useful principles for forecasting model building, evaluation, and uses.

CONCLUSION

Artificial neural networks have emerged as an important tool for business forecasting. ANNs have many desired features that are quite suitable for practical forecasting applications. This chapter provides a general overview of the neural networks for forecasting applications. Successful forecasting appli-cation areas of ANNs, as well as critical modeling issues are reviewed. It should be emphasized that each forecasting situation requires a careful study of the problem characteristics, prudent design of modeling strategy, and full consideration of modeling issues. Many rules of thumb in ANNs may not be useful for a new application, although good forecasting principles and established guidelines should be followed.

ANNs have achieved remarkable successes in the field of business forecasting. It is, however, important to note that they may not be a panacea for every forecasting task under all circumstances. Forecasting competitions suggest that no single method, including neural networks, is universally the best for all types of problems in every situation. Thus, it may be beneficial to combine several different models in improving forecasting performance. Indeed, efforts to find better ways to use ANNs for forecasting should never cease. The subsequent chapters of this book will provide a number of new forecasting applications and address some practical issues in improving ANN forecasting performance.

REFERENCES

Adya, M. & Collopy, F. (1998). How effective are neural networks at forecasting and prediction? A review and evaluation. *Journal of Forecasting,* 17, 481-495.

Agrawal, D. & Schorling, C. (1996). Market share forecasting: An empirical comparison of artificial neural networks and multinomial logic model. *Journal of Retailing*, 72, 383-407.

Aiken, M. & Bsat, M. (1999). Forecasting market trends with neural networks. *Information Systems Management*, (Fall), 42-48.

Alon, I., Qi, M., & Sadowski, R. J. (2001). Forecasting aggregate retail sales: A comparison of artificial neural networks and traditional methods. *Journal of Retailing and Consumer Services*, 8(3), 147-156.

Anandarajan, M., Lee, P., & Anandarajan, A. (2001). Bankruptcy prediction of financially stressed firms: An examination of the predictive accuracy of artificial neural networks. *International Journal of Intelligent Systems in Accounting, Finance & Management,* 10, 69-81.

Ansuj, A. P., Camargo, M. E., Radharamanan, R., & Petry, D. G. (1996). Sales forecasting using time series and neural networks. *Computers and Industry Engineering,* 31(1/2), 421-424.

Armstrong, J. S. (1988). Research needs in forecasting. *International Journal of Forecasting,* 4, 449-465.

Armstrong, J. S. (2001). *Principles of Forecasting: A Handbook for Researchers and Practitioners*. Boston, MA: Kluwer Academic Publishers.

Ashley, R. (2003). Statistically significant forecasting improvements: How much out-of-sample data is likely necessary? *International Journal of Forecasting*, 19, 229-239.

Atiya, A. F. (2001). Bankruptcy prediction for credit risk using neural networks: A survey and new results. *IEEE Transactions on Neural Networks*, 12(4), 929-935.

Azoff, E. M. (1994). *Neural Network Time Series Forecasting of Financial Markets*. Chichester, UK: John Wiley & Sons.

Bakirtzis, A. G., Petridis, V., Kiartzis, S. J., Alexiadis, M. C., & Maissis, A. H. (1996). A neural network short term load forecasting model for the Greek power system. *IEEE Transactions on Power Systems*, 11(2), 858-863.

Bansal, K. & Vadhavkar, S. (1998). Neural networks based forecasting techniques for inventory control applications. *Data Mining and Knowledge Discovery*, 2, 97-102.

Bishop, M. (1995). *Neural Networks for Pattern Recognition*. Oxford, UK: Oxford University Press.

Box, G. E. P. & Jenkins, G. (1976). *Time Series Analysis: Forecasting and Control*. San Francisco, CA: Holden-Day.

Callen, J. L., Kwan, C. Y., Yip, C. Y., & Yuan, Y. (1996). Neural network forecasting of quarterly accounting earnings. *International Journal of Forecasting*, 12, 475-482.

Charytoniuk, W., Box, E. D., Lee, W.-J., Chen, M.-S., Kotas, P., & Olinda, P. V. (2000). Neural-network-based demand forecasting in a deregulated environment. *IEEE Transaction on Industry Applications,* 36(3), 893-898.

Chatfield, C. (2001). *Time-Series Forecasting*. Boca Raton, FL: Chapman & Hall/CRC.

Chen, A.-S., Leung, M. T., & Daouk, H. (2003). Application of neural networks to an emerging financial market: Forecasting and trading the Taiwan Stock Index. *Computers & Operations Research*, 30(6), 901-924.

Chen, H., Grant-Muller, S., Mussone, L., & Montgomery, F. (2001). A study of hybrid neural network approaches and the effects of missing data on traffic forecasting. *Neural Computing & Applications*, 10(3), 277-286.

Chen, X., Racine, J., & Swanson, N. R. (2001). Semiparametric ARX neural-network models with an application to forecasting inflation. *IEEE Transactions on Neural Networks*, 12(4), 674-683.

Cheng, W., Wagner, L., & Lin, C. (1996). Forecasting the 30-year US Treasury bond with a system of neural networks. *Journal of Computational Intelligence in Finance*, 4(1), 10-16.

Chiang, W., Urban, T. L., & Baldridge, G. W. (1996). A neural network approach to mutual fund net asset value forecasting. *Omega*, 24(2), 205-215.

Church, K. B. & Curram, S. P. (1996). Forecasting consumers' expenditure: A comparison between econometric and neural network models. *International Journal of Forecasting*, 12, 255-267.

Coakley, J. R. & Brown, C. E. (1999). Artificial neural networks in accounting and finance: Modeling issues. *International Journal of Intelligent Systems in Accounting, Finance & Management*, 9, 119-144.

Connor, J. T., Martin, R. D., & Atlas, L. E. (1994). Recurrent neural networks and robust time series prediction. *IEEE Transaction on Neural Networks,* 51(2), 240-254.

Darbellay, G. A. & Slama, M. (2000). Forecasting the short-term demand for electricity: Do neural networks stand a better chance? *International Journal of Forecasting*, 16, 71-83.

de Carvalho, M. C. M., Dougherty, M. S., Fowkes, A. S., & Wardman, M. R. (1998). Forecasting travel demand: A comparison of logic and artificial neural network methods. *Journal of Operational Research Society*, 49, 717-722.

Desai, V. S. & Bharati, R., (1998). A comparison of linear regression and neural network methods for predicting excess returns on large stocks. *Annals of Operations Research*, 78, 127-163.

Dhar, V. & Chou, D. (2001). A comparison of nonlinear methods for predicting earnings surprises and returns. *IEEE Transactions on Neural Networks*, 12(4), 907-921.

Dia, H. (2001). An object-oriented neural network approach to short-term traffic forecasting. *European Journal of operation research*, 131, 253-261.

Doughetry, S. M. & Cobbett, M. R. (1997). Short-term inter-urban traffic forecasts using neural networks, *International journal of forecasting,* 13, 21-31.

Dougherty, M. (1995). A review of neural networks applied to transport. *Transportation Research, Part C,* 3(4), 247-260.

Elkateb, M. M., Solaiman, K., & Al-Turki, Y. (1998). A comparative study of medium-weather-dependent load forecasting using enhanced artificial/

fuzzy neural network and statistical techniques. *Neurocomputing*, 23, 3-13.

Fadlalla, A. & Lin, C.-H. (2001). An analysis of the applications of neural networks in finance. *Interfaces*, 31(4), 112-122.

Fahlman, S. & Lebiere, C. (1990). The cascade-correlation learning architecture. In D. Touretzky (Ed.), *Advances in Neural Information Processing Systems* (Vol. 11, pp. 524-532).

Frean, M. (1990). The Upstart algorithm: A method for constructing and training feed-forward networks. *Neural Computations*, 2, 198-209.

Gately, E. (1996). *Neural Networks for Financial Forecasting*. New York: John Wiley & Sons.

Geman, S., Bienenstock, E., & Doursat, T. (1992). Neural networks and the bias/variance dilemma. *Neural Computation*, 5, 1-58.

Goh, B.-H. (1998). Forecasting residential construction demand in Singapore: A comparative study of the accuracy of time series, regression and artificial neural network techniques. *Engineering, Construction and Architecture Management*, 5, 261-275.

Gorr, L. (1994). Research prospective on neural network forecasting. *International Journal of Forecasting*, 10, 1-4.

Granger, C. W. J. (1993). Strategies for modelling nonlinear time-series relationships. *The Economic Record*, 69(206), 233-238.

Hippert, H. S., Pedreira, C. E., & Souza, R. C. (2001). Neural networks for short-term load forecasting: A review and evaluation. *IEEE Transactions on Power Systems*, 16(1), 44-55.

Hoptroff, R. G. (1993). The principles and practice of time series forecasting and business modeling using neural networks. *Neural Computing and Applications*, 1, 59-66.

Hu, M. Y., Hung, M. S., Patuwo, B. E., & Shanker, M. S. (1999). Estimating the performance of Sino-Hong Kong joint ventures using neural network ensembles. *Annals of Operations Research*, 87, 213-232.

Hua, G. B. (1996). Residential construction demand forecasting using economic indicators: A comparative study of artificial neural networks and multiple regression. *Construction Management and Economics*, 14, 25-34.

Husken, M. & Stagge, P. (2003). Recurrent neural networks for time series classification. *Neurocomputing*, 50, 223-235.

Hwang, H. B. (2001). Insights into neural-network forecasting of time series corresponding to ARMA (p,q) structures. *Omega*, 29, 273-289.

Indro, D. C., Jiang, C. X., Patuwo, B. E., & Zhang, G. P. (1999). Predicting Mutual Fund Performance Using Artificial Neural Networks. *Omega, the International Journal of Management Science,* 27, 373-380.

Jiang, J. J., Zhong, M., & Klein, G. (2000). Marketing category forecasting: An alternative of BVAR — Artificial neural networks. *Decision Sciences,* 31, 789-812.

Kaastra, I. & Boyd, M. (1996). Designing a neural network for forecasting financial and economic time series. *Neurocomputing,* 10, 215-236.

Kaastra, I. & Boyd, M. S. (1995). Forecasting futures trading volume using neural networks. *The Journal of Futures Markets,* 15(8), 953-970.

Kermanshahi, B. (1998). Recurrent neural network for forecasting next 10 years loads of nine Japanese utilities. *Neurocomputing,* 23, 125-133.

Khotanzad, A., Afkhami-Rohani, R., Lu, T. L., Abaye, A., Davis, M., & Maratukulam, D. J. (1997). ANNSTLF — A neural-network-based electric load forecasting system. *IEEE Transactions on Neural Networks*, 8(4), 835-846.

Kirby, H. R., Watson, S. M., & Dougherty, M. S. (1997). Should we use neural networks or statistical models for short-term motorway traffic forecasting? *International Journal of Forecasting*, 13, 43-50.

Kohzadi, N., Boyd, M. S., Kermanshahi, B., & Kaastra, I. (1996). A comparison of artificial neural network and time series models for forecasting commodity prices. *Neurocomputing,* 10, 169-181.

Kolehmainen, M., Martikainen, H., & Ruuskanen, J. (2001). Neural networks and periodic components used in air quality forecasting. *Atmospheric Environment,* 35, 815-825.

Krycha, K. A. & Wagner, U. (1999). Applications of artificial neural networks in management science: A survey. *Journal of Retailing and Consumer Services*, 6, 185-203.

Kuan, C.-M. & Liu, T. (1995). Forecasting exchange rates using feedforward and recurrent neural networks. *Journal of Applied Econometrics,* 10, 347-364.

Kuo, R. J. (2001). A sales forecasting system based on fuzzy neural network with initial weights generated by genetic algorithm. *European Journal of operation research,* 129, 496-571.

Law, R. (2000). Back-propagation learning in improving the accuracy of neural network-based tourism demand forecasting. *Tourism Management,* 21, 331-340.

Lennon, B., Montague, G. A., Frith, A. M., Gent, C., & Bevan, V. (2001). Industrial applications of neural networks — An investigation. *Journal of Process Control*, 11, 497-507.

Leung, M. T., Chen, A. S., & Daouk, H. (2000). Forecasting exchange rates using general regression neural networks. *Computers and Operations Research*, 27(11), 1093-1110.

Leung, M. T., Daouk, H., & Chen, A. -S. (2000). Forecasting stock indices: A comparison of classification and level estimation models. *International Journal of Forecasting*, 16, 173-190.

Luxhoj, J. T., Riis, J. O., & Stensballe, B. (1996). A hybrid econometric-neural network modeling approach for sales forecasting. *International Journal of Production Economics*, 43, 175-192.

Maier, H. R. & Dandy, G. C. (2000). Neural networks for the prediction and forecasting of water resource variables: A review of modeling issues and applications. *Environmental Modeling and Software*, 15, 101-124.

Makridakis, S., Anderson, A., Carbone, R., Fildes, R., Hibdon, M., Lewandowski, R., Newton, J., Parzen, E., & Winkler, R. (1982). The accuracy of extrapolation (time series) methods: Results of a forecasting competition. *Journal of Forecasting*, 1(2), 111-153.

Mandic, D. & Chambers, J. (2001). *Recurrent Neural Networks for Prediction: Learning Algorithms, Architectures and Stability*. Chichester, UK: John Wiley & Sons.

Mckee, T. E. & Greenstein, M. (2000). Predicting bankruptcy using recursive partitioning and realistically proportioned data set. *Journal of forecasting*, 19, 219-230.

Medeiros, M. C. & Pedreira, C. E. (2001). What are the effects of forecasting linear time series with neural networks? *Engineering Intelligent Systems*, 4, 237-424.

Murtagh, F., Zheng, G., Campbell, J. G., & Aussem, A. (2000). Neural network modelling for environmental prediction. *Neurocomputing*, 30, 65-70.

Nag, A. K. & Mitra, A. (2002). Forecasting Daily Foreign Exchange Rates Using Genetically Optimized Neural Networks. *Journal of Forecasting*, 21(7), 501-512.

Nam, K. & Schaefer, T. (1995). Forecasting international airline passenger traffic using neural networks. *Logistics and Transportation Review*, 31(3), 239-251.

Nelson, M., Hill, T., Remus, T., & O'Connor, M. (1999). Time series forecasting using neural networks: Should the data be deseasonalized first? *Journal of Forecasting*, 18, 359-367.

Nguyen, N. & Cripps, A. (2001). Predicting Housing Value: A Comparison of Multiple Regression Analysis and Artificial Neural Networks. *Journal of Real Estate Research*, 22(3), 313-335.

Ntungo, C. & Boyd, M. (1998). Commodity futures trading performance using neural network models versus ARIMA models. *The Journal of Futures Markets,* 18(8), 965-983.

Parlos, A. G., Rais, O. T., & Atiya, A. F. (2000). Multi-step-ahead prediction using dynamic recurrent neural networks. *Neural networks,* 13, 765-786.

Partovi, F. Y. & Anandarajan, M. (2002). Classifying inventory using an artificial neural network approach. *Computers and Industrial Engineering*, 41, 389-404.

Prybutok, V. R., Yi, J., & Mitchell, D. (2000). Comparison of neural network models with ARIMA and regression models for prediction of Houston's daily maximum ozone concentrations. *European Journal of Operational Research*, 122, 31-40.

Qi, M. (1999). Nonlinear predictability of stock returns using financial and economic variables. *Journal of Business & Economic Statistics,* 17(4), 419-429.

Qi, M. (2001). Predicting US recessions with leading indicators via neural network models. *International Journal of Forecasting*, 17(3), 383-401.

Qi, M. & Zhang, G. P. (2001). An investigation of model selection criteria for neural network time series forecasting. *European Journal of Operational Research,* 132, 666-680.

Qiao, F., Yang, H., & Lam, W. H. K. (2001). Intelligent simulation and prediction of traffic flow dispersion. *Transportation Research, Part B*, 35, 843-863.

Reed, R. (1993). Pruning algorithms — A survey. *IEEE Transactions on Neural Networks,* 4(5), 740-747.

Remus, W. & O'Connor, M. (2001). Neural networks for time series forecasting. In J. S. Armstrong (Ed.), *Principles of Forecasting: A Handbook for Researchers and Practitioners* (pp. 245-256). Norwell, MA: Kluwer Academic Publishers.

Ripley, B. D. (1996). *Pattern Recognition and Neural Networks*. Cambridge: Cambridge University Press.

Ruiz-Suarez, J. C., Mayora-Ibarra, O. A., Torres-Jimenez, J., & Ruiz-Suarez, L. G. (1995). Short-term ozone forecasting by artificial neural networks. *Advances in Engineering Software*, 23, 143-149.

Rumelhard, D. E., McClelland, J. L. and the PDP Research Group. (1986). *Parallel Distributed Processing: Explorations in the Microstructure of Cognition, Volume 1: Foundations*. Cambridge, MA: MIT Press.

Saad, W. E., Prokhorov, D.V., & Wunsch, C. D. (1998). Comparative study of stock trend prediction using time delay, recurrent and probabilistic neural networks. *IEEE Transactions on Neural Networks,* 9(6), 1456-1470.

Smith, M. (1993). *Neural Networks for Statistical Modeling.* New York: Van Nostrand Reinhold.

Swanson, N. R. & White, H. (1995). A model-selection approach to assessing the information in the term structure using linear models and artificial neural networks. *Journal of Business & Economic Statistics,* 13, 265-275.

Thieme, R. J., Song, M., & Calantone, R. J. (2000). Artificial neural network decision support systems for new product development project selection. *Journal of Marketing Research,* 37, 499-507.

Tkacz, G. (2001). Neural network forecasting of Canadian GDP growth. *International Journal of Forecasting,* 17, 57-69.

Tseng, F.-M., Yu, H.-C., & Tzeng, G.-H. (2001). Applied hybrid grey model to forecast seasonal time series. *Technological Forecasting and Social Change,* 67, 291-302.

Vellido, A., Lisboa, P. J. G., & Vaughan, J. (1999). Neural networks in business: A survey of applications (1992-1998). *Expert Systems with Applications,* 17, 51-70.

Vermaak, J. & Botha, E. C. (1998). Recurrent neural networks for short-term load forecasting. *IEEE Transactions on Power Systems,* 13(1), 126-132.

Wang, J.-H. & Leu, J.-Y. (1996). Stock market trend prediction using ARIMA-based neural networks. *IEEE International Conference on Neural Networks,* 2160-2165.

Wang, S. (1999). An adaptive approach to market development forecasting. *Neural Computation & Applications,* 8, 3-8.

Weigend, A. S. & Gershenfeld, N. A. (1994). *Time Series Prediction: Forecasting the Future and Understanding the Past.* Reading, MA: Addison-Wesley.

Werbos, P. (1974). Beyond regression: New tools for prediction and analysis in the behavioral sciences. *Ph.D. thesis,* Harvard University.

West, P. M., Brockett, P. L., & Golden, L. L. (1997) A comparative analysis of neural networks and statistical methods for predicting consumer choice. *Marketing Science,* 16, 370-391.

Widrow, B., Rumelhart, D., & Lehr, M. A. (1994). Neural networks: Applications in industry, business and science. *Communications of the ACM,* 37(3), 93-105.

Wittkemper, H. & Steiner, M. (1996). Using neural networks to forecast the systematic risk of stocks. *European Journal of Operational Research,* 577-588.

Wong, B. K. & Selvi, Y. (1998). Neural network applications in finance: A review and analysis of literature (1990-1996). *Information and Management,* 34, 129-139.

Wong, B. K., Lai, V. S. & Lam, J. (2000). A bibliography of neural network business applications research: 1994-1998. *Computers and Operations Research,* 27, 1045-1076.

Yang, Z. R. (1999). Probabilistic neural networks in bankruptcy prediction. *Journal of Business Research,* 44, 67-74.

Yao, J., Li, Y., & Tan, C. L. (2000). Option price forecasting using neural networks. *Omega,* 28, 455-466.

Zhang, G. P. (2001). An investigation of neural networks for linear time-series forecasting. *Computers & Operations Research,* 28, 1183-1202.

Zhang, G. P. & Hu, M. Y. (1998). Neural network forecasting of the British Pound/US dollar exchange rate. *Omega,* 26(4), 495-506.

Zhang, G. P. & Qi, M. (2002). Predicting consumer retail sales using neural networks. In Smith & Gupta (Eds.), *Neural Networks in Business: Techniques and Applications* (pp. 26-40). Hershey, PA: Idea Group Publishing.

Zhang, G. P., Hu, M. Y., Patuwo, B. E., & Indro, D. C. (1999). Artificial neural networks in bankruptcy prediction: General framework and cross-validation analysis. *European Journal of Operational Research,* 116, 16-32.

Zhang, G.P., Keil, M., Rai, A., & Mann, J. (2003). Predicting information technology project escalation: A neural network approach. *European Journal of Operational Research,* 146, 115-129.

Zhang, G. P., Patuwo, E. P., & Hu, M. Y. (1998). Forecasting with artificial neural networks: The state of the art. *International Journal of Forecasting,* 14, 35-62.

Zhang, G. P., Patuwo, E. P., & Hu, M. Y. (2001). A simulation study of artificial neural networks for nonlinear time series forecasting. *Computers & Operations Research,* 28, 381-396.

Chapter II

Using Artificial Neural Networks to Forecast Market Response

Leonard J. Parsons, Georgia Institute of Technology, USA

Ashutosh Dixit, University of Georgia, USA

ABSTRACT

Marketing managers must quantify the effects of marketing actions on contemporaneous and future sales performance. This chapter examines forecasting with artificial neural networks in the context of model-based planning and forecasting. The emphasis here is on causal modeling; that is, forecasting the impact of marketing mix variables, such as price and advertising, on sales.

INTRODUCTION

Ever-improving information technology has changed the face of marketing research, marketing analysis, and marketing practice. Prime examples are the use of electronic point-of-sale (POS) data collected through optical scanners to improve decision-making and logistics (Ing & Mitchell, 1994). The magnitudes (in millions) of typical databases available to a brand manager in a consumer packaged goods firm are: store audit one, warehouse withdrawal 10, market-level scanner 300, chain-level scanner 500, and store-level scanner 10,000 (Blattberg, Kim, & Ye, 1994, p. 174). The data explosion makes the increased quantification of the marketing function inevitable. More sophisticated modeling approaches will be necessary. The modeling may either be descriptive for uncovering marketing phenomena, or predictive for solving problems (Little, 1994, p. 155). The basic issue addressed in this chapter is what is the role of artificial neural networks (ANNs) for forecasting and planning in this setting? To answer this question, let's begin by briefly looking at forecasting with market response models.

Market response models — also known as marketing mix models — capture the factors that drive a market. They show how controllable marketing instruments, such as price, distribution, advertising, sales promotion, and sales force effort, as well as uncontrollable environmental conditions, which capture competitive actions as well as autonomous factors such as economic climate, affect performance measures; in particular, unit sales and market share. For example, sales of umbrellas could be expressed as a function of the relative price, relative promotion expenditure, personal disposable income, and rainfall (Proctor, 1992). Relative price is the price of our umbrellas divided by the average price charged by our competitors. Relative promotion expenditure is our expenditure on promotion divided by the total spent by our competitors. We set our price and promotion. We do not control our competitors' actions or the state of the economy or the weather conditions. When market response models are directly incorporated into the planning process, the approach is called model-based planning and forecasting (Hanssens, Parsons, & Schultz, 2001, pp. 16-19). This approach is presented in Figure 1. At the heart of this process, forecasts of unit sales are made using a market response model on the basis of brand plans and budgets, along with estimates of competitive actions and environmental conditions. Responsibility for forecasts is placed on the manager who makes the decisions, not the forecaster (Parsons & Schultz, 1994).

While there is considerable evidence to support the managerial use of market response models to describe a marketplace and to provide diagnostic information, the use of response models, especially market share models, in forecasting has been more controversial. The forecasting ability of a market response model is typically benchmarked against a "naïve" time series model. The naïve model does not contain any marketing mix data but contains the lagged dependent variable, which may capture major causal effects because it

Figure 1: Model-Based Planning and Forecasting (Source: Hanssens et al., 2001, p. 17)

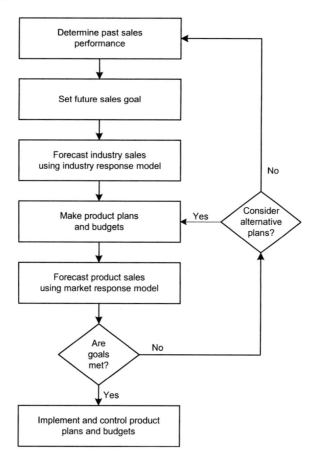

reflects the carryover effects of marketing effort and/or consumer inertia. Thus, for a market response model to be superior in forecasting, there must be strong current effects from the marketing mix. Other conditions, such as poor data quality, may blur the advantages of market response models over naïve models. Competitive behavior may or may not be taken into account in market response models depending on the importance of competitive effects on the particular brand studied.

This chapter reviews the literature on ANNs and market response models (causal models) and identifies key issues, especially in forecasting with causal models. We address using ANNs to forecast a single marketing time series (non-causal models) only in passing.

WHY ARTIFICIAL NEURAL NETWORK MODELS?

ANNs fall into the class of input-output models and, as such, may be suitable for response modeling. In addition to an observable input layer and an observable output layer, there is usually one, and possibly more, unobservable hidden layers. We focus primarily on what is known as the feedforward, multilayer perceptron model out of the larger class of all ANNs. For a brief description of ANNs, see the introduction chapter of this book. Technical details about practical considerations in conducting an ANN analysis can be found in books by authors such as Bishop (1995), Orr and Muller (1998), and Zapranis and Refenes (1999).

Nodes occurring in a hidden layer may be said to perform the role of "feature detectors" (Curry & Morgan 1997, p. 124). Hidden nodes represent latent variables. How might latent variables arise naturally in response modeling? Consider three examples. First, aggregate marketing mix models are loosely based on stimulus-response theory at the individual level. A stimulus affects what is going on inside the buyer's mind, which is impossible to observe. Only the ultimate reaction is observable. The appropriateness of ANNs in such a situation was explicitly recognized by Wartenberg and Decker (1995). Second, intermediate variables between stimulus and response may be formally postulated. For example, a household brand choice is made from its consideration set, which may not involve all brands. This consideration set is unobservable. An ANN can be constructed in which the consideration set corresponds to the hidden layer in the model (Vroomen et al., in press). See Figure 2. Third, market share models may be based on comparing the "attractiveness" of our brand to the attractiveness of all brands in the market. The attractiveness of a brand depends on its marketing mix. Assuming (1) that all brand attractions are non-negative and sum to one, (2) that a brand with zero attraction has zero market share, (3) that equal attractions imply equal market shares, and (4) a brand's share is affected the same if the attraction of any other brand is increased by a fixed amount, then market share can be shown to be a simple linear normalization of attraction (Bell, Keeney, & Little, 1975). Attraction, however, is unobservable and, therefore, is not formally modeled in market response models.

While the ability to capture latent intermediate factors is attractive, the power of ANNs is their flexible nonlinear modeling capability. ANNs can adapt to the features present in the data. ANNs have been shown to be able to provide an accurate approximation to any continuous function of the inputs if

Figure 2: Augmented Hidden-Layer ANN Model (Source: Constructed from Vroomen, Franses, & van Nierop, in press)

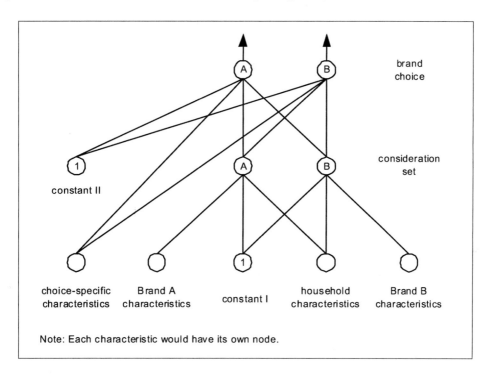

there are a sufficiently large number of units in the middle (hidden) layer (Cybenko, 1989; Funahashi, 1989; Hornik, Stichcombe, & White, 1989). Furthermore, even for discontinuous functions, at most only two hidden layers are required. As one would conjecture, ANNs should be able to approximate traditional statistical methods: ordinary and nonlinear least squares (White, 1992b; White & Stinchcombe, 1992), nonparametric regression (White, 1992a), and Fourier series (White & Gallant, 1992). A multi-output ANN can be viewed as a specialized version of a simultaneous equation nonlinear multiple regression (Kuan & White, 1994). In sum, ANNs are inherently nonlinear and can estimate nonlinear functions well.

How might nonlinearity arise naturally in response modeling? A sales response function may exhibit various properties. The most prominent of these is diminishing returns to scale. While sales will always increase with increases in marketing effort, each additional unit of marketing effort brings in less in incremental sales than the previous unit does. Occasionally a response function might be S-shaped; that is, sales initially may exhibit increasing returns to scale and then diminishing returns to higher levels of marketing effort. In addition, the sales response function may show minimum sales potential, saturation, threshold, and/or marketing mix interactions effects. Even when marketing effort is zero, base sales might occur due to loyal buyers, captive buyers, or impulse buyers. On the other hand, some positive amount of marketing effort might be necessary before any sales impact can be detected. Moreover, no matter how much marketing effort is expended, there is a finite achievable upper limit to sales. Finally, the level of effort for one marketing mix variable might affect the sensitivity of sales to changes in the level of effort in other marketing mix variables. For example, consistent theme advertising expenditures can impact a market's sensitivity to price. For more details, see Hanssens et al. (2001).

In sum, artificial neural networks are known to perform well in data-rich, knowledge-poor situations. ANNs uncover complex relationships in data and permit forecasting based on those relationships. Since market response models have been estimated for many years, a knowledge base exists (Hanssens et al., 2001). We believe that this information can aid in the construction of ANNs used for forecasting. In turn, ANNs may provide insights not captured by conventional functional forms traditionally used in market response modeling.

MODELING RESPONSE WITH ANNS

There have been indications that ANNs can forecast accurately using marketing mix variables. An ANN forecasts weekly sales of an apparel SKU (stock keeping unit) using data on historical sales, advertising history, and promotional and pricing plans. The correlation between the forecast and actual results was 0.87. A similar result was achieved in applying an ANN to a database containing daily sales history, price, promotion, and advertising data for just over a year on a single highly promotional SKU in one store. The correlation between the forecast and actual results was 0.84. The same model reportedly forecasts sales for the same SKU in other stores in the retail chain with similar accuracy (Thall, 1992).

In this section, studies that compare ANNs to traditional market response models estimated by regression and other econometric techniques will be reviewed. There will be subsections on sales response models, market share models, and brand choice models. The latter will involve aggregation to the market share level.

Sales Response Models

In the case of an Austrian consumer brand that dominated the market, competitive influences could be ignored (Hruschka, 1993). Sales in the current period t, Q_t, was the dependent variable. Retail price, current advertising budget, advertising budget lagged one period, and average monthly temperature were the sales drivers $X_{k,t}$. A linear monthly model:

$$Q_t = \beta_0 + \beta_1 X_{1,t} + \beta_2 X_{2,t} + \cdots + \beta_2 X_{K,t} + v_t \tag{1}$$

with first-order autoregressive AR(1) disturbances:

$$v_t = \rho v_{t-1} + w_t \tag{2}$$

was estimated by general least squares using the Cochrane-Orcutt procedure. See Greene (2000, pp. 546-552) for a discussion of this method and its limitations. Other functional forms were tried as well. The results indicated strong influences by price (negative) and temperature (positive). The advertising also had an effect (positive). The corresponding ANN consisted of four input variables plus a constant, four hidden units plus a second constant, and one output unit with connections between variables of neighboring layers. Simplifications of this model were considered as well. All comparisons were on the basis of fit using mean square error and mean absolute deviations. The full ANN model fitted best, but even the simplest version of the ANN model fitted better than the econometric model. The weights in the ANN model had plausible economic interpretations. This research simply attempted to identify and estimate the market response function. No comparison of the forecasting ability of the econometric and ANN models was made.

Competitive effects were also ignored in a simulation study inspired by a company in the Netherlands that imports a Scandinavian brand of high-quality saws to sell through do-it-yourself outlets (Wierenga & Kluytmans, 1994; Wierenga & Kluytmans, 1996). Promotion consists of newspaper advertisements in cities where these outlets are located and providing point-of-purchase material to these retailers. In addition to a linear model (without autocorrelated errors), a multiplicative model:

$$Q = e^{\beta_0} X_1^{\beta_1} X_2^{\beta_2} \cdots X_K^{\beta_K} \tag{3}$$

was estimated in order to take into account interactions among variables. This model is sometimes called the constant elasticity model because its power parameters can be interpreted directly as elasticities. This model is known in its estimation form as the double log (log-log) model:

$$\ln Q = \beta_0 + \beta_1 \ln X_1 + \beta_2 \ln X_2 + \cdots + \beta_K \ln X_K. \tag{4}$$

The estimation form is linear in its parameters and ordinary least squares regression can be used. The simulation study forecast sales for 13 weeks based on five or 10 years of data; that is, 65 or 130 four-week periods. Three input variables were specified. These might represent the marketing mix variables: price, advertising expenditures, and promotion expenditures, for instance. Three levels of random noise were introduced. Using root mean square error as the criterion, this exploratory study found that when the "true" relationship between the marketing instruments was linear, a neural network was hardly better than regression. However, if the "true" relationship between the marketing instruments was nonlinear, a neural network performed better than regression.

A store-level analysis of a national brand of strawberry yogurt was done for weekly scanner data from two markets (Ainscough & Aronson, 1999). Sales drivers were two measures of newspaper advertising: major ad (yes = 1, no = 0) and line ad (yes = 1, no = 0), price, average value of coupons used, special display (yes = 1, no = 0), and in-ad coupon (yes = 1, no = 0). Lagged unit sales, that is, sales during the prior week in the same store, was also included as an explanatory variable. In addition, the way the data was compiled required a control variable that specified the share of sales of a chain that came from each of its individual stores. An interaction model was estimated econometrically:

$$\begin{aligned} Q_t = &\ \beta_0 + \beta_1 X_1 + \beta_2 X_2 + \beta_3 X_3 \\ &+ \beta_{12} X_1 X_2 + \beta_{13} X_1 X_3 + \beta_{23} X_2 X_3 + \beta_4 Q_{t-1}. \end{aligned} \tag{5}$$

Higher-order interactions were assumed to have zero impact. Two-way interactions among similar variable types, e.g., types of newspaper ads, were not included because these always reduce to zero. The data were split into an 80% estimation sample and a 20% validation sample.

Two ANN configurations, a three-layer model and a four-layer model, were examined. The models had eight input units and one output unit. The lowest mean squared error for the trained three-layer model occurred when there were 12 units in the hidden layer and for the trained four-layer model when there were 12 units in the first hidden layer and eight units in the second hidden layer. The four-layer did not provide a materially better fit than the three-layer model and so the rule of parsimony would favor the three-layer model. The regression model had an R^2 of 0.50 and a mean squared error of 549 while the three-layer ANN model had an R^2 of 0.70 and a mean squared error of 326. This difference was statistically significant. Competitive effects were not addressed.

Market Share Models

In the case of a fast moving consumer good in a continental European market, the competition among five beverage brands could not be ignored (van Wezel & Baets, 1995). Fifty-one bimonthly observations were available on each brand's market share and marketing variables. The sales drivers included price, numerical distribution, weighted distribution, numerical out-of-stock, weighted out-of-stock, and advertising. Note that market share rather than unit sales is the dependent variable in this study. The market response functions for the brands were estimated separately and together. Variants of the linear and multiplicative models, which used relative (to the market) rather than absolute variables, were also examined. The emphasis of this study was on forecasting, so the sample was split into an estimation sample for econometric analysis (known also as a training sample for ANN) and a validation sample. Root mean squared errors were calculated. ANNs were trained for each brand separately and for all brands together. The first type of network had one output unit, market share of the brand, and the brand's marketing variables as inputs. The second type of network had five output units, the market shares of each brand, and all the marketing variables available as inputs. The input variables were all expressed either in absolute terms or in relative terms. All networks had one hidden layer containing five hidden units. ANNs performed better than traditional models.

The problem with this study is that the linear and multiplicative market share models may predict market shares less than one or greater than one, and the sum of predicted market shares for all brands may not add up to one; that is, they are not logically consistent.

One approach to logical consistency has been to compare the "attractiveness," A, of each of B market alternatives to yield the market share of a specific brand b (say), MS_b:

$$MS_b = \frac{A_b}{\sum\limits_{i=1}^{B} A_i}. \tag{6}$$

This model, as was mentioned earlier, has been called an attraction model (Bell, Keeney, & Little, 1975). The empirical problem is that attraction is an unobservable construct. The solution has been to use the observable variable unit sales, Q.

A model must be logically consistent if it is based upon the definition of market share. In this definition, unit sales of a brand is replaced by the brand's sales response function.

$$MS_b \equiv \frac{Q_b}{\sum\limits_{i=1}^{B} Q_i} = \frac{f_b(\mathbf{X};\beta_b)}{\sum\limits_{i=1}^{B} f_i(\mathbf{X};\beta_i)}. \tag{7}$$

By including competitors' marketing instruments in the set of explanatory variables $\mathbf{X}$ for each sales response function, cross-competitive (market share) effects can be modeled, although this would typically result in a large number of parameters. A different functional form could represent the sales response function for each brand-form combination. In practice, each combination would be assumed to have the same functional form. Not surprisingly, the most common approach is to use the multiplicative functional form, shown here in exponential form for the underlying sales response function and with $K1$ quantitative variables X (for example, price) and $K-K1$ qualitative dummy variables D (for example, the absence or presence of a display in a store):

$$Q_b = \exp\left(\beta_{b0} + \sum\limits_{i}^{B}\sum\limits_{k}^{K1} \beta_{bik} \ln[X_{ik}] + \sum\limits_{i}^{B}\sum\limits_{k=K1+1}^{K} \delta_{bik} D_{ik}\right). \tag{8}$$

The corresponding market share model belongs to the class of models called Multiplicative Competitive Interaction (MCI) models. In particular, it is known as the Cross-Effects MCI Model because it allows each item to have its unique own effects ($i = b$) while experiencing all possible cross effects ($i \neq b$). Thus, it captures market structure asymmetry. The full Cross-Effects MCI model places too many demands on the data. One approach is to set some of the parameters to zero. The problem then is to distinguish between fundamental asymmetries and those that are small enough to set equal to zero.

One could, of course, set all cross-effects parameters equal to zero *a priori*. The result would be:

$$Q_b = \exp\left(\beta_{b0} + \sum_{k}^{K1} \beta_{bk} \ln[X_{bk}] + \sum_{k=K1}^{K} \delta_{bk} D_{bk} \right). \tag{9}$$

Unit sales of an item are now only determined by its own marketing mix and not by those of its competitors. The effectiveness of a marketing instrument can still vary from one brand to another. Thus, this market share model is known as the Differential-Effects MCI Model. The parameters in this model will be biased if, in fact, large asymmetries are present in the data.

Finally, one could assume that the marketing effectiveness of any particular marketing instrument is equal across brands. In effect, a prototype brand rather than a specific brand is being estimated. Usually items are allowed to have individual "intercepts":

$$Q_b = \exp\left(\beta_{b0} + \sum_{k}^{K1} \beta_{k} \ln[X_{bk}] + \sum_{k=K1}^{K} \delta_{k} D_{bk} \right). \tag{10}$$

This is called simply the MCI Model. If all items also have the same constant, β_0, then this constant is unidentifiable because it appears in both the numerator and denominator of the market share expression and cancels out. In this situation where a prototypical relation must be estimated from cross-sectional data, a market share model shouldn't be used, but rather the sales response function should be estimated. The sales response function will give exactly the same parameters estimates as the market share model. It will also provide an estimate of the "unidentifiable" constant.

Sales and unit price data on five shampoo brands in German drugstores were collected over 11 periods using point of sale scanners (Wartenberg & Decker, 1995). An ANN was compared to the MCI-model. The ANN had five inputs, the price of each brand, and five outputs, the market share of each brand. There were three units in the hidden layer. Both approaches fit the data well as measured by Mean Relative Error and the Modified Theil inequality coefficient. The ANN approach slightly dominated the MCI model for all brands. Similar results were reported to have been found in two other data sets. (See Gaul, Decker, & Wartenberg, 1994.)

For the retail coffee market in one city, ANNs were compared to the Differential-Effects MCI model (Gruca & Klemz, 1998). The Cross-Effects MCI model could not be estimated because of lack of data. ANNs do not give the elasticities of marketing mix variables directly. They have to be calculated. For example, to calculate the price elasticity, each observed price is inputted to the ANN model having first set the non-price variables to their mean values and a predicted market share is generated. Using the resultant data series, in this case price and market share, the definition of elasticity can be used to estimate the price elasticity:

$$\varepsilon_P \equiv \frac{\Delta MS}{MS} \Big/ \frac{\Delta P}{P} = \frac{\Delta MS}{\Delta P} \times \frac{P}{MS}. \tag{11}$$

The elasticities of other sales drivers can be found in a similar manner. More than 95% of the elasticities in the Differential-Effects MCI model had the theoretically correct sign, but in the ANN model this percentage was less than 75%. While the magnitudes of the elasticities of both models were generally comparable, there were exceptions. The ANN model identified substantial cross-elasticities. These could not be detected by the MCI model, which by assumption sets the cross-effects parameters to zero. Furthermore, ANNs surpassed the MCI model in forecasting ability. Here a holdout sample was used and mean absolute percentage error (MAPE) was the criterion. One would have liked to have seen the ANN information about substantial cross-elasticities used to facilitate estimation of the Cross-Effects MCI model. Inconsequential cross-effect parameters could be set to zero reducing the data needed and perhaps making it possible to estimate the model.

Rather than using the multiplicative functional form in the market share model, one could use the exponential functional form:

$$Q_b = \exp\left(\beta_{b0} + \sum_i^B \sum_k^K \beta_{ik} X_{ik} \right). \tag{12}$$

Here the distinction between continuous and dummy variables does not have to be made explicit. The corresponding market share model belongs to the class of models called Multinomial Logit (MNL) models. The logit model, better known for its use in representing brand choice, falls in this class. Here we have the Cross-Effects MNL Model.

The associated Differential-Effects MNL Model and simple MNL Model are:

$$Q_b = \exp\left(\beta_{b0} + \sum_{k}^{K} \beta_{bk} X_{bk} \right) \qquad (13)$$

and

$$Q_b = \exp\left(\beta_{b0} + \sum_{k}^{K} \beta_{k} X_{bk} \right), \qquad (14)$$

respectively.

These models do not incorporate threshold or saturation effects. Hruschka (2001) recognized that greater flexibility could be achieved using a neural approach. He extended the attraction model version of the Differential-Effects MNL Model by adding a second summation:

$$A_{bt} = \exp\left(\beta_{b0} + \sum_{k}^{K} \beta_{bk} X_{bkt} + \sum_{h}^{H_b} \lambda_{hb} \lambda_{hbt} \right). \qquad (15)$$

The new part of attraction is equivalent to a multilayer perceptron (MLP) with one layer of H_b hidden units having values λ_{hbt} for brand b. Thus, the hidden units are brand-specific. Values of these hidden units are computed by inserting a linear combination of brand-specific predictors into the binomial logistic function $b(\bullet)$:

$$\lambda_{hbt} = b\left(-\alpha_{b0} - \sum_{k}^{K} \alpha_{hbk} X_{bkt} \right) = 1 \Big/ \left(1 + \exp\left(-\alpha_{b0} - \sum_{k}^{K} \alpha_{hbk} X_{bkt} \right) \right). \qquad (16)$$

The conventional Differential-Effects MNL Model is nested in the neural net, that is, when $H_b = 0$ for all brands.

The empirical study analyzed store-level data for four brands of a certain category of consumer nondurables (Hruschka, 2001). There were 104 weekly observations on each brand's market share, current retail price, and features (zero-one dummy variables). A variety of neural net models were fit. The best fitting model had one hidden unit for each of two brands, but no hidden units for the other two brands. The path diagram for this model is shown in Figure 3. The neural net model implied a price response qualitatively different from the Differential-Effects MNL Model.

Brand Choice Models

Brand choice models are of interest here only in so far as household choice probabilities can be aggregated to generate forecasts of brand shares for a particular marketing mix environment. Indeed, ANNs require a long purchase history to train a network and such data is not usually available at the individual household level in grocery scanner panels; consequently, ANNs are more appropriate for forecasting the more aggregate store or market-level brand shares (Agrawal & Schorling, 1996).

Consumer choice probabilities can be estimated econometrically with (binomial) logit for binary choice or multinomial logit (MNL) for polychoto-

Figure 3: Path Diagram for ANN Attraction Model (Source: Based on Hruschka, 2001, p. 33)

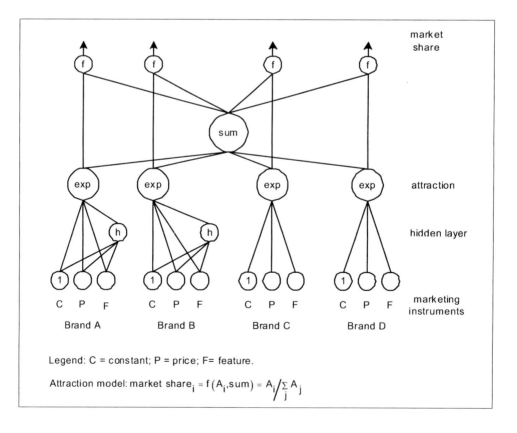

Legend: C = constant; P = price; F= feature.

Attraction model: market share$_i$ = $f(A_i, \text{sum})$ = $A_i / \sum_j A_j$

mous choice. These econometric techniques are clearly explained with detailed empirical examples in Franses and Paap (2001).

One empirical study examined three frequently purchased categories of grocery products (Agrawal & Schorling, 1996). Purchase data were merged with store environment data. The latter included weekly information on brand price in the store and whether the retailer featured the brand in its advertising or had a special display for the brand. Households were clustered into homogeneous segments based on variety seeking, the number of different brands that they purchased. The parameters of the MNL model were estimated using an estimation period, and then the brand choice probabilities were estimated using data from a prediction period. Finally, the predicted choice probabilities were averaged over all purchase occasions during a week to forecast weekly brand share. For ANNs, the number of nodes in the output layer equaled the number of brands, while the number of nodes in the input layer equaled three times the number of brands, as there are three store environmental variables for each brand. Preliminary empirical investigation suggested five nodes in the hidden layer. The results showed that ANNs forecasted brand shares better than MNL for the peanut butter and dishwashing liquid categories, and moderately better in the catsup category.

Another study looked at brands of instant coffee in various sizes from stores in five Australian towns (Bentz & Merunka, 2000). The causal variables used were marketing-mix variables (price per quantity, promotional price cut as a percent of regular price), product characteristics (dummy variables specific to each alternative) and household-specific characteristics (brand and size loyalties). The multinomial logit and ANN approaches were compared. The ANN was partially connected and with shared weights. The shared weights were necessary to keep the coefficients of the consumer utility function equal across alternatives, while the network was only partially connected so that the attributes of different alternatives cannot interact (pp. 185-186). Performance was measured by U^2 for in-sample performance and R^2 for out-of-sample performance. Choice probabilities were weighted over one-week periods into market shares. A weighted (by market share) R^2 over all the alternatives was used. Both models performed very well but the ANN slightly outperformed the multinomial logit model. This indicated that the utility function was slightly nonlinear. The utility function could be extracted from the neural network by taking the output before it entered an output unit. The relationships between the decision variables and utility were plotted and analyzed. Additional explanatory variables were created to account for the nonlinear effects uncovered. One variable was an interaction variable between brand loyalty and price cut. The second variable was a quadratic term in brand loyalty to account for a concave relation between utility and brand loyalty. The third was a dummy variable to account for the threshold effect of a promotion price cut. The logit model was respecified to take into account these nonlinear components. Model performance was only marginally improved, but the improvement was statistically significant.

FORECASTING EXPLANATORY AND OTHER VARIABLES

Construction of the sales response function is just one step in developing models of marketing systems. Meaningful forecasts can only be made on the basis of a firm's plans and expectations regarding competitive reactions or environmental conditions. In doing "what if" simulations, i.e., conditional forecasts, managers can manipulate the values of the sales drivers under their control. The managers, however, need to anticipate what competitors might do in response. One way is to estimate the reaction function for each relevant sales driver of each competitor (Hanssens et al., 2001, pp. 166-173). A reaction function describes the decision rule that each of our competitors uses to change one of its marketing instruments in response to a change in our marketing mix. Recall the umbrella manufacturer. The manufacturer would determine its price and promotion expenditure. It would need estimates of competitors' prices and promotional expenditures, as well as estimates of personal disposable income and rainfall. If competitors react to the umbrella manufacturer's actions, competitive reaction functions must be developed. One could model competitive reactions in the same way one would model market response. For example, there would be separate reaction functions for each competitor with price and promotion expenditures each being separate dependent variables and the umbrella manufacturer's price and promotion expenditures being the explanatory variables. However, if competitors don't react to the umbrella manufacturer's actions, the competitors' decision variables could simply be extrapolated from their past levels.

The manufacturer would also need extrapolative estimates for personal disposable income and rainfall, which are outside of its control. The predictions for these autonomous variables are then used along with estimates of the competitive variables in a market response model to obtain sales forecasts. Such situations, which might involve the extrapolative forecasting of competitive decision variables, are referred to as forecasting exogenous variables.

Consider a second scenario. Sometimes a product line may be so large that building individual planning models for each product is prohibitive. Nevertheless, separate sales forecasts for each item are needed. Perhaps the company will invest in a comprehensive marketing mix model for the four or five leading products, but use extrapolative methods to forecast sales of the remaining 200 or so items. The latter would be an example of forecasting performance variables (Hanssens et al., 2001, Chapter 6).

Thus, there are several situations in model-based planning and forecasting that may make it desirable to analyze a marketing time series strictly as a function of its own past. Although Box-Jenkins procedures may not be more accurate than other extrapolative techniques, e.g., Armstrong (2001, p. 231), these procedures have been commonly used for forecasting single time series needed to support model-based planning and forecasting. Perhaps this is because most market response analyses are done using weekly data rather than data with a higher interval of temporal aggregation. What is intriguing is there are indications that ANNs forecast better than traditional methods, including Box Jenkins, the shorter the time interval of analysis (Remus & O'Connor, 2001, pp. 247-248). For general discussions of extrapolative time-series forecasting using ANNs, see Zhang, Patuwo, and Hu (1998), Remus and O'Connor (2001), and Zhang (2003, in press).

DISCUSSION
Advantages and Limitation of ANNs

A succinct summary of the advantages and limitations of ANNs is provided by Gorr, Nagin and Szczypula (1994, p. 19). ANNs should perform as well as traditional econometric techniques because of their universal approximator functional form; that is, their "capacity to 'mimic' a wide variety of shapes" (Curry, Morgan, & Silver, 2002, p. 951). While being a universal approximator on a given data set does not guarantee good out-of-sample forecasts, the performance of ANNs in forecasting has been shown empirically to generally be better than traditional techniques when the data exhibit nonlinear properties, as is often the case with market response models. Furthermore, ANNs with one or more hidden layers develop an internal representation of the relationship among variables and, thus, have no need of the maintained hypotheses associated with regression analysis, such as normality of disturbances, lack of serious collinearity among the explanatory variables, and so on. ANNs also perform well with missing or incomplete data: situations that create serious problems for regression analysis (Venugopal & Baets, 1994). Gorr et al. (1994) conclude, "ANNs are appropriate for complex phenomena for which we have good measures but a poor understanding of the relationships within these phenomena. Moreover, ANNs are ideally suited for prediction and forecasting...."

On the other hand, the main deficiency of ANNs is said to be with respect to causal modeling and hypothesis testing. We, however, have shown examples of successful causal modeling with ANNs. What is true is the ease of interpretation of results. This strongly favors econometric models over ANNs. The stronger assumptions underlying econometric models permit hypothesis testing, including misspecification tests. Nonetheless, the impact of causal variables can be assessed in ANNs. Both approaches are amenable to out-of-sample validation and forecasting.

Future Research

One key to accurate forecasting in market response models is the ability to accurately forecast uncontrollable explanatory variables, including competitors' actions (Allen & Fildes, 2001, p. 309; Brodie, Danaher, Kumar, & Leeflang, 2001, pp. 605-606.). There has been no work on using ANNs in this context. However, some empirical studies that we have discussed have shown that ANNs can forecast a single time series better than Box Jenkins approaches under certain conditions. These conditions are applicable in market response modeling and so we would expect a payoff from using ANNs.

As has been shown, the typical artificial neural network exhibits three features: massive parallelism, nonlinear response to input, and processing by multiple layers. Kuan and White (1992, p. 3) stress that "Incorporation of a fourth feature, dynamic feedback among units, leads to even greater generality and richness." For example, sales may feed back on the hidden layer with time delay. Purchase may reinforce the predisposition to buy a brand. This suggests that "recurrent" neural networks might usefully be employed (van Wezel & Baets, 1995).

Conclusion

In general, ANNs work well in data-rich environments that characterize many marketing situations. One could begin with traditional explanatory models of market response. At a minimum, ANNs can be used to look for non-linearities in the data missed by traditional econometric methodologies. This suggests that a hybrid approach combining both methodologies could be beneficial.

Econometric methods will give good forecasts when (1) the causal relationship can be estimated accurately, (2) the causal variables change substantially over time, and (3) the change in the causal variables can be forecast accurately (Armstrong 1985, pp. 193-194). The same criteria apply to ANNs. We have seen some evidence that ANNs may forecast better than traditional econometric models.

Our focus has been on market-level response. One can build response models using ANNs at the individual level. This is true especially in the area of direct marketing where companies maintain large databases that are used to establish and maintain a relationship with their customers. The companies want to make specific product offers to targeted individuals. First, clustering can identify customer segments. Here unsupervised ANNs can be used. Unsupervised learning does not involve the use of target data. A special kind of ANN that can be used to detect clusters is the "self-organizing map" (SOM). Second, the segment into which prospective customers would fit can be predicted. Finally, sales to these segments can be predicted. Here supervised ANNs can be used. Supervised learning, as we have seen, involves target values for the network outputs. The distinction between supervised and unsupervised ANNs is much the same as the classification of multivariate methods into dependence techniques and interdependence techniques.

This general approach has been used by a global food giant that sells a broad line of products in an unusually wide range of markets. In conjunction with the steps above, association models were built to find the relationships among collections of products. One purpose of this market basket analysis was to discover and capitalize on opportunities for cross-couponing by placing coupons in or on packages (Edelstein, 1997).

To wrap up, market response begins with decision-making (Hanssens et al., 2001, p. 401). Market forecasts are a by-product of marketing planning. Any combination of forecasting techniques is not one of different views of the sales generation process, but one of different techniques for different parts of the overall modeling task. ANNs (and times series and other methods) have their place in forecasting economic trends, industry sales growth, competitive actions, and so on, and we would expect that any company using market response models would be one to also use complementary techniques, perhaps some of those as combined forecasts. For a particular product or brand or SKU, however, forecasting based on market response means forecasting based on a representative model of sales. Explanatory models presuppose control while extrapolative models merely indicate expectation. This chapter has indicated the promise of ANNs for causal model building in the context of marketing mix models.

REFERENCES

Agrawal, D. & Schorling, C. (1996). Market share forecasting: An empirical comparison of artificial neural networks and multinomial logit model. *Journal of Retailing, 72,* 383-407.

Ainscough, T. L. & Aronson, J. E. (1999). An empirical investigation and comparison of neural networks and regression for scanner data analysis. *Journal of Retailing and Consumer Services, 6,* 205-217.

Allen, P. G. & Fildes, R. (2001). Econometric forecasting. In J. S. Armstrong (Ed.), *Principles of Forecasting* (pp. 303-362). Boston, MA: Kluwer Academic.

Armstrong, J. S. (1985). *Long-Range Planning from the Crystal Ball to the Computer.* New York: John Wiley & Sons.

Armstrong, J. S. (2001). Extrapolation for time-series and cross-sectional data. In J. S. Armstrong (Ed.), *Principles of Forecasting* (pp. 217-243). Boston, MA: Kluwer Academic.

Baets, W. (1998). *Organizational Learning and Knowledge Technologies in a Dynamic Environment.* Boston, MA: Kluwer.

Bell, D. E., Keeney, R. E., & Little, J. D. C. (1975). A market share theorem. *Journal of Marketing Research, 12,* 136-141.

Bentz, Y. & Merunka D. (2000). Neural networks and the multinomial logit for brand choice modelling: A hybrid approach. *Journal of Forecasting, 19,* 177-200.

Bishop, C. M. (1995). *Neural Networks for Pattern Recognition.* Oxford: Clarendon Press.

Blattberg, R. C., Kim, B. D., & Ye, J. (1994). Large-scale databases: The new marketing challenge. In R. C. Blattberg, R. Glazer & J. D. C. Little (Eds.), *The Marketing Information Revolution* (pp. 173-203). Boston, MA: Harvard Business School Press.

Brodie, R. J., Danaher, P., Kumar, V., & Leeflang, P. S. H. (2001). Econometric models for forecasting market share. In J. S. Armstrong (Ed.), *Principles of Forecasting* (pp. 597-611). Boston, MA: Kluwer Academic.

Coates, D., Doherty, N., French, A., & Krikup, M. (1995). Neural networks for store performance forecasting: An empirical comparison with regression. *International Review of Retail, Distribution and Consumer Research, 5*, 415-432.

Curry, B. & Morgan, P. (1997). Neural networks: A need for caution. *Omega, 25*, 123-133.

Curry, B., Morgan, P., & Silver, M. (2002). Neural networks and non-linear statistical methods: An application to the modeling of price-quality relationships. *Computers & Operations Research, 29*, 951-969.

Cybenko, G. (1989). Approximation by superpositions of sigmoid function. *Mathematics of Control, Signals, and Systems, 2*, 303-314.

Edelstein, H. (1997). Predicting consumer behavior. *DB2magazine,* (Spring).

Fok, D. & Franses, P. H. (2001). Forecasting market shares from models for sales. *International Journal of Forecasting, 17*, 121-128.

Fok, D., Franses, P. H., & Paap, R. (2002). Econometric analysis of the market share attraction model. In P. H. Franses & R. Paap (Eds.), *Econometric Models in Marketing* (pp. 223-256). Amsterdam: JAI.

Franses, P. H. & Paap, R. (2001). *Quantitative Models in Marketing Research.* Cambridge: Cambridge University Press.

Funahashi, K. (1989). On the approximate realization of continuous mappings by neural networks. *Neural Networks, 2*, 183-192.

Gaul, W., Decker, R., & Wartenberg, F. (1994). Analyse von panel- und POS-scanner-daten mit neuronalen. *Jahrbuch der Absatz- und Verbrauchsforchung, 40*, 281-306.

Gorr, W. P., Nagin, D., & Szczpula, J. (1994), Comparative study of artificial neural network and statistical models for predicting student grade point averages. *International Journal of Forecasting, 10*, 17-34.

Greene, W. H. (2000). *Econometric Analysis.* Upper Saddle River, NJ: Prentice-Hall.

Grey Tedesco, B. (1993). Neural networks: Artificial intelligence neural networks applied to single source and geodemographic data. In *ESOMAR/ EMAC/AFM Symposium on Information Based Decision Making in Marketing* (pp. 83-93). Amsterdam: ESOMAR.

Gruca, T. S. & Klemz, B. R. (1998). Using neural networks to identify competitive market structures from aggregate market response data. *Omega, 21*, 49-62.

Hanssens, D. M., Parsons, L. J., & Schultz, R. L. (2001). *Market Response Models.* Boston, MA: Kluwer.

Hornik, K., Stinchcombe, M., & White, H. (1989). Multi-layer feedforward networks are universal approximators. *Neural Networks, 2*, 359-366.

Hruschka, H. (1993). Determining market response functions by neural network modeling: A comparison to econometric techniques. *European Journal of Operations Research, 66*, 27-35.

Hruschka, H. (1993). Einsatz künstlicher neural netzwerke zur datenanalyse in marketing. *Marketing ZFP, 4*, 217-225.

Hruschka, H. (2001). An artificial neural net attraction model (ANNAM) to analyze market share effects of marketing instruments. *Schmalenbach Business Review, 53*, 27-40.

Ing, D. & Mitchell, A. A. (1994). Point-of-sale data in consumer goods marketing: Transforming the art of marketing into the science of marketing. In R. C. Blattberg, R. Glazer & J. D. C. Little (Eds.), *The Marketing Information Revolution* (pp. 30-57). Boston, MA: Harvard Business School Press.

Kuan, C. M. & White, H. (1994). Artificial neural networks: An econometric perspective. *Econometric Reviews, 13*, 1-91.

Little, J. D. C. (1994). Modeling market response in large customer panels. In R. C. Blattberg, R. Glazer & J. D. C. Little (Eds.), *The Marketing Information Revolution* (pp. 150-172). Boston, MA: Harvard Business School Press.

McMenamin, J. S. (1967). A primer on neural networks for forecasting. *Journal of Business Forecasting, 16*, 17-22.

Natter, M. & Hruschka, H. (1998). Using artificial neural nets to specify and estimate aggregate reference price models. In J. M. Aurifeille & C. Deissenberg (Eds.), *Bio-Mimetic Approaches in Management Science* (pp. 101-118). Boston, MA: Kluwer Academic.

Orr, G. B. & Muller, K. R. (1998). *Neural Networks: Tricks of the Trade*. Berlin: Springer.

Pandelidaki, S. & Burgess, A. N. (1998). The potential of neural networks evaluated within a taxonomy of marketing applications. In J. M. Aurifeille, & C. Deissenberg (Eds.), *Bio-Mimetic Approaches in Management Science* (pp. 1-12). Boston, MA: Kluwer Academic.

Parsons, L. J. & Schultz, R. L. (1994). Forecasting market response. *International Journal of Forecasting, 10*, 181-189.

Proctor, R. A. (1992). Marketing decision support systems: a role for neural networking. *Marketing Intelligence & Planning, 10*, 21-26.

Remus, W. & O'Connor, M. (2001). Neural networks for time-series forecasting. In J. S. Armstrong (Ed.), *Principles of Forecasting* (pp. 245-258) Boston, MA: Kluwer Academic.

Thall, N. (1992). Neural forecasts: A retail sales booster. *Discount Merchandiser, 32*, 41-42.

van Wezel, M. C. & Baets, W. (1995). Predicting market responses with neural network: The case of fast moving consumer goods. *Marketing Intelligence & Planning, 13*, 23-30.

Venugopal, V. & Baets, W. (1994). Neural networks and statistical techniques in marketing research: A conceptual comparison. *Marketing Intelligence & Planning, 12*, 30-38.

Vroomen, B., Franses, P. H., & van Nierop, E. (in press). Modeling consideration sets and brand choice using artificial neural networks. *European Journal of Operational Research*.

Wartenberg, F. & Decker, R. (1995). Analysis of sales data: A neural network approach. In W. Gaul & D. Pfeifer (Eds.), *From Data to Knowledge* (pp. 326-333). Berlin: Springer.

White, H. (1992a). Connectionist nonparametric regression: Multilayer feedforward networks can learn arbitrary mappings. In H. White (Ed.), *Artificial Neural Networks: Approximations and Learning Theory*, (pp. 160-190). Oxford, UK: Blackwell.

White, H. (1992b). Consequences and detection of misspecified nonlinear regression models. In H. White (Ed.), *Artificial Neural Networks: Approximations and Learning Theory* (pp. 224-258). Oxford, UK: Blackwell.

White, H. & Gallant, A. R. (1992). There exists a neural network that does not make avoidable mistakes. In H. White (Ed.), *Artificial Neural Networks: Approximations and Learning Theory* (pp. 5-11). Oxford, UK: Blackwell.

White, H. & Stinchcombe, M. (1992). Approximating and learning unknown mappings using multilayer feedforward networks with bounded weights. In H. White (Ed.), *Artificial Neural Networks: Approximations and Learning Theory* (pp. 41-54). Oxford, UK: Blackwell.

White, H., Hornik, K. & Stinchcombe, M. (1992). Universal approximation of an unknown mapping and its derivatives. In H. White (Ed.), *Artificial Neural Networks: Approximations and Learning Theory* (pp. 55-77). Oxford, UK: Blackwell.

Wierenga, B. & Kluytmans, J. (1994). Neural nets versus marketing models of time series analysis: A simulation study. In J. Bloemer, J. Lemmink & H. Kasper (Eds.), *Proceedings of the 23rd Annual European Marketing Academy Conference* (pp. 1139-1153). Maastricht.

Wierenga, B. & Kluytmans, J. (1996). *Prediction with Neural Nets in Marketing*. Rotterdam, The Netherlands: Erasmus Universiteit, School of Management.

Zapranis, A. & Refenes, A.P. (1999). *Principles of Neural Model Identification, Selection, and Adequacy: With Applications to Financial Econometrics*. London: Springer.

Zhang, G. P. (2003). Time series forecasting using a hybrid ARIMA and neural network model. *Neurocomputing, 50*, 159-175.

Zhang, G. P. (in press). Business forecasting with artificial neural networks: An overview. In G. P. Zhang (Ed.), *Neural Networks for Business Forecasting* (this volume). Hershey, PA: Idea Group.

Zhang, G. P., Patuwo, B. E., & Hu, M. Y. (1998). Forecasting with artificial neural networks: The state of the art. *International Journal of Forecasting, 14*, 35-62.

Chapter III

Forecasting Stock Returns with Artificial Neural Networks

Suraphan Thawornwong, Thailand Securities Depository, Thailand

David Enke, University of Missouri - Rolla, USA

ABSTRACT

During the last few years there has been growing literature on applications of artificial neural networks to business and financial domains. In fact, a great deal of attention has been placed in the area of stock return forecasting. This is due to the fact that once artificial neural network applications are successful, monetary rewards will be substantial. Many studies have reported promising results in successfully applying various types of artificial neural network architectures for predicting stock returns. This chapter reviews and discusses various neural network research methodologies used in 45 journal articles that attempted to forecast stock returns. Modeling techniques and suggestions from the literature are also compiled and addressed. The results show that artificial neural networks are an emerging and promising computational technology that will continue to be a challenging tool for future research.

INTRODUCTION

Over the past two decades, many important trends have changed the environment of the financial markets. Investors are becoming more dependent on advanced computer algorithms and technologies to benefit from a wider range of investment choices (Elton & Gruber, 1991). One of the techniques that has caused the most excitement in the financial environment is artificial neural networks (ANNs). ANNs are interesting techniques that approximate nonlinear continuous functions on a compact domain to any designed degree of accuracy (Cybenko, 1989). The novelty of ANNs lies in their ability to model nonlinear processes without a priori assumptions about the nature of the generating process (Hagen et al., 1996). This is useful in security investment and other financial areas where much is assumed and little is known about the nature of the processes determining asset prices (Burrell & Folarin, 1997).

In the past, several studies have reviewed the use of ANNs in a wide range of business problems. These studies include Burrell and Folarin (1997), O'Leary (1998), Wong et al. (1997), Vellido et al. (1999), and Zhang et al. (1998). However, each study did not provide an in-depth analysis of a specific number of financial areas. This chapter provides a more in-depth review of ANN applications for forecasting stock returns and makes a result comparison among alternative parametric methods used as benchmarks reported in the academic journals. The review draws from 45 journal articles published from 1996 to 2002 that investigated the use of ANNs for stock return forecasting.[1] The presentation is highlighted on summary tables compiling a variety of datasets, network modeling, modeling benchmarks, and performance measurements adopted in the literature. This review should shed some light on whether the well-documented nonlinearity of the financial markets can be modeled by way of ANNs to provide accurate forecasts of stock return.

BACKGROUND

Stock return forecasting is an important financial topic. This is because once the prediction of returns is successful, monetary rewards will be substantial. However, predicting stock returns is very difficult since it depends on several known and unknown factors, and frequently the data used for prediction is noisy, uncertain, and incomplete. Two techniques typically used during stock price analysis are fundamental analysis and technical analysis. Readers interested in fundamental and technical analysis may refer to Ritchie (1996) and Murphy (1999), respectively. Most studies attempt to capture the relationship between the available data and the stock return using linear assumptions.

Practically, there is no evidence that the relationship between stock returns and the financial and economic variables is perfectly linear. This is because there is significant residual variance of the predicted return from the actual return. Therefore, it is possible that nonlinear models will be more useful in explaining the residual variance and will produce more reliable predictions of stock return (Mills, 1990).

In recent years, the discovery of nonlinearity in the financial markets has been emphasized by various researchers and financial analysts (see Abhyankar et al., 1997). Even though a number of nonlinear statistical techniques have been used to produce better predictions of stock returns or prices, most techniques (model-driven approaches) require that the nonlinear model be specified before the estimation of parameters can be determined. In contrast, ANNs (data-driven approaches) do not require a pre-specification during the modeling process because they independently learn the relationships inherent in the variables. Thus, ANNs are capable of performing nonlinear modeling without a priori knowledge about the relationship between input and output variables. Readers interested in greater detail may refer to Trippi and Turban (1996) for an overview of the application of ANNs used in financial analysis and investment.

ISSUES, PROBLEMS, AND RECOMMENDATIONS

In retrospect, the literature on stock return forecasting falls into two groups. The first group reports that ANNs were not useful and were unable to improve the explanation of the residual variance as compared to traditional linear models (see Faber & Sidorowich, 1988). The second group reports that ANNs provided excellent techniques for enhanced forecasting. In recent years, many studies have come to a conclusion that the relationship between the financial and economic variables and the stock returns is nonlinear, and that ANNs can be accurately used to model problems involving nonlinearities (see Abhyankar et al., 1997). Nevertheless, not many successes were reported in full detail, probably due to commercial intelligence and competitive advantage factors. With this limitation in mind, this study will examine relevant research methods involving stock return forecasting that were reported in published articles. The studies will be examined under the following categories: Data Sets, Input Variables, ANN Methodology, Model Enhancement, and Performance Evaluation.

Data Sets

A list of articles that used ANNs to forecast returns on a single stock market index is presented in Table 1. The S&P 500 and the DJIA were among the most popular stock indices. There are also several studies that tested the robustness of ANNs using multiple stock indices. These studies include Cogger et al. (1997), Darrat and Zhong (2000), Dropsy (1996), Leung et al. (2000), and Motiwalla and Wahab (2000). While stock return forecasting was the main objective, a few researchers incorporated other financial instruments. Poddig and Rehkugler (1996) modeled ANNs on three asset classes (stocks, bonds, and currencies) of three countries — the US, Japan, and Germany. The S&P 500, small stock fund, and T-bonds were used by Desai and Bharati (1998b).

Table 1: Studies Using a Single Stock Market Index

Index	Article
Euronext Paris Stock Exchange (CAC)	Refenes et al. (1997)
German Stock Exchange (DAX)	Hochreiter et al. (1997), Siekmann et al. (2001)
Dow Jones Industrial Average (DJIA)	Brown et al. (1998), Gencay (1996), Gencay et al. (1997), Gencay et al. (1998), Gencay (1998)
Financial Times Stock Exchange 100 Share (FTSE 100)	Brownstone (1996)
Hang Seng Stock Exchange in Hong Kong (HSI)	Lam et al. (2000)
Korea Stock Exchange (KOSPI)	Kim (1998), Kim et al. (2000), Oh et al. (2002)
Madrid Stock Exchange in Spain	Fernandez-Rodriguez et al. (2000)
Morgan Stanley USA Capital Market (MSCI)	Wood et al. (1996)
New York Stock Exchange (NYSE)	Leigh et al. (2002)
Standard and Poor's 500 Stock Exchange (S&P 500)	Austin et al. (1997), Chenoweth et al. (1996a, 1996b), Desai et al. (1998a), Dorsey et al. (1998), Qi (1999), Qi et al. (1999), Tsaih et al. (1998)
Singapore Stock Price	Kim et al. (1998)
Tokyo Stock Exchange Price in Japan (TOPIX)	Kohara et al. (1996, 1997)
Taiwan Stock Exchange Weighted Index (TSEW)	Kuo (1998)
Wilshi 5000 Stock Exchange (Wilshi)	Chandra et al. (1999)
Warsaw Stock Exchange (WSE)	Zemke (1999)

There are a few studies that placed interest in developing ANNs for individual companies. Pantazopoulos et al. (1998) presented an ANN for predicting prices of IBM stock. Saad et al. (1998) applied ANNs for predicting the price changes of ten stocks. Kishikawa and Tokinaga (2000) used the ANNs with one hundred stocks in the electronics, machinery, and trading industries.

The selection of stock portfolios using ANNs was also investigated by several studies. Deboeck and Ultsch (2000) performed stock selection on 7,730 securities. Hung et al. (1996) determined the optimal portfolios from 51 outstanding stocks listed in TSEW. Longo and Long (1997) selected the 50 best and worst stocks from approximately 1,000 to 1,500 US companies available per year. Quah and Srinivasan (1999) used an ANN to select the stocks that outperformed and under-performed the Singapore SES ALL Index by 5%. Steiner and Wittkemper (1997) selected the eight best and worst performing stocks from the 31 heavily traded stocks of the Frankfurt Stock Exchange in Germany.

In the review, most studies (37 articles) based their predictions on the stock market indices. This may be due to the fact that a stock index represents the performance of all stocks listed in a particular market. It provides investors with a general idea of how the market performed as a whole. Consequently, the impacts of unexpected firm-specific events on the return of particular stocks are believed to cancel each other out.

In financial time series, an ANN that outperforms other models can be easily found by experimentation with a single test case. On the other hand, a model that outperforms the ANN could also be found from another experiment. To avoid such disputes in terms of model comparison, more than one test case must be required, or a dataset of the test case should at least be partitioned into several subsets under different time periods. This would reassure researchers that the ANN does not just work for one single dataset. Several researchers, such as Wood and Dasgupta (1996), Qi and Maddala (1999), and Pantazopoulos et al. (1998) did not test the ANN on more than one dataset.

Input Variables

A summary of important input variables reported in the articles is presented in Table 2. Essentially, the input variables can be divided into two categories: fundamental analysis and technical analysis. Beyond the two categories, qualitative variables extracted from newspapers were also selected by Kohara et al. (1996, 1997) and Kuo (1998). In the literature, there is an

Table 2: Summary of Input Variables

Article	Input variables
Austin et al. (1997)	S&P 500 div, stock/bond spread, commercial bank prime rate, discount rate, advance/decline, up/down volume, Arms index, short sales ratio
Brown et al. (1998)	DJIA index, DJIA return, up/down indicator
Brownstone (1996)	FTSE index, exchange rate, interest rate, futures market, etc.
Chandra et al. (1999)	Index values
Chenoweth et al. (1996a)	T-bill, S&P 500 return, T-bond, consumer price, S&P 500 index
Chenoweth et al. (1996b)	T-bill, S&P 500 return, T-bond
Cogger et al. (1997)	Index return, day of week variable, holiday variable
Darrat et al. (2000)	Stock prices
Deboeck et al. (2000)	Earning per share, relative strength, % stocks held by funds, % stocks owned, shares outstanding, market capitalization, debt-to-equity
Desai et al. (1998a, 1998b)	T-bill, default and term spreads, NYSE return, S&P 500 index, yields (S&P 500 div, T-bond, and earning)
Dorsey et al. (1998)	S&P 500 return, S&P 500 index, DJIA index, NYSE volume, DJ 20 Bond, DJUA, standard deviation
Dropsy (1996)	Excess return, government spending ratio, money growth rate, interest rate, trade balance to GDP ratio, inflation rate, currency depreciation
Fernandez et al. (2000)	Index returns
Gencay (1996) and Gencay et al. (1997)	Return signal, buy-sell signal
Gencay et al. (1998)	Return signal, buy-sell signal, volume average rule
Hochreiter et al. (1997)	Industrial production/money supply, business sentiment, foreign order, tendency ratio, interest rate, div rate, DAX index, RSI, MACD
Hung et al. (1996)	Inputs derived from the factor analysis of the arbitrage pricing theory
Kim (1998)	Index values
Kim et al. (1998)	Index value and return, div yield, turnover by volume, P/E ratio
Kim et al. (2000)	Oscillator, momentum, stochastic, disparity, commodity channel index

apparent uncertainty in selecting the input variables that are used to forecast stock returns. In fact, the inputs selected to model the ANNs are often different even when the same test case for prediction was examined (see Table 1). When each study was examined more closely, it was found that different study periods may be partly responsible for this diversity. This observation suggests that the behaviors of the data change as time changes. Another finding was that most studies employed a series of input variables without justification as to why they were chosen, other than that these inputs were effective during modeling

Table 2: Summary of Input Variables (continued)

Article	Reported input variables
Kishikawa et al. (2000)	Fractal dimension, stock trend variance, wavelet coefficient
Kohara et al. (1996, 1997)	Event-knowledge, TOPIX index, DJIA index, exchange rate, CD, crude oil price
Kuo (1998)	Event-knowledge, technical indicators, remaining quota, physical line, financing buying and selling, index volume and value
Lam et al. (2000)	Moving average level and return differences
Leigh et al. (2002)	Price values derived from a bull flag technical analysis pattern
Leung et al. (2000)	Interest rate, index return, consumer price level, industrial production level
Longo et al. (1997)	Myers variable, payout rate, RSI, price differences, market capitalization, various fundamental ratios
Motiwalla et al. (2000)	T-bill, commercial paper rate, default and term spreads (T-bond, T-bill, Baa-bond, and AAA-bond)
Oh et al. (2002)	Index values
Pantazopoulos et al. (1998)	Index values
Poddig et al. (1996)	Return, price, macroeconomic data, other important time series
Qi et al. (1999)	Div yield, T-bill, interest rate, industrial production growth rate, inflation rate, money growth rate
Qi (1999)	Div yield, P/E ratio, T-bill, T-bond, inflation rate, industrial production rate, money growth rate
Quah et al. (1999)	P/E ratio, cashflow yield, market capitalization, earning per share, return on equity, momentum factor
Refenes et al. (1997)	P/E ratio, stock return, interest rate, earning per share, exchange rate
Saad et al. (1998)	Stock price values derived from specific formula
Siekmann et al. (2001)	DJIA index, T-bond, exchange rate, interest rate, Morgan Stanley Capital Index Europe
Steiner et al. (1997)	Fundamental estimates, level estimates, relative stock performance, market portfolio return
Tsaih et al. (1998)	Upward and downward linear regression slopes, market tend, RSI
Wood et al. (1996)	Index moving averages
Zemke (1999)	Index returns

efforts. Motiwalla and Wahab (2000) and Longo and Long (1997) were the only researchers who reported that the selected input variables were from a larger available dataset. Obviously, a systematic approach to determining what inputs are important is necessary.

The selection of input data is an important decision that can greatly affect the model performance. One needs relevant data that will allow the ANNs to extract valuable information hidden in the data. There are hundreds of financial variables available for analysis. However, many of the variables may be irrelevant or redundant to the prediction of stock returns. Leaving out relevant variables or including irrelevant variables in the input data may be detrimental, causing confusion to the ANNs. The added volume of irrelevant or redundant variables can also slow down the network learning process.

To minimize the potential impact of data snooping, all variables provided to ANNs must contain explanatory meaning to the return series of the test case. Recently, there have been many studies in various areas of machine learning on variable relevance analysis for data understanding (Han & Micheline, 2000). The general idea behind variable relevance analysis is to compute some measures that can be used to quantify the relevance of variables from a large dataset. One interesting technique involves the use of an information gain analysis to measure how much information each variable provides towards stock return performance (Thawornwong & Enke, 2003). This technique removes the less information-producing variables and collects the relevant variables containing explanatory information.

To further improve network performance, principal component analysis (PCA) can also be performed on the relevant variables (Thawornwong & Enke, 2002). PCA has proven to be a valuable tool not only for reducing the dimensionality of the relevant variables, but also for smoothing out part of the noise that is contained in the data (Huang & Antonelli, 2001). By using PCA, dimensionality reduction is achieved without throwing away useful information. Thus, the use of PCA helps accelerate network training by eliminating the curse of dimensionality, further improving network performance. The two supporting technologies seem attractive in performing the variable relevance analysis and dimensionality reduction.

ANN Methodology

The ANN methodology will be examined under the following categories: network outputs, data preprocessing, network types, network structures, network generalization, and network training. The summary of key modeling techniques, including data preprocessing, data frequency and size, network type, network layers, transfer functions, network generalization, network validation, and training method are presented in Table 3 (abbreviations in the table are given in the respective categories).

Network Outputs

To forecast stock returns, a price series (P_t) must be transformed into a return series (R_t). Three of the most common transformation techniques used

Table 3: Summary of Modeling Techniques

Article	Data preprocessing	Frequency: size	ANN type	Network layers	Transfer functions	Network generalization	Validation set	Training method
Austin et al. (1997)	N/P	W: ≈610	BPN	8-15-10-1	N/P	N/P	No	Re
Brown et al. (1998)	N/P	D: 25,111	RNN	49-?-1	N/P	N/P	No	Fix
Brownstone (1996)	0~1	D: 1,800	BPN	54-?-1	N/P	N/P	No	Fix
Chandra et al. (1999)	N/P	M: 300	BPN	?-?-?-1 ?-?-1	N/P	N/P	No	Fix
Chenoweth et al. (1996a)	Yes	D: 2,273 M: 232	BPN	6-4-1 8-3-1	Tan-Tan	N/P	No	Mw
Chenoweth et al. (1996b)	Yes	D: ≈3,036	BPN	6-4-1 2-2-1	Tan-Tan	N/P	No	Mw
Cogger et al. (1997)	N/P	D: ≈212	ALN	12-?-1	N/P	Yes	No	Fix
Darrat et al. (2000)	N/P	W: 402 W: 383	BPN	2-?-1	N/P	N/P	No	Fix
Deboeck et al. (2000)	N/P	Q: ≈12	SOM	N/A	N/A	N/P	No	Fix
Desai et al. (1998a)	N/P	M: 384	BPN	11-15-15-1	Sig-Sin-Sig	Yes	No	Mw
Desai et al. (1998b)	N/P	M: 420	BPN	11-26-1	N/P	Yes	No	Mw
Dorsey et al. (1998)	N/P	D: ≈3,026	BPN	19-5-1	?-Lin	Yes	No	Fix
Dropsy (1996)	N/P	M: 240	BPN	9-?-1	?-Sig	Yes	No	Re
Fernandez et al. (2000)	N/P	D: 6,931	BPN	9-4-1	Tan-Sig	N/P	No	Re
Gencay (1996)	N/P	D: 6,409	BPN	{1~4}-10-1	Sig-Sig	N/P	No	Mw

in the literature are price differencing, return continuous compounding, and return periodic compounding. Price differencing (C) is regarded as the profit/loss obtained from trading during the observation period. At the very least, this method can be used to remove a linear trend from the output data. In modeling financial time series, it is important to eliminate the trend so that ANNs can focus on the other important details necessary for an accurate prediction.

Return continuous compounding refers to the use of logarithmic transformation on the relative price change during the observation period. Return

Table 3: Summary of Modeling Techniques (continued)

Article	Data preprocessing	Frequency: size	ANN type	Network layers	Transfer functions	Network generalization	Validation set	Training method
Gencay et al. (1997)	N/P	D: 6,404	BPN	{1~5}-{1~10}-1	Sig-Sig	Yes	No	Mw
Gencay et al. (1998)	N/P	D: 6,409	BPN	{1~6}-{1~10}-1	Sig-Sig	Yes	No	Mw
Gencay (1998)	N/P	D: 6,409	BPN	?-{1~10}-1	Sig-Sig	Yes	No	Mw
Hochreiter et al. (1997)	N/P	Q: 92 M: 328 W: 420	BPN	3-8-1 5-8-1 12-9-1	N/P	Yes	No	Fix
Hung et al. (1996)	N/P	D: ≈767	BPN	{3,4}-5-{3,4}	N/P	N/P	No	Mw
Kim (1998)	N/P	D: 400	TRNN ATNN TNN	?-?-1	N/P	N/P	No	Fix
Kim et al. (1998)	log, z-m, differencing	D: 3,056	RNN BPN APN	5-{5,10,15,20}-1 5-{5,10,15,20}-1 5-N/A	Sig-Sig Sig-Sig N/A	N/P	No	Fix
Kim et al. (2000)	Yes	D: 2,928	BPN	12-?-1	Sig-Sig	Yes	No	Fix
Kishikawa et al. (2000)	Yes	D: 1,000	BPN	9-6-1	N/P	N/P	N/P	N/P
Kohara et al. (1996)	0~1	D: 408	BPN	{5,6}-{5,6}-1	Sig-Sig	Yes	Yes	Fix
Kohara et al. (1997)	0~1	D: 408	BPN RNN	{5,6}-{5,6,20}-1	Sig-Sig	Yes	Yes	Fix
Kuo (1998)	0~1	N/P	BPN	42-60-60-1 14-29-1	N/P	N/P	N/P	N/P
Lam et al. (2000)	differencing	D: ≈1,983	BPN	6-5-1	Tan-Tan	Yes	No	Fix
Leigh et al. (2002)	z-m	D: ≈4,761	BPN	22-8-2	N/P	N/P	No	Fix
Leung et al. (2000)	differencing	M: 348	BPN PNN	5-{6,10}-1 5-N/A	N/P N/A	N/P	Yes	Fix
Longo et al. (1997)	N/P	N/P	N/P	25-N/P	N/P	N/P	N/P	N/P

periodic compounding, on the other hand, defines the transformation as the holding period return of the observation period. Nonetheless, the difference between continuous compounding and periodic compounding is usually small on relatively high frequency data (i.e., daily or weekly observations). Excess

Table 3: Summary of Modeling Techniques (continued)

Article	Data preprocessing	Frequency: size	ANN type	Network layers	Transfer functions	Network generalization	Validation set	Training method
Motiwalla et al. (2000)	Yes	M: 99	BPN	20-9layers-1	9Tans-Sig	N/P	No	Mw
Oh et al. (2002)	N/P	D: 3,069	BPN	N/P	N/P	N/P	No	Fix
Pantazopoulos et al. (1998)	log	D: N/P	RNN	13-?-?-1	N/P	N/P	N/P	N/P
Poddig et al. (1996)	N/P	M: 143	GRNN BPN RNN	N/P	N/P	Yes	Yes	Fix
Qi et al. (1999)	N/P	M: 468	BPN	6-?-1	N/P	N/P	No	Fix
Qi (1999)	N/P	M: 468	BPN	9-8-1	Sig-Sig	Yes	No	Re
Quah et al. (1999)	N/P	Q: 16	BPN	7-{4,8,10,12,14}-1	N/P	N/P	No	Fix
Refenes et al. (1997)	Yes	D: 1,000	BPN	6-?-1	Sig-Sig	N/P	No	Mw
Saad et al. (1998)	N/P	D: 175~2,650	TNN RNN PNN	{5~10}-{3~7}-1 1-8-1 29-N/A	Tan-Tan Tan-Tan N/A	Yes	No	Fix
Siekmann et al. (2001)	N/P	N/P	BPN	2-6-N/P-1	N/P	N/P	N/P	N/P
Steiner et al. (1997)	N/P	D: ≈667	PNN GRNN	6-N/A	N/A	N/P	No	Fix
Tsaih et al. (1998)	-1~1	D: ≈2,520	RN PN BPN	6-N/A 6-N/P 6-N/P	N/A	N/P	No	Mw
Wood et al. (1996)	Yes	M: 142	BPN	8-3-1	Sig-Sig	Yes	No	Mw
Zemke (1999)	0.2~0.8	D: 1,200	BPN	10-1 10-5-1 10-{5,8,20}-{3,5}-1	Sig Sig-Sig Sig-Sig-Sig	N/P	Yes	Fix

N/P   = *not provided in the article*
N/D   = *not developed in the article*
N/A   = *not available for modeling*
x~y   = *from* x *to* y
»   = *approximate*
?   = *not reported*

stock return (ER) is also one of the outputs used as an alternative to return compounding. It is simply the difference between the stock periodic compounding return and the risk-free rate for the observation period.

From the literature, 16 studies selected the periodic compounding method for their return calculation, while continuous compounding was used as the stock return in 12 studies. Price differencing was chosen as the network output in seven studies. Two studies selected the network output based on special calculations. That is, three trading calls as interpreted by Hamilton were used in Brown et al. (1998), while the combination of risk-free return and stock risk factors derived from the arbitrage pricing theory was selected in Hung et al. (1996). Unfortunately, the specific types of network output were not clarified in eight studies. Six studies also included the dividend as part of their return calculation.

It is well known that most trading strategies adopted by financial analysts rely on accurate predictions of the price levels of financial instruments. Nonetheless, some recent studies have discussed benefits of forecasting the directional price change, as opposed to a strict numerical price level prediction (Aggarwal & Demaskey, 1997; Wu & Zhang 1997). Leung et al. (2000) also found that the classification models based on the direction of stock return outperformed the models based on the level of stock return in terms of both predictability and profitability. These studies demonstrate the usefulness of forecasting the directional change in the price or return level by means of a gain or loss. The results of these findings are reasonable because accurate price estimation, as determined by the residual variance, may not be a good predictor for the directional price change of financial instruments.

Data Preprocessing

Data preprocessing includes data cleaning and data transformation. The objective is to remove noise, resolve inconsistencies, and accentuate important relationships in the input variables. This is necessary since the raw data in the financial environment are noisy, missing, and incomplete, which prevent ANNs from focusing on the important information. A normalization technique where input variables are scaled so as to fall within a specified range (e.g., between 0 and 1 or -1 and 1) is particularly useful for modeling the ANNs. It minimizes the effect of magnitude among the inputs and thus facilitates the ANNs in learning the relevant relationships.

First differencing (absolute and percentage) and taking the natural log of the variables are also common. In addition, the values of variables can be normalized based on the mean and standard deviation. This process is called a zero-mean normalization (z-m). There are also several other methods developed in the literature. For instance, Chenoweth and Obradovic (1996a, 1996b) developed a data filter for separating the training patterns. Siekmann et al. (2001) used fuzzy rules to split inputs into increasing, stable, and decreasing trend variables. Kim and Han (2000) used a genetic algorithm to transform continuous input values into discrete ones. Kishikawa and Tokinaga (2000) used a wavelet transform to extract the short-term feature of stock trends.

The size and frequency of the data depend mostly on the data availability and research objective. Technical data is normally easy to access from various sources, while fundamental data is somewhat more difficult to obtain. To forecast a short-term movement of stock returns, daily (D) data is likely to be selected. Researchers focused on a longer-term horizon are likely to use weekly (W) or monthly (M) data as inputs to the ANNs. Studies relying on economic variables would likely be restricted to monthly or quarterly (Q) data. This is due to the lag associated with the publication of economic indicators. According to the review, 26 studies modeled the ANNs using daily data, whereas monthly data was used in 10 studies. In addition, two studies examined the predictability of ANNs on data of different time frequencies, while quarterly and weekly data were each selected by two studies.

Network Types

Consistent with Vellido et al. (1999), the backpropagation neural network (BPN) was designed and developed in 37 out of the 45 studies being considered. Specifically, the BPN was the only type of network architecture selected to forecast stock returns in 32 studies. Beyond modeling the BPN, several researchers expressed interest in exploring other types of ANNs for stock return predictions. The recurrent neural network (RNN) seems to be the next promising candidate. It has the ability to retain short-term memory by recirculation of previous outputs back to the inputs. The RNN was selected by Brown et al. (1998), Kim and Chun (1998), Kohara et al. (1997), Pantazopoulos et al. (1998), Poddig and Rehkugler (1996), and Saad et al. (1998).

Another type of ANN receiving attention is the time-delay neural network (TNN). Unlike the RNN, the TNN exhibits the characteristic of short-term memory as controlled by a finite-duration impulse response filter. The TNN was examined by Saad et al. (1998) and Kim (1998). In addition, two sophisticated types of TNN, including time-delay recurrent neural network (TRNN) and adaptive time-delay neural network (ATNN), were also included in Kim (1998). Other types of ANNs include adaptive logic neural network

(ALN), arrayed probabilistic neural network (APN), generalized regression neural network (GRNN), probabilistic neural network (PNN), perceptron neural network (PN), reasoning neural network (RN), and the self-organizing map neural network (SOM).

Network Structures

The structures of ANNs are mainly based on the number of neurons in each layer and the type of transfer functions. The number of input and output neurons can be easily determined by the number of input and output variables. However, the number of hidden layers and hidden neurons is unrestricted. In the past, ANNs with one hidden layer and with a sufficient number of hidden neurons have been successfully used for financial classification and prediction (Swales & Yoon, 1992). In this review, a majority of studies (29 articles) relied only on a single hidden layer BPN, while a two hidden layer BPN was developed in seven studies. In addition, three studies compared the predictive performance between one and two hidden layer networks. The ANNs developed by Motiwalla and Wahab (2000) contained nine hidden layers.

Transfer functions are used to control the output of neurons. Four of the transfer functions reported in the reviewed articles are the hyperbolic-tangent function (Tan), the log-sigmoid transfer function (Sig), the sine transfer function (Sin), and the linear transfer function (Lin). Designing the architectures and training the networks involves much trial and error (Murphy et al., 1997). There are typically no strict procedures or rules for making these critical choices, although a few recent studies suggest that genetic algorithms can be applied to optimize network configurations (Gupta & Sexton, 1999; Ignizio & Soltys, 1996). Yoon et al. (1993) found that the optimal learning rate and the number of epochs required to train the network vary for different applications. Computing time is also proportional to the number of neuron units in the network and the complexity of the transfer functions.

Network Generalization

The danger of over-fitting can occur during network training. A polynomial function approximation having too many free parameters allows ANNs to over-fit the training data. The over-fitting is detrimental because the network will not only capture the relationships inherent in data, but will also learn the existing noise. This over-fitted network, while making better predictions for within-sample data, makes poor predictions for out-of-sample data. Generally, too many neurons in the hidden layers and, therefore, too many connections, produce ANNs that memorize the data and lack the ability to generalize. The only way to avoid over-fitting and improve generalization is to use a network size that is just large enough to provide an adequate fit. The problem is that it is difficult to know beforehand how large the network should be for a specific task.

During the past decade, several valuable approaches for improving network generalization have been suggested. Weight-elimination minimizes the complexity of the network by adjusting the weights according to the resulting gradient of the performance measure (Weigend et al., 1991). Network pruning checks the network at periodic intervals and permanently eliminates certain weights whose absolute values fall below a certain cutoff after the network has been trained (Hassibi et al., 1993). Bayesian regularization involves modifying the performance function that will force the network response to be smoother and less likely to over-fit (MacKay, 1992). Early stopping involves dividing the available data into three subsets: training, validation, and testing (Demuth & Beale, 1998). In this approach, the validation set is used to decide when training should be stopped. Cross-validation randomly partitions data into v equal-sized folds and the network is trained v times (Peterson et al., 1995). In each of the training passes, one fold is omitted from the training data and the resulting model is validated on the cases in the omitted fold.

Network Training

For stock return forecasting, three common techniques are used to split data for training the network: fixed sample, recursive training, and moving window. The fixed sample training technique (Fix) was used in 23 studies. It refers to the specified period of the sample that is constantly used for training the network. This trained network is then used to generate all of the out-of-sample forecasts. Regarding the recursive training technique (Re) that was selected in four studies, all historical available data are employed to make a one-step-ahead forecast. The recursive forecasts of the out-of-sample period are, therefore, made by repeatedly adding the latest available data into the training sample. This process assumes that additional data is required for a more accurate forecast.

For the moving window training technique (Mw) a specified period of sample is also required for training the network. However, only a one-step-ahead forecast is calculated. The sample is then rolled forward by removing the first data of the sample and adding the latest one to the end. Another one-step-ahead forecast is then made. This process is repeated until all the forecasts of the out-of-sample period have been made. Used in 13 studies, this technique assumes that old data is no longer relevant to the current structural change of rapidly evolving market conditions.

Proven to be relatively robust to data noise, ANNs are trained to predict the desired goals given an exact set of training inputs. Thus, the network performance is sensitive to the amount of historical data provided. By giving more training data, the ANN will be forced into generalizations rather than specifics. However, there is one problem with the historical data when dealing with a fundamental change in the market dynamics. As more data is presented, some historical relationships that are no longer relevant to the present market conditions are also given to the ANNs. In this case, the network may not be able to generalize successfully, either because a lower priority is placed on the current conditions, or because of conflicting information present in the data (e.g., two sets of training data having matching inputs but different outputs).

More than a half of the reported literature (23 of 40 studies) used a fixed sample training technique to train the ANNs. These networks, therefore, learned to predict stock returns based on a dynamic set of market forces and constraints that are valid over a finite period of time. However, there are times when those forces and constraints quickly change, such as during a dot.com boom, a dot.com crash, or a credibility crisis that reduces the trust in the accuracy of financial reports. Due to the market dynamics, it would be reasonable to expect that these models would perform poorly after a fundamental change in the market. It is suggested that ANNs be frequently remodeled with input variables that are relevant to the present market conditions to help overcome this problem.

Model Enhancement

This section summarizes new and modified network architectures devoted to improving the predictive abilities of ANNs, as well as hierarchical and hybrid systems developed to tackle limitations of ANNs in forecasting stock returns.

New and Modified Network Architectures

A number of existing network architectures have been modified by several researchers. In particular, many of these attempts have been devoted to improving the learning sequences of the financial time-series and for penalizing the network when prediction errors have been made. This is because structural changes of the stock market and price are so complex that researchers have not been able to identify an appropriate neural network for accurate stock predictions.

Hochreiter and Schmidhuber (1997) presented a new training algorithm called Flat Minimum Search (FMS) for improving the generalization ability of the BPN. The algorithm searched for a flat minimum of the error function. The authors concluded that the FMS outperformed the previously developed algorithms. Kim (1998) presented the time-delay recurrent network (TRNN) for temporal correlation and prediction. It has both adaptive time delays and recurrent connections combined for processing temporal information of input sequences. It was concluded in the article that the TRNN efficiently learned the temporal correlations between current data and past events by using dynamic time delays and recurrences. Kim and Chun (1998) developed the arrayed probabilistic network (APN). The APN involves an architecture comprised of an array of elementary PNNs with bipolar output. The authors concluded that the APN exhibited the best overall classification performance.

Refenes et al. (1997) proposed a simple modification to the backpropagation procedure for dealing with changing input-output relations. The procedure was based on the principle of Discounted Least Squares whereby learning was biased towards more recent observations. The results were promising for financial environments where it was believed that structural relationships tend to change gradually over time. Saad et al. (1998) integrated a penalty factor punishing the network for false predictions more than for missed profit opportunities. This strategy was tested on three networks including the PNN, TNN, and RNN. The authors concluded that the penalty factor worked effectively for investors seeking conservative predictions.

Hierarchical and Hybrid Systems

The integration of ANNs with other technologies or techniques has been investigated in the past years due to various limitations (e.g., selection of optimal network architectures) when modeling with ANNs. This is because the assistance of other techniques, such as rule-based systems, fuzzy logic, genetic algorithms, chaos theory, and wavelets, are believed to help overcome these limitations. Accordingly, several researchers attempted to use these techniques to develop more reliable systems for predicting stock returns.

Chenoweth and Obradovic (1996a) proposed a stock market prediction system consisting of statistical feature selection for identifying the relevance data, a data filtering component for splitting the data, two specialized BPNs (one trained on positive return and the other trained on negative return), and a decision rule base for determining trading actions. Chenoweth and Obradovic (1996b) combined the average direction index (ADX) and moving average convergence/divergence (MACD) indicators into the previous system. A third BPN (called combiner BPN) was also developed to further take predictions from each specialized BPN. A genetic algorithm was used in Dorsey and Sexton (1998) for searching and eliminating unnecessary connections and irrelevant variables of the BPN. Kim and Han (2000) used the genetic algorithm to determine connection weights of the BPN and transform continuous input values into discrete ones in accordance with certain thresholds.

Oh and Kim (2002) used a chaotic analysis to determine time-lag size in input variables. Leigh et al. (2002) identified bull flag technical analysis image values by using a pattern recognition technique. Tsaih et al. (1998) proposed a hybrid AI system integrating the rule-based technique and the reasoning neural network (RN) previously developed by the authors. Kuo (1998) developed a stock market trading system that uses the modified fuzzy delphi with the help of stock market experts to decide the qualitative effects on the stock market. Pantazopoulos et al. (1998) presented a neurofuzzy approach for predicting the prices of IBM stock. Siekmann et al. (2001) implemented a network structure that contains the adaptable fuzzy parameters in the weights of the connections between the first and second hidden layers.

Performance Evaluation

To quantify the success of ANNs for stock return prediction, a number of alternative models were developed and used as benchmarks in the literature. Key modeling benchmarks adopted in each study are given in Table 4. They include other neural network types, autoregressive integrated moving average (ARIMA), buy-and-hold account (B&H), genetic algorithm (GA), generalized autoregressive conditional heteroskedasticity (GARCH), multiple linear regression (MLR), random walk (RW), and nearest neighbor (NN). The total number of times that each benchmark was selected for modeling comparisons is given in the last row of the table.

Surprisingly, no comparison was made with the RNN developed in Pantazopoulos et al. (1998). Also, Hochreiter and Schmidhuber (1997), Kim and Han (2000), Kohara et al. (1996), Kuo (1998), and Refenes et al. (1997) did not compare their BNN against the other types of benchmark. These researchers did, however, redevelop their network from different modeling techniques. The technique that produces the highest network performance was concluded as the best model in the studies. A comparison among forecasting techniques is a critical process that helps evaluate the success of the model. MLR is a simple statistical technique that can be easily developed for perfor-

Table 4: Summary of Modeling Benchmarks

Article	ANNs	MLR	ARIMA	GA	GARCH	NN	RW	B&H	Others
Austin et al. (1997)								✓	
Brown et al. (1998)								✓	
Brownstone (1996)		✓							
Chandra et al. (1999)								✓	
Chenoweth et al. (1996a)								✓	
Chenoweth et al. (1996b)								✓	✓
Cogger et al. (1997)		✓	✓						
Darrat et al. (2000)			✓		✓		✓		
Deboeck et al. (2000)								✓	
Desai et al. (1998a)		✓							
Desai et al. (1998b)		✓			✓			✓	
Dorsey et al. (1998)		✓							
Dropsy (1996)		✓					✓		
Fernandez et al. (2000)								✓	
Gencay (1996)		✓			✓				
Gencay et al. (1997)					✓	✓	✓		
Gencay et al. (1998)		✓			✓				
Gencay (1998)								✓	
Hung et al. (1996)			✓					✓	

mance comparison. Additional statistical models used for financial time-series should also be used to determine whether an adoption of the ANNs leads to performance improvement. Unfortunately, these models were used by only a few studies (see Table 4).

There are some studies that included other types of modeling techniques developed for comparison. Forecasting and trading based on the MACD indicator were included in Chenoweth and Obradovic (1996b). Kim and Chun

Table 4: Summary of Modeling Benchmarks (continued)

Article	ANNs	MLR	ARIMA	GA	GARCH	NN	RW	B&H	Others
Kim (1998)	✓								
Kim et al. (1998)	✓								✓
Kishikawa et al. (2000)				✓					
Kohara et al. (1997)	✓	✓					✓		
Lam et al. (2000)								✓	
Leigh et al. (2002)								✓	✓
Leung et al. (2000)	✓		✓					✓	✓
Longo et al. (1997)								✓	
Motiwalla et al. (2000)		✓						✓	
Oh et al. (2002)								✓	
Poddig et al. (1996)	✓	✓					✓		
Qi et al. (1999)		✓					✓	✓	
Qi (1999)		✓						✓	
Quah et al. (1999)								✓	
Saad et al. (1998)	✓								✓
Siekmann et al. (2001)		✓					✓	✓	
Steiner et al. (1997)	✓							✓	
Tsaih et al. (1998)	✓							✓	
Wood et al. (1996)		✓	✓						
Zemke (1999)				✓			✓		✓
Total	8	15	5	2	5	2	7	22	6

ANNs = Two ANN types or more were developed for model comparison

(1998) employed a case based reasoning system as one of the benchmarks. Linear discriminant analysis, logit and probit, adaptive exponential smoothing, and vector autoregression were included in Leung et al. (2000). Saad et al. (1998) used a conventional linear classifier for comparisons. A pattern recognition approach was included in Leigh et al. (2002). A naive Bayesian classifier was compared in Zemke (1999).

To accept that the performance of the ANNs is better than those of the other forecasting techniques, evaluation criteria for assessing the prediction accuracy given by various models are required. There were many performance measures used in the literature. A collection of the key performance measures is presented in Table 5. The last column in Table 5 provides the best performing model concluded from the article.[2] Some of the traditional performance measures included in Table 5 are correlation (CORR), mean absolute error (MAE), mean absolute percentage error (MAPE), mean squared error (MSE), mean square prediction error (MSPE), normalized mean squared error (NMSE), normalized root mean squared error (NRMSE), root mean squared error (RMSE), root mean square prediction error (RMSPE), prediction mean (MEAN), and prediction standard deviation (STD).

As observed in 19 studies, the proportion of correctly predicted directions of future stock returns was one of the highlighted performance measures. This is because forecasting performance based on the directional measure (HIT) is believed to match more closely to the profit performance than do traditional criteria (Leitch & Tanner, 1991). There is also evidence in finance literature suggesting that the traditional measures of forecasting performance may not be strongly related to profits from trading (Pesaran & Timmermann, 1995). Superior predicting performance does not always guarantee the profitability of the forecasting models.

There has also been a growing interest in assessing profits from trading guided by the forecasts of ANNs and their benchmarks. The results from trading can help isolate the best model if predictive performances are not statistically different. It was found that 27 studies reported the financial results obtained from the simulated trading. Three profitability results that are often used include trading return (RETURN), standard deviation of the return (STD-R), and Sharpe ratio. Essentially, there were four strategies used to measure trading performances: (1) buy stock index, or buy T-bill, (2) buy stock index, or short stock index, (3) buy stock index, or say out of the market, and (4) select the best/worst performing stocks to form portfolios.

Trading returns obtained from forecasts directed by the ANNs and key benchmarks are presented in Table 6. Note that the last three rows in Table 6 were based on trading profits. A simple arithmetic calculation is used to calculate average annual returns and profits for comparable evaluations among different articles. One interesting observation was that many of the studies ignored the costs of performing the transaction to simplify modeling complexity.

Table 5: Summary of Performance Measures

Article	Model performance measures	Best model
Austin et al. (1997)	RETURN, STD-R, Alpha and Beta[3], Shape and Treynor ratios[4]	BPN
Brown et al. (1998)	RETURN, STD-R	RNN
Brownstone (1996)	MSE, RMSE, PA	BPN
Chandra et al. (1999)	RETURN	B&H
Chenoweth et al. (1996a)	RETURN, RETURN per trade	BPN
Chenoweth et al. (1996b)	RETURN, RETURN per trade	BPN
Cogger et al. (1997)	MSE, Theil[5]	ALN
Darrat et al. (2000)	RMSE, MAE, Theil	BPN
Deboeck et al. (2000)	RETURN	SOM
Desai et al. (1998a)	MSE, CORR, R^2	BPN
Desai et al. (1998b)	RETURN, STD-R, MSE, CORR, MAE, MAPE	BPN
Dorsey et al. (1998)	HIT, MSE, NRMSE, % up correct, % down correct	BPN
Dropsy (1996)	HIT, RMSE, MAE, U statistic[6], DBS[7], PT[8]	LR
Fernandez et al. (2000)	HIT, RETURN, Sharpe ratio, IP[9], PT	BPN
Gencay (1996)	MSPE	BPN
Gencay et al. (1997)	RMSPE	BPN
Gencay et al. (1998)	HIT, MSPE	BPN
Gencay (1998)	HIT, RETURN, Sharpe ratio, IP, HM[10], PT	BPN
Hochreiter et al. (1997)	MSE, correct-incorrect ratio	N/C
Hung et al. (1996)	RETURN, STD-R	BPN
Kim (1998)	NMSE	N/C
Kim et al. (1998)	HIT, CORR, Hypothesis testing (Types I & II)	APN
Kim et al. (2000)	HIT	N/C

In reality, a profitable trade cannot be assured if profits obtained from trading are not large enough to cover the transaction costs (TCs). Under this scenario, it would be more beneficial if investors perform trading only when the profits from doing so exceed the costs.

Table 5: Summary of Performance Measures (continued)

Article	Model performance measures	Best model
Kishikawa et al. (2000)	HIT	GA
Kohara et al. (1996)	Index profit, MAE	N/C
Kohara et al. (1997)	Index profit, MAE, CORR	RNN
Kuo (1998)	Index profit, other financial measures, MSE	N/C
Lam et al. (2000)	RETURN, STD-R, Index profit	BPN
Leigh et al. (2002)	Index profit, HIT (% good buys)	BPN
Leung et al. (2000)	HIT, RETURN	PNN
Longo et al. (1997)	RETURN, STD-R	ANN
Motiwalla et al. (2000)	HIT, RETURN, STD-R, Sharpe ratio, CORR	BPN
Oh et al. (2002)	RMSE, MAE, MAPE, Index profit	BPN
Pantazopoulos et al. (1998)	RETURN	N/C
Poddig et al. (1996)	HIT, RETURN, STD-R, Sharpe ratio, Index profit, MSE, CORR, Theil	RNN
Qi et al. (1999)	HIT, RETURN, STD-R, Sharpe ratio, Index profit, RMSE, MAE, MAPE, CORR, PT	LR
Qi (1999)	HIT, RETURN, STD-R, Sharpe ratio, RMSE, MAE, MAPE, CORR, PT	BPN
Quah et al. (1999)	RETURN, Portfolio-market return ratio	BPN
Refenes et al. (1997)	RMSE	N/C
Saad et al. (1998)	HIT (% good buys)	RNN
Siekmann et al. (2001)	HIT, RETURN, RMSE	BPN
Steiner et al. (1997)	RETURN, STD-R	GRNN
Tsaih et al. (1998)	HIT, RETURN	RN
Wood et al. (1996)	HIT, CORR, RMSE, MEAN, STD	BPN
Zemke (1999)	HIT	NN

N/C = no comparison with other benchmarks

DISCUSSION AND FUTURE TRENDS

When ANNs are properly configured, they offer superb abilities that can be used for predicting stock returns. However, the development of ANNs is still an art rather than a science. ANNs have numerous parameters and

Table 6: Summary of Average Annual Returns (%) from Trading Guided by ANNs and Key Benchmarks

Article	Others	RW	ARIMA	MLR	GARCH	ANN	B&H	TCs
Austin et al. (1997)						26.47	13.35	No
Brown et al. (1998)						7.94	7.07	No
Chandra et al. (1999)						23.80	40.56	No
Chenoweth et al. (1996a)						14.87	10.00	No
Chenoweth et al. (1996b)						14.07	11.05	No
Deboeck et al. (2000)						123.48	49.68	No
Desai et al. (1998b)				11.37	8.52	12.11	9.66	No
Fernandez et al. (2000)						34.67	1.40	No
Gencay (1998)						22.33	-8.17	Yes
Hung et al. (1996)			7.67			12.36	3.36	No
Lam et al. (2000)						24.46	20.93	Yes
Leung et al. (2000)[E]	8.79		6.46			11.02	2.73	No
Longo et al. (1997)						31.80[F]	21.60	Yes
Motiwalla et al. (2000)				9.09		26.28	21.08	Yes
Poddig et al. (1996)		35.04		30.84		43.11		No
Qi et al. (1999)		7.89		16.55		13.84	15.37	Yes
Qi (1999)				12.37		14.23	11.13	Yes
Quah et al. (1999)[E]						62.41	<39.22	No
Siekmann et al. (2001)		22.17		24.68		47.18	37.07	No
Steiner et al. (1997)						27.33[F]	12.88	No
Tsaih et al. (1998)						11.91	8.23	Yes
Kohara et al. (1997)		109		324.50		390.50		No
Leigh et al. (2002)	0.004					0.005	0.003	No
Oh et al. (2002)						18.57	6.77	Yes

[E] = *indicate an excess stock return*
[F] = *based on the HEDGE portfolio*

architectures, and no confirmed theory has been established for specifying the optimal network architecture. This can be observed by a wide variety of research methods reported in the literature. The trial-and-error methodology is usually adopted by most researchers. In addition, network performance is usually not very stable since the training process may depend on the choice of a random start. Network training is also computationally expensive in terms of the time used to figure out the appropriate network structure. The degree of success, therefore, may fluctuate from one training pass to another. It may be for this reason that inconsistencies in the literature still exist.

The functioning of ANNs is also hardly transparent to the developer. This limitation is due to the fact that they function as a black box. The knowledge acquired during network training is encoded within the internal structure of the ANNs. Currently, there is no explicit technique to extract the relationship between input and output variables, causing difficulty in interpreting results from the networks. Before jumping on the bandwagon, it is suggested that practitioners not only understand their strengths and weaknesses, but also make a careful modeling decision for constructing, training, and testing the ANNs based on a particular problem domain.

Driven by the fact that predictability with small forecasting errors does not necessarily imply profitability, there is a need to develop more rigorous trading strategies under realistic investment assumptions. As discussed in Qi and Maddala (1999), whether investors can make a profit, how much profit investors can make, and how much risk investors have to bear depend not only on how accurate the forecasts are, but also on what investment strategy the investors use. The magnitude of the transaction costs and individual taxes incurred also has to be considered for measuring the true investment performances. In reality, profitability may be easily washed out, especially when stock trading is excessive. It is possible that such investment may incur higher costs and may not be as profitable as the buy-and-hold strategy.

Among numerous types of ANNs, BPN has been shown to be the most often used network to model financial and business applications. Nonetheless, we find that interest in exploring other types of ANNs for stock return prediction has increased. Both RNN and TNN may be more appropriate than the BPN for stock return predictions because they have the ability to learn previous behavior of inputs that may influence future behavior. However, more stringent research is required to determine the appropriate type of ANN that is best suited for stock return forecasting. Several advanced techniques and technologies have also been shown to be successful for building hybrid systems. Genetic algorithms can be used to identify network training parameters. Fuzzy logic provides the ability to account for some uncertainty produced by the ANN predictions. A wavelet transform can be used to extract features of time series data. Instead of separately using these methods, their use in conjunction with ANNs could provide a tremendous improvement for stock return predictions.

Ultimately, investors need dynamic forecasting systems that can adapt to changes in market conditions. These systems also need to be able to process qualitative events (e.g., political situations, international situations, and business prospects) that have influence on the stock market. There have been studies in the field of emerging technologies that attempt to build autonomous agents that can not only interact with the environment, but can also adapt their own capabilities in order to survive/thrive in the changing environment (Mueller, 1998). Advances in this technology will help improve our understanding of the dynamic behaviors and underlying mechanisms of the stock markets (Wan et al., 2002). Future research directions might include the integration of ANNs with the aforementioned technologies to create autonomous systems that are adaptive to dynamic fundamental changes in the market environment, as well as in their own predicting and trading strategies. The systems should also continuously explore new strategies via a modeling simulation, which is changing over time to better match the environment, and dynamically update the knowledge on the basis of the results.

CONCLUSION

This chapter has compiled and addressed the current development of ANNs for forecasting stock returns as reported in academic journals. A majority of the studies (33 of 38 articles) concluded that ANNs were the best models when compared against the benchmarks. In addition, most studies that performed trading simulation (22 of 24 articles) reported that trading returns directed by ANNs were higher than those given by the benchmarks. This finding suggests that ANNs can be used not only to generate more accurate forecasts, but also to arrive at higher trading results. However, this does not mean that the simple buy-and-hold strategy and other parametric forecasting models can be totally ignored since they can also be very profitable. As compared to the buy-and-hold account, the profitability obtained from some of the ANN forecasts will likely be less if transaction costs are taken into consideration.

As seen from many successful results, the traditional strong form version of the efficient market hypothesis is doubtful. Nonetheless, when market inefficiencies are clearly discovered, as well as when examples of the successful ANN and the accompanying trading strategies have been developed, investors will have a better understanding of the relationships between available information and future stock returns. Once a method for identifying and taking advantage of these relationships becomes general public knowledge, all investors will attempt to profit by exploiting these inefficiencies. This will result in an elimination of the existing relationships and eventually create a more complex, albeit better understood, market. In the long run, investors acquiring these relationships may not receive an abnormal rate of return as the market becomes more efficient.

It is also observed that most studies were done by researchers in academia. This does not imply that financial companies are not exploring neural network technology in the private sector. One interesting thought is that if one succeeds in developing a technology that can correctly predict future stock returns, he/she is unlikely to seek publication of the research results (Pantazopoulos et al., 1998). On the contrary, if something is published, the technology might not be used to generate profits. In fact, the benefit of this advanced technology may have already been used in some financial companies without record in the academic journals. Commercial advantages and competitive factors may be a publishing barrier of this challenging computational technology. In the end, the review finds that ANNs are an emerging and challenging computational technology that should continue to be a promising tool for future research.

ENDNOTES

[1] The search for relevant articles was done on the following databases: Current Contents, ProQuest, and Compendex.

[2] The best model was concluded in the article. If no decisive conclusion was made, the best model is selected based on the RETURN, HIT, RMSE, or MSE, respectively.

[3] The Alpha and Beta can be calculated by running a regression of the return based on trading guided by the forecasting model against the market return.

[4] The Sharpe ratio uses standard deviation of return to measure risk, while the Treynor ratio uses Beta as its measure of risk.

[5] Theil (Theil decomposition) partitions the MSE into bias (U^M), regression (U^R), and disturbance (U^D) components.

[6] U statistic refers to the ratio of one model's RMSE to another model's RMSE.

[7] DBS (Diebold-Mariano Sign) is a non-parametric test designed to assess the equality of forecasting accuracy between two models.

[8]   PT (Pesaran-Timmermann market timing) is a non-parametric test designed to assess the accuracy of forecasts in terms of directional changes.

[9]   IP (Ideal Profit) measures the returns based on trading against a perfect predictor.

[10]   HM (Henriksson-Morton) refers to the number of forecasts that have a hypergeometric distribution under the null hypothesis of no market timing ability.

REFERENCES

Abhyankar, A., Copeland, L. S., & Wong, W. (1997). Uncovering nonlinear structure in real-time stock-market indexes: The S&P 500, the DAX, the Nikkei 225, and the FTSE-100. *Journal of Business & Economic Statistics*, 15, 1-14.

Aggarwal, R. & Demaskey, A. (1997). Using derivatives in major currencies for cross-hedging currency risks in Asian emerging markets. *Journal of Future Markets*, 17, 781-796.

Austin, M., Looney, C., & Zhuo, J. (1997). Security market timing using neural network models. *New Review of Applied Expert Systems*, 3, 3-14.

Brown, S. J., Goetzmann, W. N., & Kumar, A. (1998). The Dow theory: William Peter Hamilton's track record reconsidered. *Journal of Finance*, 53, 1311-1333.

Brownstone, D. (1996). Using percentage accuracy to measure neural network predictions in stock market movements. *Neurocomputing*, 10, 237-250.

Burrell, P. R. & Folarin, B. O. (1997). The impact of neural networks in finance. *Neural Computing & Applications*, 6, 193-200.

Chandra, N. & Reeb, D. M. (1999). Neural networks in a market efficiency context. *American Business Review*, 17, 39-44.

Chenoweth, T. & Obradovic, Z. (1996a). A multi-component nonlinear prediction system for the S&P 500 Index. *Neurocomputing*, 10, 275-290.

Chenoweth, T. & Obradovic, Z. (1996b). Embedding technical analysis into neural network based trading systems. *Applied Artificial Intelligence*, 10, 523-541.

Cogger, K. O., Koch, P. D., & Lander, D. M. (1997). A neural network approach to forecasting volatile international equity markets. *Advances in Financial Economics*, 3, 117-157.

Cybenko, G. (1989). Approximation by superpositions of a sigmoidal function. *Mathematics of Control, Signals, and Systems*, 2, 303-314.

Darrat, A. F. & Zhong, M. (2000). On testing the random-walk hypothesis: A model-comparison approach. *The Financial Review*, 35, 105-124.

Deboeck, G. J. & Ultsch, A. (2000). Picking stocks with emergent self-organizing value maps. *Neural Network World*, 10, 203-216.

Demuth, H. & Beale, M. (1998). *Neural Network Toolbox: For Use with MATLAB* (5th edition). Natick, MA: The Math Works, Inc.

Desai, V. S. & Bharati, R. (1998a). A comparison of linear regression and neural network methods for predicting excess returns on large stocks. *Annals of Operations Research*, 78, 127-163.

Desai, V. S. & Bharati, R. (1998b). The efficiency of neural networks in predicting returns on stock and bond indices. *Decision Sciences*, 29, 405-425.

Dorsey, R. & Sexton, R. (1998). The use of parsimonious neural networks for forecasting financial time series. *Journal of Computational Intelligence in Finance*, 6, 24-31.

Dropsy, V. (1996). Do macroeconomic factors help in predicting international equity risk premia?: Testing the out-of-sample accuracy of linear and nonlinear forecasts. *Journal of Applied Business Research*, 12, 120-133.

Elton, E. J. & Gruber, M. J. (1991). *Modern Portfolio Theory and Investment Analysis* (4th edition). New York: John Wiley & Sons.

Farber, J. D. & Sidorowich, J. J. (1988). Can new approaches to nonlinear modeling improve economic forecasts? In P. W. Anderson, K. J. Arrow, and D. Pines (Eds.) *The Economy as an Evolving Complex System* (pp. 99-115). Redwood City, CA: Addison-Wesley.

Fernandez-Rodriguez, F., Gonzalez-Martel, C., & Sosvilla-Rivero, S. (2000). On the profitability of technical trading rules based on artificial neural networks: Evidence from the Madrid stock market. *Economic Letters*, 69, 89-94.

Gencay, R. (1996). Nonlinear prediction of security returns with moving average rules. *Journal of Forecasting*, 15, 165-174.

Gencay, R. (1998). Optimization of technical trading strategies and the profitability in securities markets. *Economics Letters*, 59, 249-254.

Gencay, R. & Stengos, T. (1997). Technical trading rules and the size of the risk premium in security returns. *Studies in Nonlinear Dynamics and Econometrics*, 2, 23-34.

Gencay, R. & Stengos, T. (1998). Moving averages rules, volume and the predictability of security returns with feedforward networks. *Journal of Forecasting*, 17, 401-414.

Gupta, J. N. D. & Sexton, R. S. (1999). Comparing backpropagation with a genetic algorithm for neural network training. *Omega-International Journal of Management Science*, 27, 679-684.

Hagen, M. T., Demuth, H. B., & Beale, M. (1996). *Neural Network Design*. Boston, MA: PWS Publishing Company.

Han, J. & Micheline, K. (2000). *Data Mining: Concepts and Techniques*. San Francisco, CA: Morgan Kaufmann.

Hassibi, B., Stork, D. G., & Wolff, G. J. (1993). Optimal brain surgeon and general network pruning. *Proceedings of the IEEE International Joint Conference on Neural Networks* (Volume 1, pp. 293-299).

Hochreiter, S. & Schmidhuber, J. (1997). Flat minima. *Neural Computation*, 9, 1-42.

Huang, H. L. & Antonelli, P. (2001). Application of principal component analysis to high-resolution infrared measurement compression and retrieval. *Journal of Applied Meteorology*, 40, 365-388.

Hung, S., Liang, T., & Liu, V. W. (1996). Integrating arbitrage pricing theory and artificial neural networks to support portfolio management. *Decision Support Systems*, 18, 301-316.

Ignizio, J. P. & Soltys, J. R. (1996). Simultaneous design and training of ontogenic neural network classifiers. *Computers & Operations Research*, 23, 535-546.

Kim, K. J. & Han, I. (2000). Genetic algorithms approach to feature discretization in artificial neural networks for the prediction of stock price index. *Expert Systems with Applications*, 19, 125-132.

Kim, S. H. & Chun, S. H. (1998). Graded forecasting using an array of bipolar predictions: Application of probabilistic neural networks to a stock market index. *International Journal of Forecasting*, 14, 323-337.

Kim, S. S. (1998). Time-delay recurrent neural network for temporal correlations and prediction. *Neurocomputing*, 20, 253-263.

Kishikawa, Y. & Tokinaga, S. (2000). Prediction of stock trends by using the wavelet transform and the multi-stage fuzzy inference system optimized by the GA. *IEICE Transactions on Fundamentals of Electronics Communications & Computer Sciences*, E83-A, 357-366.

Kohara, K., Fukuhara, Y., & Nakamura, Y. (1996). Selective presentation learning for neural network forecasting of stock markets. *Neural Computing & Applications*, 4, 143-148.

Kohara, K., Ishikawa, T., Fukuhara, Y., & Nakamura, Y. (1997). Stock price prediction using prior knowledge and neural networks. *International Journal of Intelligent Systems in Accounting, Finance, and Management*, 6, 11-22.

Kuo, R. J. (1998). A decision support system for the stock market through integration of fuzzy neural networks and fuzzy delphi. *Applied Artificial Intelligence*, 12, 501-520.

Lam, K. & Lam, K. C. (2000). Forecasting for the generation of trading signals in financial markets. *Journal of Forecasting*, 19, 39-52.

Leitch, G. & Tanner, J. E. (1991). Economic forecast evaluation: Profits versus the conventional error measures. *American Economic Review*, 81, 580-590.

Leigh, W., Paz, M., & Purvis, R. (2002). An analysis of a hybrid neural network and pattern recognition technique for predicting short-term increases in the NYSE composite index. *Omega-International Journal of Management Science*, 30, 69-76.

Leung, M. T., Daouk, H., & Chen, A. S. (2000). Forecasting stock indices: A comparison of classification and level estimation models. *International Journal of Forecasting*, 16, 173-190.

Longo, J. M. & Long, M. S. (1997). Using neural networks to differentiate between winner and loser stocks. *Journal of Financial Statement Analysis*, 2, 5-15.

MacKey, D. J. C. (1992). Bayesian interpolation. *Neural Computation*, 4, 415-447.

Mills, T.C. (1990). Nonlinear time series models in economics. *Journal of Economic Surveys*, 5, 215-241.

Motiwalla, L. & Wahab, M. (2000). Predictable variation and profitable trading of US equities: A trading simulation using neural networks. *Computer & Operations Research*, 27, 1111-1129.

Mueller, J. P. (1998). Architectures and applications of intelligent agents: A survey. *Knowledge Engineering Review*, 13, 353-380.

Murphy, C. M., Koehler, G. J., & Fogler, H. R. (1997). Artificial stupidity. *Journal of Portfolio Management*, 23, 24-30.

Murphy, J. J. (1999). *Technical Analysis of the Financial Markets: A Comprehensive Guide to Trading Methods and Applications*. New York: New York Institute of Finance.

O'Leary, D. E. (1998). Using neural networks to predict corporate failure. *International Journal of Intelligent Systems in Accounting, Finance & Management*, 7, 187-197.

Oh, K. J. & Kim, K. (2002). Analyzing stock market tick data using piecewise nonlinear model. *Expert Systems with Application*, 22, 249-255.

Pantazopoulos, K. N., Tsoukalas, L. H., Bourbakis, N. G., Brun, M. J., & Houstis, E. N. (1998). Financial prediction and trading strategies using neurofuzzy approaches. *IEEE Transactions on Systems, Man, and Cybernetics-Part B: Cybernetics*, 28, 520-530.

Pesaran, M. H. & Timmermann, A. (1995). Predictability of stock returns: Robustness and economic significance. *Journal of Finance*, 50, 1201-1227.

Peterson, G. E., St. Clair, D. C., Aylward, S. R., & Bond, W. E. (1995). Using Taguchi's method of experimental design to control errors in layered perceptrons. *IEEE Transactions on Neural Networks*, 6, 949-961.

Poddig, T. & Rehkugler, H. (1996). A world of integrated financial markets using artificial neural networks. *Neurocomputing*, 10, 251-273.

Qi, M. (1999). Nonlinear predictability of stock returns using financial and economic variables. *Journal of Business & Economic Statistics*, 17, 419-429.

Qi, M. & Maddala, G. S. (1999). Economic factors and the stock market: A new perspective. *Journal of Forecasting*, 18, 151-166.

Quah, T. & Srinivasan, B. (1999). Improving returns on stock investment through neural network selection. *Expert Systems with Applications*, 17, 295-301.

Refenes, A. N., Bentz, Y., Bunn, D. W., Burgess, A. N., & Zapranis, A. D. (1997). Financial time series modeling with discounted least squares backpropagation. *Neurocomputing*, 14, 123-138.

Ritchie, J. C. (1996). *Fundamental Analysis: A Back-to-the-Basics Investment Guide to Selecting Quality Stocks*. Chicago, IL: Irwin Professional Pub.

Saad, E. W., Prokhorov, D. V., & Wunsch, D. C. (1998). Comparative study of stock trend prediction using time delay, recurrent and probabilistic neural networks. *IEEE Transactions on Neural Networks*, 9, 1456-1470.

Siekmann, S., Kruse, R., & Gebhardt, J. (2001). Information fusion in the context of stock index prediction. *International Journal of Intelligent Systems*, 16, 1285-1298.

Steiner, M. & Wittkemper, H. (1997). Portfolio optimization with a neural network implementation of the coherent market hypothesis. *European Journal of Operational Research*, 100, 27-40.

Swales, G. S. & Yoon, Y. (1992). Applying artificial neural networks to investment analysis. *Financial Analysts Journal*, 48, 78-80.

Thawornwong, S. & Enke, D. (2002). A computational approach for selecting the performing stocks of the Dow. *Intelligent Engineering Systems through Artificial Neural Networks*, 12, 695-700.

Thawornwong, S. & Enke, D. (2003). The adaptive selection of financial and economic variables for use with artificial neural networks. *Neurocomputing*, in press.

Trippi, R. R. & Turban, E. (1996). *Neural Networks in Finance and Investing*. Chicago, IL: Irwin Professional Publishing.

Tsaih, R., Hsu, Y., & Lai, C. C. (1998). Forecasting S&P 500 stock index futures with a hybrid AI system. *Decision Support Systems*, 23, 161-174.

Vellido, A., Lisboa, P. J. G., & Vaughan, J. (1999). Neural networks in business: A survey of application (1992-1998). *Expert Systems with Applications*, 17, 51-70.

Wan, H. A., Hunter, A., & Dunne, P. (2002). Autonomous agent models of stock markets. *Artificial Intelligence Review*, 17, 87-128.

Weigend, A. S., Rumelhart, D. E., & Huberman, B. A. (1991). Generalization by weight-elimination applied to currency exchange rate prediction. *Proceedings of the IEEE International Joint Conference on Neural Networks* (Vol. 3, pp. 2374 –2379).

Wong, B. K., Bodnovich, T. A., & Selvi, Y. (1997). Neural network applications in business: A review and analysis of the literature. *Decision Support Systems*, 19, 301-320.

Wood, D. & Dasgupta, B. (1996). Classifying trend movements in the MSCI U.S.A. capital market index — A comparison of regression, ARIMA, and neural network methods. *Computers & Operations Research*, 23, 611-622.

Wu, Y. & Zhang, H. (1997). Forward premiums as unbiased predictors of future currency depreciation: A non-parametric analysis. *Journal of International Money and Finance*, 16, 609-623.

Yoon, Y., Swales, G., & Margavio, T. (1993). A comparison of discriminant analysis versus artificial neural networks. *Journal of Operational Research Society*, 44, 51-60.

Zemke, S. (1999). Nonlinear index prediction. *Physica A.*, 269, 177-183.

Zhang, G., Patuwo, B. E., & Hu, M. Y. (1998). Forecasting with artificial neural networks: The state of art. *International Journal of Forecasting*, 14, 35-62.

Chapter IV

Forecasting Emerging Market Indexes with Neural Networks

Steven Walczak, University of Colorado at Denver, USA

ABSTRACT

Forecasting financial time series with neural networks is problematic. Multiple decisions, each of which affects the performance of the neural network forecasting model, must be made, including which data to use and the size and architecture of the neural network system. While most previous research with neural networks has focused on homogenous models, that is, only using data from the single time series to be forecast, the ever more global nature of the world's financial markets necessitates the inclusion of more global knowledge into neural network design. This chapter demonstrates how specific markets are at least partially dependent on other global markets and that inclusion of heterogeneous market information will improve neural network forecasting performance over similar homogeneous models by as much as 12 percent (i.e., moving from a near 51% prediction accuracy for the direction of the market index change to a 63% accuracy of predicting the direction of the market index change).

INTRODUCTION

Neural network models are widely used for evaluating and solving business problems (Li, 1994; Widrow et al., 1994), with applications in accounting (Etheridge & Brooks, 1994; Falas et al., 1994; Walczak et al., 1998), finance (West, 2000; White, 1993; Zahedi, 1996; Zhang & Hu, 1998), and other business domain problems. Additionally, neural networks have demonstrated significantly superior performance over more traditional statistical forecasting models of business problems (Bansal et al., 1993; León, 1994; Piramuthu et al., 1994; Walczak et al., 1998; West, 2000). Although still outperforming random walk and statistical forecasting models, empirical research evidence has indicated that standard neural network forecasting of financial time series values typically does not fare very well, with performance at or below 60% accuracy (Lequarré, 1993, Tahai et al., 1998).

Why have neural network financial time series forecasting models been unable to achieve the 90% and above accuracy levels of neural network business classification models? Several explanations have been offered including: time series are dynamic in nature and thus are less representable by static models, financial time series are essentially a random walk following the weak form efficient market hypothesis and thus would be unpredictable, and current neural network design philosophy does not accurately capture necessary knowledge for modeling time series (Walczak & Cerpa, 1999). While the former arguments may ultimately limit the long term usage of a single neural network model, retraining of the model on more current data should overcome the limitations of a static model (Walczak, 2001).

A commonly employed neural network design heuristic is to use homogeneous input data sets, that is, only use the time series values or other values that may be calculated directly from the time series itself (e.g., lags or trends). Research by Walczak et al. (1998) has demonstrated that heterogeneous data sets that contain not only the time series but other relevant data values are critical for improving a financial time series neural network's forecasting performance (specifically, forecasting the correct direction of change to a financial time series). Additionally, the ever more global economy causes interaction effects among the various economies around the world.

Well established capital markets, such as the New York or London or Tokyo stock exchanges may be better insulated against disruptive signals received from other global markets or they may have an efficient means for incorporating external signals into their respective time series. The growth of telecommunication infrastructure has investors and business planners looking more globally for opportunity and this includes many markets that are considered to be emerging or new. However, emerging capital markets are known to have thin trading and lack of information efficiencies (Leal & Austin, 1996; Urrutia, 1995). Lack of information may cause external signals from stronger economies to have a significant effect on the performance of the emerging market. If a cause and effect relationship exists between external signals or other market related information and the directional movement of the market (as indicated by composite index or other individual stock values), then nonparametric modeling techniques such as neural networks may be able to exploit this information to develop arbitrage opportunities for investors.

The research reported in this chapter will examine the effect of incorporating external global market signals into neural network input vectors for neural network models that forecast the market performance of specific emerging markets. The emerging market performance is measured through the change to a market specific index value that reflects the overall growth in the emerging market. Various neural network models utilizing different levels of global information are constructed to forecast the Singapore, Malaysian, and Mexican stock market indexes. Results indicate that emerging markets appear to behave as efficient markets when only homogeneous information is utilized. However, as global information is introduced, the forecasting performance of the neural network models for each emerging market index improves. Thus, especially with emerging markets, neural network developers must incorporate global economic information into the input vector variable set to achieve optimal performance when forecasting financial time series.

BACKGROUND

Market Inefficiencies

Emerging markets have been an increasingly popular choice for investors (Posner, 1998). What factors produce the opportunity for extraordinary gains? Various researchers have shown that specific emerging markets have thin trading and inadequacy of financial information and claim that these factors may make the markets less efficient (Huang, 1995; Leal & Austin, 1996; Urrutia, 1995; Yadav et al., 1996). While these researchers claim that emerging markets are less efficient than their more established counterparts, the existence of long-term cointegration effects does not appear to exist in the emerging Pacific Rim markets (Kwok, 1995).

Several simple statistical tests are available that may be used to reject an efficient market hypothesis (based on the assumption that an efficient market will follow a random walk) and confirm the potential for trading advantages through the exploitation of any inefficiencies. These tests include a nonparametric runs test (Urrutia, 1995) and the variance ratio test (Lo & MacKinlay, 1988). Nonparametric runs tests are performed by examining the number of times two consecutive periods of trading move in the same direction (have a run) versus the number of times that they do not move in the same direction. A nonparametric runs test on a market following a random walk model will produce the results that approximately 50% of the total observations occur in runs. The variance ratio test compares the variances over different lag periods with a random walk model having variance ratios equal to the ratio of the lags.

Urrutia (1995) uses both the nonparametric runs test and the variance ratio test to reject a random walk model for three South American equity markets and the Mexico equity market. Huang (1995) also uses a variance ratio test, among others, to examine the behavior of nine Asian markets, including Singapore and Malaysia. Using the variance ratio test with homoscedastic error terms, the null hypothesis of a random walk model is rejected only for markets in Korea and Malaysia, with partial rejections (for at least one of the seven holding periods examined) for the markets in Hong Kong and the Philippines. However, Walczak (1999) demonstrates that using both a nonparametric runs test and a variance ratio test on slightly more modern data, an efficient market hypothesis (a market that appears to follow a random walk) cannot be rejected for the Singapore market.

Hence, there appears to be some inconsistent results on whether emerging markets are less than efficient, at least with respect to the homogeneous market index values. Trading advantages achievable from exploiting any inadequacies of financial information may still be available even if the emerging markets are efficient, however the interaction of internal and external indicators may be very complex. Various external factors appear to influence the Pacific Rim emerging stock markets in general and the Singapore and Malaysian markets specifically. The most significant external effect appears to come from anticipated production levels in the US and Japan, with the United States values having the largest impact (Cheung & Ng, 1995; Yoda, 1994). There also appears to be short-term cointegration effects (movement in one market is reflected by movements in another "cointegrated" market) between the different Pacific Rim markets (including Hong Kong, Malaysia and Singapore) (Kwok, 1995; Rowley, 1987). Since no long-term cointegration exists (Kwok, 1995), this implies that the inter-relationships between the various Pacific Rim emerging markets are dynamic and frequently changing. A very strong and persistent link exists between the Singapore and Malaysian stock markets (Rowley, 1987), possibly due to their long history as a joint exchange (George, 1989) and the co-listing of many stocks on both exchanges. Traders in Singapore have confirmed this by indicating that external signals do in fact have a significant impact on Singapore's market performance, but that the impact of various signals changes on a daily basis and it is difficult to predict which external signals will dominate (Walczak, 1999).

Neural Networks For Market Index Forecasting

Neural networks are an ideal tool for modeling complex variable interactions and, thus, may be the most efficient choice for modeling the future values of emerging markets (Smith, 1993). The backpropagation learning algorithm has been shown to be able to model arbitrary associations (White, 1990) and to be a universal approximator (Hornik, 1991; Hornik et al., 1989). While various other neural network learning algorithms exist, the backpropagation algorithm is the most widely used (Fu, 1994; Walczak & Cerpa, 1999; Widrow et al., 1994). Therefore, the backpropagation algorithm is the only neural network training algorithm utilized for the neural network models reported in this chapter in order to enable evaluation of the interaction effects of external signals and to facilitate comparison with other reported research.

Besides selecting the training protocol for the neural network forecasting model, another problem associated with financial time series forecasting in general is how to evaluate the model's predictions. Commonly, researchers evaluate neural network forecasting models through the RMSE (Root Mean Square Error) or MAD (Mean Average Difference). As Walczak (2001) and others (Green & Pearson, 1994; Levich, 1981; Tahai et al., 1998) have noted, even very small errors that are made in the wrong direction of change may cause significant negative returns and these measures are, therefore, misleading at best and often just wrong. Hence, predicting the correct direction of change to an existing market index value is the primary criterion for financial forecasting models and a proper evaluation should analyze the proportion of predictions that correctly indicate the direction of change to the current market value.

NEURAL NETWORK MODEL DESIGN

Input variable selection is a critical factor in maximizing neural network forecasting performance (Pakath & Zaveri, 1995; Smith, 1993; Tahai et al., 1998; Walczak & Cerpa, 1999). Previous research has indicated that multiple time lags facilitate encoding of knowledge regarding the movement patterns of a time series (Cornell & Dietrich, 1978; Levich & Thomas, 1993). Further research (Walczak, 1999, 2001; Walczak et al., 1998) has demonstrated empirically that the use of multiple time lag values in the input vector increases the domain knowledge available to neural networks and consequently produces superior forecasting results. Lags are calculated using the following equation:

$$\text{Lag}_k = x_t - x_{t-k}, \tag{1}$$

where x_t is the closing value for the specified index on day t, such that a one day lag is the difference between the closing index value from yesterday and the day before.

While the Cornell and Dietrich (1978) research provides a comprehensive statistical analysis of time lags for various foreign exchange rates and their correlation to future values, such an analysis has not currently been performed for the emerging market indexes used in the research reported in this chapter. A nominal starting point for any forecasting model is to include the lag that is equivalent in time to the forward forecast, e.g., a neural network model forecasting a one-day future value would need a one day lag (Lag_1) in its input vector, while a neural network model forecasting a one week future value would require either a five-day or a seven-day (depending on the trading days available for the particular time series) lag value in the input vector. Therefore, all of the input vectors evaluated for the Singapore neural networks include the five-day lag and the Malaysian and Mexican neural networks all include a one-day lag in the input vector. A full-factorial design is performed using the homogenous index value with lags up to five days from the corresponding emerging market to select the lags to be used as input to predict the future value of the corresponding index (this equates to 16 different models for each index). Each of the 16 models is trained and tested separately for the homogeneous input and output of the corresponding emerging market index values, which may bias the results slightly in favor of the homogeneous model (since it is possible that a different set of lags would work more optimally for the various combinations of external signals). However, the use of a consistent set of lags for all input variables for a particular market forecasting problem reduces extraneous effects from data latency across the various index values and enables a more straightforward comparison of forecasting performance across the various index models. For all three emerging market index forecasting problems, a one-day, two-day, and five-day (one week) lag produced the best results and, therefore, for each of the presented neural network forecasting models the values of k from equation (1) come from the set $\{1, 2, 5\}$.

As indicated in the previous section, various local market and large global markets will have dynamically changing effects on an emerging market. Market indexes are classified as either local and emerging or global and mature. For the Singapore market, index values from Singapore (DBS50), Malaysia (KLSE), Hong Kong (Hang Seng), Japan (Nikkei), and the US (DJIA) from October 1994 through December 1995 are used to predict the five-day future value of the index. The selection of a five-day forecasting horizon was done at the personal request of Singapore traders. The Malaysia index forecasting problem uses the same data as the Singapore neural network models, but to forecast the one-day future index value. The training set consists of those values in the date range of October 1994 through June 1995, with the validation set consisting of the remaining data, yielding 116 to 125 validation data samples.

The Mexican index forecasting neural network models utilize index values from Mexico (IPC), Brazil (Bovespa), and the US (DJIA) from November 1993 through April of 2002, with the training set containing values from 1993 through December 2000 and the validation set containing 323 values from 2001 through April 2002. Similar to the Malaysian neural network models, the Mexico IPC forecasting neural networks attempt to forecast the one-day future value of the index to enable more aggressive investment trading.

Each market index forecasting neural network model begins with the market's homogenous index lag values. Additional neural network forecasting models are then constructed to incorporate either local or global/mature heterogeneous index values or a combination of both types of external market signals. As new index values are added to the input vector of the neural network forecasting models, the ratio of input to hidden layer nodes is maintained to further reduce extraneous effects.

Both one and two hidden layer architectures are initially implemented for the homogeneous (single index) neural network models. The additional hidden layer enables the neural network to model a more convoluted solution surface (Fu, 1994) and since the complexity of the emerging market index forecasting problem is not known, both types of architecture are tested. Only a single type of architecture is used when comparing the effect of different (increasingly more global) input vectors on the index forecasting problem. The homogeneous basis for determining the architecture will necessarily bias the result towards the use of a homogenous input vector, but saves significant time, as well as reduces the difficulty of comparing different neural network hidden layer architectures.

For the homogeneous input vector of three elements (six elements for the Singapore model as lagged volume information for the indexes is also used in this model only), hidden layers of two, three, four, six, eight, nine, and 12 nodes are used (and also 15 and 18 for the Singapore models). The best hidden node architecture for all three index forecasting problems is a single hidden layer that is identical in size to the input vector as shown in Figure 1. Hence, a three-node single hidden layer is used for the three-node input vectors for both the Malaysian and Mexican index forecasting models. Once the hidden node architecture is determined, the same ratio of hidden nodes to input nodes is maintained for all additional heterogeneous models.

Figure 1: Neural Network Homogeneous Architecture for Forecasting DBS 50 (Singapore), KLSE (Malaysia), and IPC (Mexico) Index Future Values

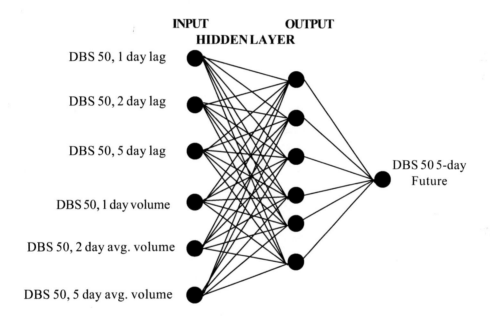

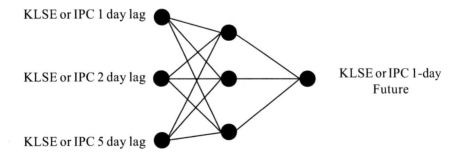

Once the neural network architecture is selected, each neural network index forecasting model presented in the next section is trained for 50,000 iterations over the training data (50,000 randomly selected with replacement samples) and then validated a single time against the validation data. Financial time series forecasting neural networks may be evaluated in many different ways. Evaluating the efficacy of financial time series forecasting neural networks by minimizing the mean standard error may well produce non-optimal neural network forecasting models, since even very small errors that are incorrect in the direction of change will result in a capital loss for an investor following the advice of the neural network model. Instead of measuring the mean standard error of a forecast, Green and Pearson (1994), and others (Levich, 1981; Taylor, 1988; Walczak, 2001) argue that a better method for measuring the performance of neural networks is to analyze the direction of change. Therefore, all of the reported results in the next section will be based on accuracy or percentage of correct predictions with regard to direction of change. Once a neural network forecasting model produces the correct direction of change, it may be argued that minimizing the standard error for degree or size of change would be useful to most investors (for determining the size of an investment), but this is a topic for future research.

RESULTS

First an evaluation for the presence of possible market inefficiencies is performed using both the nonparametric runs test and the variance ratio test for each of the three markets. Recall that an efficient market will have runs approximately 50% of the time and that the variance ratio for a multi-day lag compared to a one-day lag should approximate the size of the lag. Furthermore, the ratio of the variances for the five-day lag and two-day lag should have a value of approximately 2.5. The results for the variance ratio values

Table 1: Variance Ratio and Nonparametric Runs Tests for Singapore, Malaysia, and Mexico

Market/Index	VR 2/1	VR 5/1	Ratio of VR 5/2	Runs Percent
Singapore/DBS50	2.40	6.05	2.52	50.50 %
Malaysia/KLSE Composite	2.41	6.52	2.71	53.58 %
Mexico/IPC	2.24	5.83	2.60	55.59 %

compared to the one-day lag variance and the nonparametric runs test are given in Table 1. The runs test for both the Singapore and Malaysian market indexes is not statistically different from 50% and the variance ratio test for both the Singapore and Mexican stock market indexes is also not statistically significant from an "efficient" market. Based on these tests, it would not appear that any advantage would be gained simply due to the emerging nature of these capital markets.

The statistical results above are further supported by examining the movement of the DBS 50 (Singapore) and IPC (Mexico) index values over the time of the research, as displayed in Figure 2. Values for the Malaysian capital market index, KLSE, are very similar to the DBS 50. Figure 2 provides inferential empirical evidence of random walk appearing behavior in these markets.

The homogeneous neural network models (with a single hidden layer containing the same number of neurodes as the input vector) for all three emerging stock market indexes are displayed in Table 2, which shows that both the Singapore and Mexico homogeneous models support a random walk interpretation of their corresponding market index. Only the Malaysian market appears to have an exploitable inefficiency (meaning any factor that enables a forecasting advantage through nonrandom walk or predictable behavior), but this is at the 0.10 level and still bears further investigation.

The subsequent sections examine each of the three emerging market index forecasting experiments individually. The Singapore experiment presents a comprehensive comparison model. Both the Malaysia and Mexico neural network models abbreviate the experimental approach and examine only a limited number of possible input vectors (which is comprehensive for the Mexico market case due to the limited number of external index values available

Table 2: Homogeneous Neural Network Forecasting Performance for Three Emerging Markets

Market / Index	Forecasting Performance	p-value (significance)
Singapore / DBS 50	50.81%	0.4286
Malaysia / KLSE	56.52%	**0.0778**
Mexico / IPC	53.42%	0.2946

Figure 2: (a) DBS 50 Values, 25/10/94 – 31/12/95, (b) MXSE IPC Values, 4/11/93 – 3/5/02

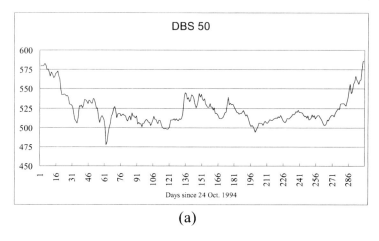

(a)

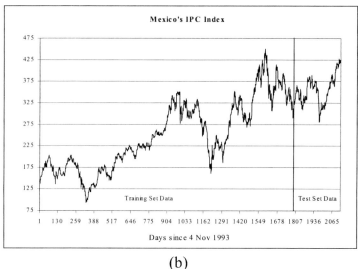

(b)

at the time of the research) in order to clarify the results of the reported research.

Results for Forecasting the Singapore DBS 50 Five-Day Future

A homogeneous neural network forecasting model that uses only the three lagged index values and also the three lagged volume average values is constructed first. The volume average values are calculated using the sigma distance from the population average for each day's trading (Walczak, 1999). As explained above, the hidden node architecture (ratio of hidden units to input units) to be used for all of the subsequent neural network forecasting models is determined from the optimal evaluated architecture for the homogeneous model.

Next, each of the other four Pacific Rim and the US index values and volumes is added individually to the Singapore stock market index and volume input vector. The third stage of the research examined two different intermediate models: one using the Singapore values combined with the KLSE and the Hang Seng (the local emerging markets) and the other using the Singapore values combined with the Nikkei and DJIA (the mature global markets). Three final forecasting models are developed for forecasting the five-day future value of the DBS 50 (Singapore's) index value by using either of the Japan or US global market values or a combination of both with the collection of emerging market values. Results for the 10 described forecasting models are displayed in Table 3.

From Table 3, adding a single external knowledge point appears to have mixed results. The Hang Seng and Nikkei index and volume values improve the DBS 50 forecasting performance over the homogeneous model, but the KLSE

Table 3: Neural Networks to Predict DBS50 (Singapore Index) Five-Day Future

Indexes used as input to the neural network	Prediction Accuracy
DBS 50 (Singapore) only	50.81 %
DBS 50 and KLSE (Malaysia)	45.69 %
DBS 50 and Hang Seng (Hong Kong)	51.72 %
DBS 50 and DJIA (U.S.)	47.97 %
DBS 50 and Nikkei (Japan)	52.59 %
DBS 50, Hang Seng, and KLSE (local only model)	51.72 %
DBS 50, DJIA, and Nikkei (global only model)	54.17 %
DBS 50, Nikkei, Hang Seng, and KLSE	55.17 %
DBS 50, DJIA, Hang Seng, and KLSE	60.50 %
DBS 50, DJIA, Nikkei, Hang Seng, and KLSE	**62.93 %**

and DJIA values actually decrease the neural network model's forecasting performance. The DBS 50 index value forecasting performance continues to improve as the two global index and volume values are combined. However, using the p-value, none of these neural network forecasting results is significantly different from chance (with the DBS 50, DJIA, and Nikkei model having a p-value of 0.1814).

Adding additional global knowledge by combining the KLSE and Hang Seng index and volume values with either the Nikkei or DJIA continues to improve the overall forecasting performance of the DBS 50 index forecasting neural network models, with the DJIA model finally achieving a statistically significant improvement over chance (p-value of 0.0110, significant at the 0.05 level). The final model, which utilizes input values from all five markets, achieves the highest forecasting performance (recall that the performance measures the percentage of neural network forecasts that are in the same direction, up or down, as the actual index for the forecast period).

These results indicate that for the emerging Pacific Rim market in Singapore, addition of external values definitely influences the performance of a neural network forecasting model. While the advantage of utilizing external values is contradictory at the single value level, as additional global information or knowledge is added to the neural network models that forecast the DBS 50 five-day future value, the performance of the corresponding neural network models continues to increase (or remains the same for the case of adding the KLSE to the Hang Seng values in the DBS 50 forecasting model).

Is this result, that increasing the quantity of global capital market information available to a neural network forecasting model generally increases the overall forecasting performance, uniform across all neural network capital market forecasting models or is this effect only realized in emerging capital markets? While much research is still needed to completely answer this question, the next two sections examine the effect of increasing global capital market information for two other emerging markets.

The effect of global information on well established markets, such as London or New York or Tokyo, may be quickly examined by comparing the performance of a homogeneous input value neural network forecasting model to one that utilizes a collection of both established and emerging market index values. The results of these two neural network models (homogeneous and heterogeneous) for forecasting both the DJIA and Nikkei are displayed in Table 4. From Table 4, it can be seen that global information actually detracts from the performance of the neural network DJIA forecasting model and only provides marginal improvement to the neural network Nikkei forecasting

Table 4: Intermarket Neural Networks Predicting DJIA and Nikkei

Neural Network Model:	Prediction Accuracy
DJIA only	56.56%
DJIA + all Pacific Rim (including Nikkei)	52.17%
Nikkei only	41.53%
Nikkei + all Pacific Rim and DJIA	42.98%

model. Hence, well established markets appear to have less of a reaction to global heterogeneous input values. As stated earlier, these markets may be better insulated against minor shocks caused from external markets or may have a better way of dynamically encapsulating the "state of the world" into their own market index value and, thus, do not require any additional information. This may explain why the DJIA neural network forecasting model suffered such a decrease in forecasting performance. If the DJIA does in fact incorporate global knowledge efficiently into its own valuation, then other external values would be highly correlated to the DJIA value itself (the value that the neural network is attempting to forecast) and the presence of correlated values in an input vector may cause sub-optimal performance (Smith, 1993).

Results for Forecasting the Malaysian KLSE One-Day Future

The development of the neural network models to forecast the Malaysian KLSE stock index has several differences. First, the KLSE forecasting neural networks will forecast only a one-day future instead of a five-day future. This is done to enable more aggressive trading and to verify if the global information effect seen in the Singapore DBS 50 forecasting neural network models may be translated to a shorter time frame. Another difference in the experiment design is that only the stock market index values for the KLSE, DBS 50, Hang Seng, Nikkei, and DJIA will be used with no volume information. In general, the KLSE results are similar to the DBS 50 results for all 10 models, so to clarify the presentation only the homogeneous, one of the smaller heterogeneous, and the complete five index models are discussed.

Forecasting results for predicting the direction of change to the KLSE index one day in the future are displayed in Table 5. In contrast to the DBS 50 models discussed in the previous section (and shown in Table 3), the addition

Table 5: Neural Networks to Predict KLSE One-Day Future

Indexes used as input to neural network	Prediction Accuracy
KLSE only	56.52%
KLSE and DBS 50	57.61%
KLSE, DBS 50, DJIA, Nikkei, and Hang Seng	**60.87%**

of the DBS 50 local index values to the KLSE local index values improves the overall performance. This may be due to the fact that Singapore is a more industrialized and global economy compared to the more agrarian culture in Malaysia (George, 1989).

Finally, the full five index neural network model to forecast the KLSE one-day future outperforms all other models (both displayed in Table 5 and those not reported) and is statistically better than chance at the 0.01 level and statistically better than the homogeneous model at the 0.10 level (p-value of 0.05764). Again, the addition of both the local and established global heterogeneous capital market information directly improves the neural network forecasting model's performance for predicting the KLSE composite index.

Results for Forecasting the Mexican IPC One-Day Future

Design of the Mexico IPC index forecasting neural networks is very similar to the design of the Malaysian KLSE composite index forecasting neural network models reported in the previous section. Since the Mexican capital market exists in the Americas, a new collection of local or emerging market indexes is needed to better represent economic, political, and cultural differences from the Pacific Rim. Technical difficulties prevented the researcher from obtaining desired values from the Venezuelan stock market, hence only the Brazilian stock market index, Bovespa, values are used to represent other local influential markets and the DJIA is used to represent global well established markets.

Results for the four different combinations of index values, one homogeneous and three heterogeneous, are displayed in Table 6. Similar to the Singapore neural network forecasting performance, the homogeneous input vector neural network forecasting model for the IPC one-day future value is not significantly different from the performance of a random walk model.

Table 6: Neural Networks to Predict MXSE IPC One-Day Future

Indexes used as input to neural network	Prediction Accuracy
IPC (Mexico) only	53.42%
IPC and Bovespa (Brazil)	60.59%
IPC and DJIA	59.61%
IPC, Bovespa, and DJIA	**63.84%**

At either a local, Brazil Bovespa, or global, DJIA, index value is added to the input vector the forecasting performance of the neural network model improves significantly over the homogeneous model, with both models forecasting at or near 60% accuracy (for direction of change in the index). Finally, the combination of all three index values, which supplies the greatest quantity of global capital market information, further improves the neural network's forecasting performance (with a p-value less than 0.01). The significant and rapid improvement of the Mexican IPC index forecasting neural network with the addition of any relevant external information may serve as an indicator that Mexico's capital market is more closely dependent on the corresponding local (and global) economies than the Pacific Rim examples given earlier.

DISCUSSION AND CONCLUSION

The three emerging markets for Singapore, Malaysia, and Mexico have served to demonstrate that at least with neural network models the inclusion of heterogeneous input values from both local markets and established global markets significantly improves the forecasting performance of the corresponding models. Preliminary evidence has also been provided that demonstrates the independence or at least the insulation of well established markets from external shocks or signals. Therefore, neural network researchers working in emerging capital markets must include heterogeneous market values from both local capital markets and well established (more global) capital markets to achieve optimal forecasting performance.

Two issues affect the viability of utilizing heterogeneous market input vectors to emerging market neural network forecasting models. The first is the question: which local and global market values should be used as input values to the neural network models? Previous research has demonstrated that selection of the appropriate input variables is critical to maximizing neural network performance and selection of unrelated input values may significantly decrease the output performance of the neural network model (Pakath & Zaveri, 1995; Smith, 1993; Tahai et al., 1998; Walczak & Cerpa, 1999). Care must be taken to ensure that the selected market index values come from an external economy that has a definite, although possibly varying as in the case of Singapore (Walczak, 1999), impact on the local economy and consequently the local capital market.

The other factor affecting external market index (or other market values) value inclusion is one of cost. An ongoing cost is associated with the procurement and utilization of input variable data (Bansal et al., 1993). As mentioned in the Mexico IPC Results section, cost and other difficulties prevented this research study from obtaining index values for the Venezuelan capital market, which is thought to have a definite economic impact on the economy of Mexico. Additionally, the cost of any additional heterogeneous variable values must be surpassed by the corresponding benefit derived from utilization of the corresponding input values.

One method for evaluating the contribution of input variables on forecasting performance is to simulate the use of the neural network forecasts to perform capital market investment trades. Using the homogeneous input vector neural network model to predict the DBS 50 future value and assuming a long or short position based upon the forecast movement produces a net gain of 3.84 points per share during the six month test period, which translates into less than a one percent gain in the value of the investment portfolio (assuming only Singapore index shares are held). Similarly, using identical conditions, the full five-index input vector neural network model for forecasting the DBS 50 produces a net gain of 61.32 points per share or a net gain of over 12% in the value of the investment portfolio over the six month test period.

A similar simulation is performed for investments in both the Malaysian KLSE composite index and the Mexican IPC index. Enough capital is assumed to enable trades (buying or selling of shares this time) every day based upon the forecast recommendation of the corresponding neural networks. The KLSE forecasting homogeneous input vector model produces a net gain of 99.09 per share, while the full five index heterogeneous input vector model produces a net gain of 151.19 per share or an advantage over the homogeneous model of over 52%. The Mexican IPC index neural network models perform similarly and their portfolio gains during the trading simulation are displayed in Figure 3. The homogeneous input vector neural network model produces a final gain in the

Figure 3: Net Performance of the Four Different IPC Forecasting Neural Network Models

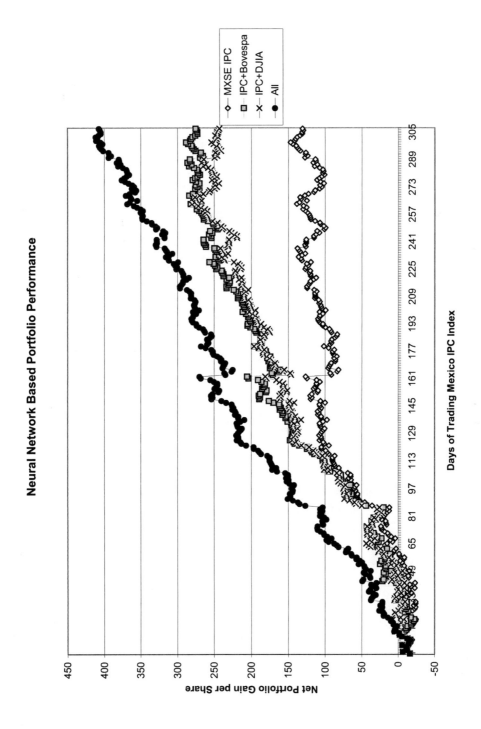

portfolio during the simulation period of 130.96, while the fully heterogeneous three index input vector neural network model produces a 407.14 net gain or a relative advantage of over 210%.

As seen from the trading simulations, the full heterogeneous input vector neural network models provide a distinct advantage over their homogeneous (and also smaller heterogeneous) input vector neural network forecasting model counterparts. Ultimately the cost of the variables must be less than the potential gains made from utilizing the additional global market information, but due to the very large trading advantages afforded by these more global neural networks and the ever-decreasing costs of data within our global information infrastructure, these advantages should not be difficult to realize.

REFERENCES

Bansal, A., Kauffman, R. J., & Weitz, R. R. (1993). Comparing the modeling performance of regression and neural networks as data quality varies: A business value approach. *Journal of Management Information Systems*, 10(1), 11-32.

Cheung, Y. W. & Ng, L. (1995). Equity price variations in Pacific Basin countries. In T. Bos & T.A. Fetherston (Eds.), *Advances in Pacific Basin Financial Markets* (Vol. 1, pp. 211-227). Greenwich, CT: JAI Press.

Cornell, W. B. & Dietrich, J. K. (1978). The efficiency of the market for foreign exchange under floating exchange rates. *The Review of Economics and Statistics*, 60, 111-120.

Etheridge, H. L. & Brooks, R. C. (1994, March). Neural networks: A new technology. *The CPA Journal*, 36-39 and 52-55.

Falas, T., Charitou, A., & Charalambous, C. (1994). The application of artificial neural networks in the prediction of earnings. *Proceedings IEEE International Conference on Neural Networks* (pp. 3629-3633).

Fu, L. (1994). *Neural Networks in Computer Intelligence*. New York: McGraw-Hill.

George, R. L. (1989). *A Guide to Asian Stock Markets*. Quarry Bay, Hong Kong: Longman Financial Services.

Green, H. & Pearson, M. (1994). Neural nets for foreign exchange trading. In G.J. Deboeck (Ed.), *Trading on the Edge* (pp. 123-129). New York: John Wiley & Sons.

Hornik, K. (1991). Approximation Capabilities of Multilayer Feedforward Networks. *Neural Networks*, 4, 251-257.

Hornik, K., Stinchcombe, M., & White, H. (1989). Multilayer feedforward networks are universal approximators. *Neural Networks*, 2(5), 359-366.

Huang, B. N. (1995). Do Asian stock market prices follow random walks? Evidence from the variance ratio test. *Applied Financial Economics*, 5, 251-256.

Kwok, R. H. F. (1995). Market integrations in the four newly industrialized economies of Asia. In T. Bos & T. A. Fetherston (Eds.), *Advances in Pacific Basin Financial Markets* (Vol. 1, pp. 199-209). Greenwich, CT: JAI Press.

Leal, R. & Austin, M. (1996). Time series properties of Asian emerging markets. In T. Bos & T. A. Fetherston (Eds.), *Advances in Pacific Basin Financial Markets* (Vol. 2, pp. 379-394). Greenwich, CT: JAI Press.

León, M. A. (1994). Binary response forecasting: Comparison between neural networks and logistic regression analysis. *World Congress on Neural Networks, San Diego*, 244-247.

Lequarré, J. Y. (1993). Foreign currency dealing: A brief introduction. In N. A. Gershenfeld & A. S. Weigend (Eds.), *Time Series Prediction: Forecasting the Future and Understanding the Past* (pp. 131-137). Reading, MA: Addison-Wesley.

Levich, R. M. (1981, August). How to compare chance with forecasting expertise. *Euromoney*, 61-78.

Levich, R. M. & Thomas, L. R. (1993). The significance of technical trading-rule profits in the foreign exchange market: A bootstrap approach. *Journal of International Money and Finance*, 12, 451-474.

Li, E. Y. (1994). Artificial neural networks and their business applications. *Information and Management*, 27(5), 303-313.

Lo, A. W. & MacKinlay, A. C. (1988). Stock market prices do not follow random walks: Evidence from a simple specification test. *Review of Financial Studies*, 1(1), 41-66.

Pakath, R. & Zaveri, J. S. (1995). Specifying critical inputs in a genetic algorithm-driven decision support system: An automated facility. *Decision Sciences*, 26(6), 749-779.

Piramuthu, S., Shaw, M., & Gentry, J. (1994). A classification approach using multi-layered neural networks. *Decision Support Systems*, 11(5), 509-525.

Posner, M. (1998). *Profiting from Emerging Market Stocks.* Paramus, NJ: Prentice Hall Press.

Rowley, A. (1987). *Asian Stockmarkets: The Inside Story.* Homewood, IL: Dow Jones-Irwin.

Smith, M. (1993). *Neural Networks for Statistical Modeling.* New York: Van Nostrand Reinhold.

Tahai, A., Walczak, S., & Rigsby, J. T. (1998). Improving artificial neural network performance through input variable selection. In P. Siegel, K. Omer, A. deKorvin & A. Zebda (Eds.), *Applications of Fuzzy Sets and The Theory of Evidence to Accounting II* (pp. 277-292). Stamford, CT: JAI Press.

Taylor, S. J. (1988). *Modelling Financial Time Series.* New York: John Wiley & Sons.

Urrutia, J. L. (1995). Tests of random walk and market efficiency for Latin American emerging equity markets. *Journal of Financial Research,* 18(3), 299-309.

Walczak, S. (1999). Gaining competitive advantage for trading in emerging capital markets with neural networks. *Journal of Management Information Systems,* 16(2), 177-192.

Walczak, S. (2001). An empirical analysis of data requirements for financial forecasting with neural networks. *Journal of Management Information Systems,* 17(4), 203-222.

Walczak, S. & Cerpa, N. (1999). Heuristic principles for the design of artificial neural networks. *Information And Software Technology,* 41(2), 109-119.

Walczak, S., Tahai, A., & Khondar, K. (1998). Improved cash flows using neural network models for forecasting foreign exchange rates. In P. Siegel, K. Omer, A. deKorvin & A. Zebda (Eds.), *Applications of Fuzzy Sets and The Theory of Evidence to Accounting II* (pp. 293-310). Stamford, CT: JAI Press.

West, D. (2000). Neural network credit scoring models. *Computers and Operations Research,* 27(11/12), 1131-1152.

White, H. (1990). Connectionist nonparametric regression: Multilayer feedforward networks can learn arbitrary mappings. *Neural Networks,* 3(5), 535-549.

White, H. (1993). Economic prediction using neural networks: The case of IBM daily stock returns. In R. R. Trippi & E. Turban (Eds.), *Neural Networks in Finance and Investing* (pp. 315-328). New York: Irwin.

Widrow, B., Rumelhart, D. E., & Lehr, M. A. (1994). Neural networks: Applications in industry, business and science. *Communications of the ACM, 37*(3), 93-105.

Yadav, P. K., Paudyal, K, & Pope, P. F. (1996). Nonlinear dependence in daily stock index returns: Evidence from Pacific Basin Markets. In T. Bos & T. A. Fetherston (Eds.), *Advances in Pacific Basin Financial Markets* (Vol. 2, pp. 349-377). Greenwich, CT: JAI Press.

Yoda, M. (1994). Predicting the Tokyo stock market. In G. J. Deboeck (Ed.), *Trading on the Edge: Neural, Genetic, and Fuzzy Systems for Chaotic Financial Markets* (pp. 66-79). New York: John Wiley & Sons.

Zahedi, F. (1996). A meta-analysis of financial applications of neural networks. *International Journal of Computational Intelligence and Organizations, 1*(3), 164-178.

Zhang, G. & Hu, M. Y. (1998). Neural network forecasting of the British pound/US dollar exchange rate. *Omega, International Journal of Management Science, 26*(4), 495-506.

Chapter V

Predicting Wastewater BOD Levels with Neural Network Time Series Models

David West, East Carolina University, USA

Scott Dellana, East Carolina University, USA

ABSTRACT

The quality of treated wastewater has always been an important issue, but it becomes even more critical as human populations increase. Unfortunately, current ability to monitor and control effluent quality from a wastewater treatment process is primitive (Wen & Vassiliadis, 1998). Control is difficult because wastewater treatment consists of complex multivariate processes with nonlinear relationships and time varying dynamics. Consequently, there is a critical need for forecasting models that are effective in predicting wastewater effluent quality. Using data from an urban wastewater treatment plant, we tested several linear and nonlinear models, including ARIMA and neural networks. Our results provide evidence that a nonlinear neural network time series model achieves the most accurate forecast of wastewater effluent quality.

INTRODUCTION

It is a common practice today in most nations to discharge treated wastewater into the ecosystem. Because wastewater treatment is a costly process, wastewater is not typically purified to be safe for human consumption. The aquatic environment is often utilized to help in the "cleansing" process. As populations increase, higher quantities of treated wastewater are discharged into the environment which can overload ecosystems, leading to unsafe conditions for humans and animals. This has actually happened in the Narragansett Bay in Rhode Island, US, which has several wastewater treatment facilities discharging along its shores. The bay has been closed to commercial fishing and recreation on many occasions when residents have become ill from food caught in the bay or from exposure to the water. Unfortunately, it is currently very difficult to predict when a body of water will become unsafe. Thus, public health is under a constant threat from potentially unclean waters (Yeung & Yung, 1999).

The present ability to monitor and control the effluent quality from a wastewater treatment process is described by researchers as primitive and notoriously difficult (Wen & Vassiliadis, 1998; Boger, 1997). Wastewater treatment has been characterized as a complex multivariate process with highly variable inputs, nonlinear time varying dynamics, and an autocorrelated time series structure that is subject to large disturbances (Lindberg, 1997). In addition, wastewater measurement systems can be unreliable and require lead times as long as five days to measure biochemical oxygen demand (BOD). The effluent BOD level is an important indication of the quantity of oxygen that will be depleted from the aquatic environment. Recently it has become possible to exercise more effective control of wastewater processes based on (1) the development of advanced forecasting models, (2) more accurate and timely measurement of process variables (Parkinson, 1998), and (3) wireless technology that provides a real time view of the treatment process (Cheek & Wilkes, 1994).

In this research we investigate the accuracy of neural network time series models to forecast wastewater effluent BOD from an urban wastewater treatment plant. We also benchmark the performance of an Autoregressive Integrated Moving Average (ARIMA) model which includes intervention terms. Our results provide evidence that the nonlinear neural network time series model achieves a substantially more accurate forecast of wastewater BOD than does the ARIMA model.

In the next section we review recent applications of time series neural network forecasting models. We then describe design considerations for short term and long term memory components of time series neural network models, the wastewater treatment data, and the experimental methodology followed in this research. The performance of each forecasting model is then evaluated for the prediction of wastewater effluent BOD. We conclude with some insight for practitioners who develop advanced monitoring and control systems for wastewater treatment facilities.

NEURAL NETWORK
TIME SERIES MODELS

Selection of an appropriate forecasting model is generally guided by the principle that parsimonious models are preferred. For example, exponential smoothing is a model that is popular for its simplicity and its ability to generate accurate forecasts (Makridakis & Hibon, 1979). However, more complex models such as neural networks may be justified in forecasting applications where the domain to be modeled is complex in nature (e.g., nonlinear relationships, interactions, and time varying dynamics). In this section we document some recent applications of nonlinear neural network models in complex forecasting domains. The reader is referred to Zhang, Patuwo and Hu (1998) for an extensive review of the application of neural networks to forecasting applications. We will describe a few recent uses of neural networks in complex forecasting environments similar to the wastewater treatment problem.

Coulibaly, Anctil and Bobee (2000) used a feed forward neural network to forecast daily inflow to a Northern Quebec reservoir, a multivariate hydrological time series. Their results suggest that the neural network is effective for improved prediction accuracy of water inflow. The observation that short term electricity demand exhibits nonlinear behavior has motivated several authors to investigate neural network forecasting models (Darbellay & Slama, 2000; Hobbs, Helman, Jitprapaikulsarn, Sreenivas, & Maratukulam, 1998). Jorquera et al. (1998) studied neural networks to predict the maximum ozone levels in Santiago, Chile. In a similar study, Prybutok, Yi and Mitchell (2000) concluded that neural networks provide better forecasts of the maximum ozone concentration in Houston, Texas. The forecast of rainfall amounts is also extremely difficult, involving both temporal and spatial outcomes that are dependent on many variables and complex atmospheric processes. Luk, Ball and Sharma (2001) forecast one time-step rainfall using recurrent and time delay neural networks and found that these models produce reasonable predictions.

There have been several attempts to model wastewater treatment applications with neural networks. Zhu, Zurcher Rao and Meng (1998) used a time delay neural network (TDNN) to predict BOD and several other process measurements in the effluent of a wastewater treatment plant, but they do not report any forecasting performance metrics or comparative analysis. Wen and Vassiliadis (1998) integrated a neural network into a hybrid wastewater treatment model to study the large temporal variations that occur in wastewater composition, concentration, and flow rate. Boger (1997) employed a neural network model to predict ammonia levels in the effluent of a wastewater treatment process. Gontarski, Rodrigues, Mori and Prenem (2000) developed a neural network simulation model for a wastewater treatment plant and concluded that an artificial neural network can be used to establish improved operating conditions.

Since the data for the wastewater treatment process is nonlinear and dynamic (i.e., the statistical properties change over time), a network with a short term memory is required for modeling the temporal patterns in the data. The traditional multilayer perceptron neural network (MLP) can only learn a static mapping of input variables to a forecast value. This is of limited utility for forecasting wastewater BOD since the MLP alone cannot model the temporal or dynamic aspects of the wastewater system where the transport (retention time in system) is not a constant, but changes with flow rate of water and drifting of the process to new operating conditions or states. Two major subcomponents (see Figure 1) are necessary for the development of a neural network time series model, *short term memory*, for representing the time series structure of the data, and *long term memory*, the traditional static mapping from the time series representation to a predicted output value. We discuss aspects of each in the following subsections.

Short Term Memory

The purpose of the short term memory is to capture the time series structure of the data in a low dimensional space that preserves the dynamic properties of the system. Two important properties of short term memory are the memory depth, D, (i.e., how many data values are necessary) and memory resolution (i.e., the precision of the representation of these data values). The selection of the memory depth, D, is an important determinant of the neural network forecasting accuracy. A large value for the memory depth increases the dimensionality of the subsequent MLP neural network and the number of network weights to be optimized during network training. A small memory

Figure 1: Neural Network Time Series Model

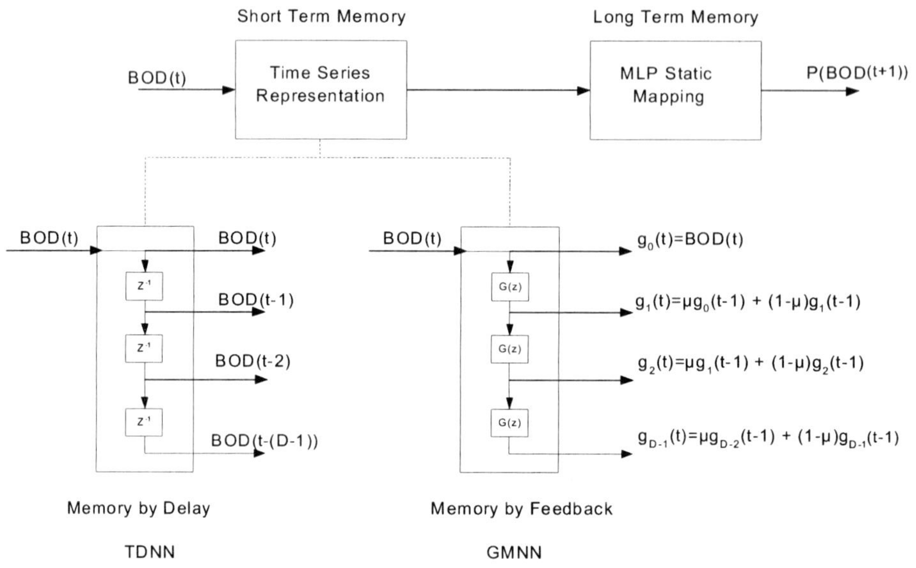

depth risks the loss of critical information necessary to define the system dynamics. Figure 1 includes two alternative strategies for representing the time series structure, *memory by delay* and *memory by feedback*. We will see in the following discussion that *memory by delay* is actually a special case of *memory by feedback*.

The TDNN architecture uses *memory by delay* for the short term memory representation. The input to the TDNN memory by delay structure is the current time series value (in this application BOD(t)); the output is a window of time-lagged input values of fixed size, D (see Figure 1). This output includes the current time series observation at time t and values for the previous D-1 time periods. This set of time delayed observations can be implemented by either partitioning the input data into sequences of length D, or including the delay mechanism in the network input layer. There is no free parameter in the memory by delay structure, so traditional backpropagation cannot be used to adapt the TDNN memory structure to the input data.

The Gamma memory implements a *memory by feedback* which is detailed in Figure 2 (De Vries & Principe, 1992). The advantage of Gamma memory is that the parameter μ can be adapted jointly with the long term memory weights during network training. The adaptation process means that the memory depth and memory resolution will be determined by the data as

Figure 2: Definition of G(Z)

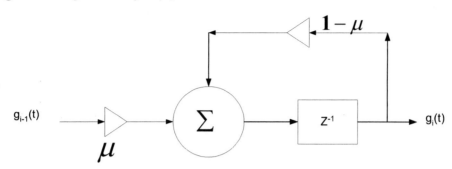

opposed to the more arbitrary decision required for the TDNN memory implementation. Adaptation of the short term memory requires a modification to the traditional backpropagation of error method to account for the fact that the error surface has time gradients. The resulting algorithm is referred to as backpropagation through time (Haykin, 1994).

Figure 3 demonstrates a TDNN with a memory depth $D = 3$. For any given time period, a vertical line projection on Figure 3 identifies the current and two lagged observations that would be input to the long term static mapping component of the time series neural network. The lagged nature of the TDNN memory is evident in Figure 3. The TDNN short term memory maintains perfect resolution of the time series data and a finite memory depth equal to D. It is also clear that any process or measurement noise in the time series will be transmitted to the network's long term memory mapping. In contrast to the TDNN, where the time series is represented by the current and D-1 lagged values, the Gamma memory neural network represents the time series with the current value and D-1 exponentially smoothed averages. Figure 4 shows the corresponding short term memory output for GMNN with $\mu = 0.3$. The first output, $g_0(t)$, is the time series observation at time t. The second and third outputs ($g_1(t)$ and $g_2(t)$, respectively) of the GMNN, are exponentially smoothed values. We notice from Figure 4 that the GMNN creates a smoother output function, with the ability to filter noise present in the time series. This concept is also evident in Figure 5, which contrasts $g_1(t)$ of the GMNN with the corresponding lagged value BOD(t-1) from the TDNN. It is also true that the information contained in the GMNN exponential averaging process has less resolution than the TDNN memory (actual observations are replaced by exponential averages). The GMNN memory depth is determined by the value of the parameter μ. For $\mu = 0$, the memory depth is limited to the current observation; as μ increases, the memory depth increases (the exponential weights go further back into the time series history). When μ = 1, the GMNN reduces to the TDNN, a *memory by delay*. The reader may note that the values plotted in Figures 3 through 5 have not been re-scaled, a process necessary before training the neural network.

Long Term Memory

The outputs of the short term memory are propagated to an MLP hidden layer and output layer to determine a predicted BOD level. The design of the long term MLP structure involves familiar issues in neural modeling that focus primarily on the configuration of the hidden layer. This involves determining the number of hidden layers, the number of neurons for each hidden layer, and the form of the nonlinear transformation (i.e., sigmoid for multilayer perceptron or Gaussian for radial basis function). For this chapter, we will use the popular MLP architecture with a hyperbolic tangent activation function and a single hidden layer. We will examine hidden layers with the number of neurons varying from two to 14 in increments of four. A mean squared error (MSE) criterion is used for the adaptive training of network weights.

Figure 3: TDNN Memory Output

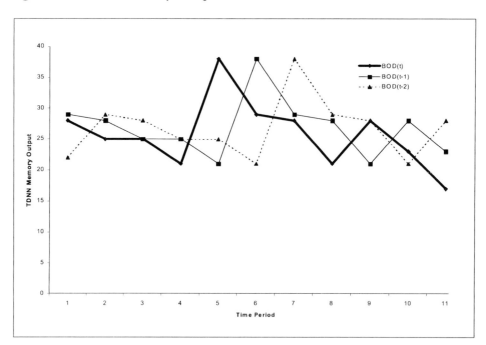

Figure 4: Gamma Memory Output

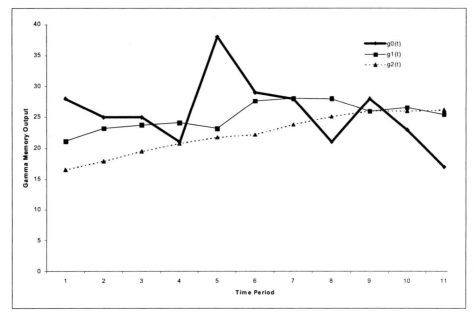

Figure 5: Comparison of Gamma Memory and TDNN Memory Output

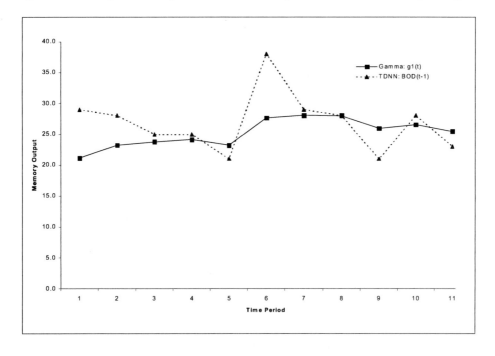

DATA DESCRIPTION AND EXPERIMENTAL METHODOLOGY

The wastewater treatment data used for our study consists of 638 daily measurements of BOD from an urban wastewater treatment plant as reported by Poch, Bejar and Cortes (1993). The BOD values for daily measurements are plotted in Figure 6. It is obvious that this data has a time series structure and periods of significant disturbances to the process.

The following methodology was used to create forecasts and determine forecast errors. The parameters of each forecast model are first estimated from a series of consecutive daily BOD observations. We refer to the series used to estimate model parameters as a data window. The size of the data window selected for this research consists of 150 observations, representing approximately five months of historical data. Two facts motivate this choice. First, many wastewater treatment plants must record BOD effluent levels to meet regulatory requirements and, therefore, a significant amount of data is available. Secondly, both the ARIMA and neural network models require this minimum quantity of data to estimate model parameters effectively. Once the parameters are estimated, the forecast models generate one-step forecasts. These forecasts are predicted values of the BOD level for the daily BOD observation immediately following the data window. This is an independent hold out

Figure 6: Wastewater Treatment Effluent BOD

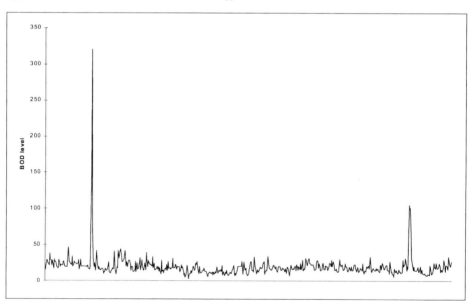

prediction since this BOD value was not used to estimate model parameters. For example, a data window made up of the first 150 observations (one through 150) is used to forecast BOD one day into the future (i.e., day 151). The data window moves iteratively through the data generating 480 cycles of estimation and forecast. We refer to a single estimation-forecast activity as a forecast cycle. The forecast accuracy of each model is measured by the mean absolute percent error (MAPE, equation 1), the mean squared error (MSE, equation 2), and Theil's U statistic (U, equation 3). Makridakis and Hibon (1979) report these metrics to be the most common measures of forecast accuracy.

$$MAPE = \frac{1}{N}\sum_{t=1}^{N}\frac{|y_t - \hat{y}_t|}{y_t}(100) \tag{1}$$

$$MSE = \frac{1}{N}\sum_{t=1}^{N}(y_t - \hat{y}_t)^2 \tag{2}$$

$$U = \frac{\sqrt{\frac{1}{N}\sum_{t=1}^{N}(y_t - \hat{y}_t)^2}}{\sqrt{\frac{1}{N}\sum_{t=1}^{N}(y_t - y_{t-1})^2}} \tag{3}$$

To assess the relative performance of the neural network time series models, we also include benchmark results for several linear forecast models including: a naïve forecast, an exponential smoothing forecast, and an ARIMA with intervention forecast.

BENCHMARK FORECASTS

The BOD effluent data depicted in Figure 6 was analyzed for trend and seasonal patterns. No evidence to support a trend or seasonal pattern was found in this data. Therefore, simple exponential smoothing and ARIMA models (without differencing time series observations) serve as appropriate benchmarks. It is also clear from Figure 6 that outliers exist in the time series data. Any observations with distances greater than ±3 sigma are replaced by interpolated values. The only exception to this outlier policy is the ARIMA intervention model, since this model jointly estimates outliers with the model parameters. All benchmark models were implemented with the SAS® system.

The one step forecast of the wastewater BOD, $\hat{y}_{it+1}$ for the naïve model is simply the most recently measured level, y_{it}. The forecast for the exponential smoothing model is determined by adding a fraction of the forecast error to the most recent forecast (equation 4), where $\hat{y}_{i_{t+1}}$ is the one-step forecast.

$$\hat{y}_{it+1} = \hat{y}_{it} + \alpha(y_{it} - \hat{y}_{it}) \quad i \in (1,2) \tag{4}$$

The coefficient, α, is a smoothing constant with a value between 0 and 1. For each forecast cycle the smoothing constant, α, is optimized to minimize the mean squared error subject to the constraints $0.1 \leq \alpha \leq 0.5$.

Autocorrelation is a fairly common characteristic of wastewater treatment time series data and motivates the inclusion of an ARIMA model in the group of benchmark forecasts. If a variable, Z_t, has a time series structure, an ARIMA (p,d,q) model of the following general form can represent the random variation (Chen & Liu, 1993):

$$\phi(B)\alpha(B)Z_t = \theta(B)a_t \qquad t = 1, 2, \ldots, n \tag{5}$$

where n is the number of observations for the series, B represents the back-shift operator, where $B(Z_t) = Z_{t-1}$. The value of $\phi(B)$ represents the polynomial expression $(1-\phi_1 B - \ldots - \phi_p B^p)$, which models the autoregressive (AR) structure of the time series. The value of $\theta(B)$ represents the polynomial $(1-\theta_1 B - \ldots - \theta_q B^q)$, which models the moving average (MA) structure of the time series. The value of $\alpha(B)$ represents the expression $(1-B)^d_1 (1-B^s)^d_2$, where $d = d_1 + sd_2$. This quantity is a polynomial in B that expresses the degree of differencing required to achieve a stationary series and any seasonal pattern in the time series. Finally, a_t is a white noise series with distribution $N(0, \sigma^2_a)$.

If the historical time series Z_t includes periods where disturbances are present, the ARIMA model may be incorrectly specified (Chang, Tiao, & Chen, 1988). This can be avoided by specifically modeling the disturbances with intervention terms as described by Box and Tiao (1973). The *observed* wastewater effluent variable is now y_{it}, and the ARIMA-I (ARIMA with intervention) model is summarized in equation 6.

$$y_{it} = \frac{\omega(B)}{\delta(B)} I_{it} + \frac{\theta(B)}{\phi(B)} a_{it} \quad i \in (1,2) \tag{6}$$

The first term, $\dfrac{\omega(B)}{\delta(B)} I_{it}$, is the intervention term and identifies periods of time when disturbances are present in the process. Here I_{it} is an indicator variable with a value of zero when the process is undisturbed and a value of one when a disturbance is present in the process. See, for example, Box, Jenkins, and Reinsel (1994), page 462, for details of the intervention term. The rational coefficient term of I_{it} is a ratio of polynomials that defines the nature of the disturbance as detailed in Box et al. (1994), page 464. The second term,

$\dfrac{\theta(B)}{\phi(B)} a_{it}$, is the basic ARIMA model of the undisturbed process from equation 5. See West, Dellana, and Jarrett (2002) for more information on the application of ARIMA intervention models in wastewater treatment.

We conducted a forecasting competition of ARIMA-I models, including AR(1), MA(1), ARMA(1,1) and the Berthouex and Box (1996) model, an MA(1) model of first differences applied to a natural log transformation of the time series data. The ARMA(1,1) model had slightly lower measures of MSE and Bayesian Information Criteria for the BOD series. This ARIMA model form was used in the subsequent development of ARIMA-I models.

The forecast accuracy measures of Theil's U, MSE, and MAPE for these models are given in Table 1. Their results will serve as benchmarks to assess the relative improvement in forecast accuracy of the nonlinear neural network time series models. For the one period forecast of BOD, the exponential smoothing model is slightly more accurate than the ARIMA-I model with a Theil's U of 0.920, compared to 0.940 for the ARIMA-I model. While the ARIMA-I model and exponential smoothing model represent a modest improvement in forecasting ability relative to the naïve model, they are not of sufficient accuracy for effective monitoring and control of a wastewater treatment plant.

NEURAL NETWORK TIME SERIES MODEL RESULTS

Several investigators have speculated about the presence of nonlinear relationships in the autocorrelation functions of wastewater treatment time series data (Lindberg, 1997; Spall & Cristion, 1997). Therefore, it is likely that we will find the neural network time series models are more accurate than the benchmark results reported in the previous section.

The TDNN and GMNN neural networks reported in this section are implemented in software by NeuroSolutions. We start with the more flexible GMNN trained for 300 epochs for each of the 480 forecast cycles. The adapted values obtained for the short term memory weight, μ, were not significantly different from 1.0. The implication of values of μ approaching 1 is that the feedback component in the GMNN is not necessary to define the BOD time series structure and a TDNN is, therefore, appropriate for this application. We speculate that TDNN is reasonable because the data consists of low frequency, daily observations that require high resolution, and because the noise in the form of outliers has already been identified and adjusted.

We, therefore, focus exclusively on the use of the TDNN to predict BOD levels, varying the number of time delays, D, from 2 to 12 in increments of two and the number of hidden neurons from 2 to 14 by increments of four. The three error measures for all TDNN configurations are given in Table 2 and the MSE results are plotted in Figure 7. The MSE performance indicates that lower error levels are achieved with a fairly large number of neurons in the hidden layer. There is a significant reduction in MSE from models with two hidden neurons to models with six hidden neurons. There is also a meaningful MSE reduction as the number of hidden nodes increase from six to 10, and a further modest reduction going from 10 to 14 hidden nodes. It is also evident from Figure 7 that for any of the long term memory structures, there is a gradual increase in error as the number of short term memory delays increases. This is a fairly shallow linear relationship that is independent of the long term memory structure.

Table 1: Forecast Accuracy by Model

Forecast Model	MAPE	MSE	Theil's U
Benchmark Models			
Naïve Forecast	25.3	31.8	1.000
Exp. Smoothing	24.0	25.7	0.920
ARIMA-I	25.7	26.6	0.940
Optimal Neural Network			
TDNN-14N-2T	**17.7**	**9.97**	**0.608**

14N = 14 hidden nodes, 2T = 2 short term memory delays

Figure 7: MSE vs. Number of Delays

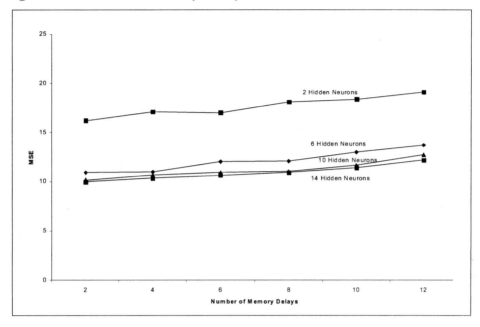

The optimal neural network time series model for forecasting BOD effluent is now identified as a TDNN with $D = 2$ and a hidden layer of 14 neurons. If we examine the one-step BOD forecast, the Theil's U coefficient of the TDNN is 0.608 compared to values of 0.920 and 0.940 for the exponential smoothing and ARIMA-I models (see Table 1 for comparisons of TDNN with benchmark models). The MSE and MAPE for the one step BOD forecasts also demonstrate the superiority of the TDNN forecast. The neural network MSE is just under 10.0 versus 25.7 for exponential smoothing and 26.6 for ARIMA-I. The TDNN's MAPE is 17.7 versus 24.0 for exponential smoothing and 25.7 for ARIMA-I.

These results indicate that the TDNN is significantly more accurate than the traditional benchmark models for predicting wastewater BOD levels. Time series neural network models are shown in this study to have a powerful advantage for forecasting wastewater effluent BOD, a complex application domain with nonlinear relationships and time varying dynamics.

CONCLUDING REMARKS

There is a current need for more effective monitoring and control of wastewater treatment plants; the current level of control has been characterized

Table 2: TDNN Results

Forecast Model	MAPE	MSE	Theil's U
TDNN-2N-2T	22.9	16.2	0.778
TDNN-2N-4T	22.9	17.1	0.790
TDNN-2N-6T	22.7	17.0	0.786
TDNN-2N-8T	23.5	18.1	0.814
TDNN-2N-10T	23.8	18.4	0.826
TDNN-2N-12T	24.7	19.1	0.860
TDNN-6N-2T	18.6	10.9	0.638
TDNN-6N-4T	18.5	11.0	0.639
TDNN-6N-6T	19.3	12.0	0.668
TDNN-6N-8T	19.1	12.1	0.664
TDNN-6N-10T	20.0	13.0	0.696
TDNN-6N-12T	20.6	13.7	0.719
TDNN-10N-2T	17.8	10.2	0.612
TDNN-10N-4T	18.1	10.7	0.623
TDNN-10N-6T	18.5	10.9	0.636
TDNN-10N-8T	18.4	11.0	0.639
TDNN-10N-10T	19.2	11.7	0.663
TDNN-10N-12T	19.8	12.7	0.688
TDNN-14N-2T	**17.7**	**10.0**	**0.608**
TDNN-14N-4T	18.0	10.4	0.618
TDNN-14N-6T	18.2	10.6	0.628
TDNN-14N-8T	18.3	10.9	0.630
TDNN-14N-10T	18.9	11.4	0.642
TDNN-14N-12T	19.0	12.2	0.664

14N = 14 hidden nodes, 2T = 2 short term memory delays

as primitive by Wen and Vassiliadis (1998). An effective forecasting model for predicting BOD levels is a necessary prerequisite for an improved control system. While simple forecasting models such as exponential smoothing are generally preferred in forecasting applications, our results show such methods lack the power to forecast wastewater BOD accurately. Wastewater treatment requires a more sophisticated forecasting approach because it is a complex process with highly variable inputs, nonlinear time varying dynamics, and an autocorrelated time series structure.

A TDNN neural network is developed to model these nonlinear relationships. This neural network time series model achieves significantly more accurate forecasts than the linear models, with a Theil's U coefficient of 0.608. The other forecasting models investigated had U values in the range 0.92-0.94. The forecast accuracy of the neural network, as measured by MSE and MAPE, is also significantly better. We conclude that the nonlinear TDNN neural network model has the accuracy to support the future development of advanced monitoring and control systems for wastewater treatment plants.

While our focus is on one-step forecasts, multi-step forecasts may also be obtained from the neural network time series model. This can be accomplished by incorporating a feedback from the output of the network to the short term memory structure. This feedback would replace the external input BOD(t) shown in Figure 1 during the generation of multi-step forecasts.

Wastewater treatment plant managers may consider implementing a wastewater quality monitoring system with near real-time feedback control and a TDNN neural network forecast model. Quick turn-around BOD measurements can be fed to the neural network software system, providing a process analyst with a forecast of expected BOD values for one or more future periods. With the aid of a forecast monitoring strategy, the data analyst can decide whether or not to take action to adjust the process or to warn relevant officials of the potential for high effluent BOD. The result is a highly responsive system that facilitates more effective management of water quality and its impact on human health.

The reader is cautioned that the results of this research may not generalize to other nonlinear data sets. For example, processes related to the chemical and pharmaceutical industries, as well as industries in the biological sciences (e.g., hospital infection rates), may be characterized as nonlinear. Although these processes share similarities to wastewater treatment, they are sufficiently different to warrant separate investigations. Thus, further research is required to confirm the effectiveness of neural network modeling under a variety of circumstances. However, we believe that some form of neural network modeling will typically out-perform linear statistical models in such cases. The issue is more likely to be one of selecting the best neural network configuration for the nonlinear process under investigation.

REFERENCES

Berthouex, P. M. & Box, G. E. (1996). Time series models for forecasting wastewater treatment plant performance. *Water Resources*, 30(8), 1865-1875.

Boger, Z. (1997). Experience in industrial plant model development using large-scale artificial neural networks. *Information Sciences*, 101, 203-216.

Box, G. E. & Tiao, G. C. (1973). Intervention analysis with applications to economic and environmental problems. *Journal of the American Statistical Association*, 70, 70-79.

Box, G. E. P., Jenkins, G. M., & Reinsel, G. C. (1994). *Time Series Analysis and Forecasting Control*. Englewood Cliffs, NJ: Prentice Hall Press.

Chang, I., Tiao, G.C., & Chen, C. (1988). Joint estimation of model parameters in the presence of outliers. *Technometrics*, 30, 193-204.

Cheek, S. & Wilkes, R. (1994). Monitoring processes using wireless data acquisition. *Water Engineering and Management*, 141(10), 17-18.

Chen, C. & Liu, L. M. (1993). Joint estimation of model parameters and outlier effects in time series. *Journal of the American Statistical Association*, 88(421), 284-297.

Coulibaly, P., Anctil, F., & Bobee, B. (2000). Daily reservoir inflow forecasting using artificial neural networks with stopped training approach. *Journal of Hydrology*, 230, 244-257.

Darbellay, G. A. & Slama, M. (2000). Forecasting the short-term demand for electricity: Do neural networks stand a better chance? *International Journal of Forecasting*, 16(1), 71-83.

De Vries, B. & Principe, J. C. (1992). The gamma model: A new neural network for temporal processing. *Neural Networks*, 5, 565-576.

Gontarski, C. A., Rodrigues, P. R., Mori, M., & Prenem, L. F. (2000). Simulation of an industrial treatment plant using artificial neural networks. *Computers and Chemical Engineering*, 24, 1719-1723.

Haykin, S. (1994). *Neural Network: A Comprehensive Foundation*. Englewood Cliffs, NJ: Macmillan.

Hobbs, B. F., Helman, U., Jitprapaikulsarn, S., Sreenivas K., & Maratukulam, D. (1998). Artificial neural networks for short-term energy forecasting: Accuracy and economic value. *Neurocomputing*, 23(1-3), 71-84.

Jorquera, H., Perez, R., Cipriano, A., Espejo, A., Victoria Letelier, M., & Acuna, G. (1998). Forecasting ozone daily maximum levels at Santiago, Chile. *Atmospheric Environment*, 32(20), 3415-3424.

Lindberg, C. F. (1997). *Control and Estimation Strategies Applied to the Activated Sludge Process.* Ph.D. Thesis, Uppsala University, Finland.

Luk, K. C., Ball, J. E., & Sharma, A. (2001). An application of artificial neural networks for rainfall forecasting. *Mathematical and Computer Modeling*, 33, 683-693.

Makridakis, S. & Hibon, M. (1979). Accuracy of forecasting: An empirical investigation. *Journal of the Royal Statistical Society*, A, 142, 97-145.

Parkinson, G. (1998). BOD measurement in real time. *Chemical Engineering*, 105(11), 25.

Poch, M., Bejar, J., & Cortes, U. (1993). Wastewater treatment data source information. Universitat Autonoma de Barcelona and Universitat Politecnica de Catalunya, Barcelona, Spain.

Prybutok, V. R., Yi, J., & Mitchell, D. (2000). Comparison of neural network models with ARIMA and regression models for prediction of Houston's daily maximum ozone concentrations. *European Journal of Operational Research*, 122(1), 31-40.

Spall, J. C. & Cristion, J. A. (1997). A neural network controller for systems with unmodeled dynamics with applications to wastewater treatment. *IEEE Transactions on Systems, Man, and Cybernetics-Part B Cybernetics*, 37(3), 369-375.

Wen, C. H. & Vassiliadis, C. A. (1998). Applying hybrid artificial intelligence techniques in wastewater treatment. *Engineering Applications of Artificial Intelligence*, 11, 685-705.

West, D., Dellana, S., & Jarrett, J. (2002). Transfer function modeling of processes with dynamic inputs. *Journal of Quality Technology*, 34(3), 312-323.

Yeung, I. & Yung, Y. (1999). Intervention analysis on the effect on two sewage screening plants on the BOD5 levels in the Hong Kong Victoria harbor and vicinity. *Environmental Monitoring and Assessment*, 58, 79-93.

Zhang, G., Patuwo, B., & Hu, M. Y. (1998). Forecasting with artificial neural networks: The state of the art. *International Journal of Forecasting*, 14(1), 35-62.

Zhu, J., Zurcher, J., Rao, M., & Meng, M. Q. H. (1998). An on-line wastewater quality prediction system based on a time-delay neural network. *Engineering Applications of Artificial Intelligence, 11*, 747-758.

Chapter VI

Tourism Demand Forecasting for the Tourism Industry: A Neural Network Approach

Rob Law, The Hong Kong Polytechnic University, Hong Kong

Ray Pine, The Hong Kong Polytechnic University, Hong Kong

ABSTRACT

Practical tourism forecasters concentrate primarily on quantitative causal-relationship and time series methods. Although these traditional quantitative forecasting techniques have attained a certain level of success in tourism research, it is generally unknown whether they are able to simulate the relationship of demand for tourism as accurately as multiprocessing node-based artificial neural networks (ANNs). This research attempts to incorporate ANNs to develop accurate forecasting techniques for international demand for travel to a particular destination. In this study the destination featured is Hong Kong and historical data of arrivals for the period of 1970 to 1999 from Japan, UK, USA, and Taiwan, and 1984 to 1999 from China. These five countries/origins have consistently produced the largest number of inbound tourists to Hong Kong. Comparing the forecasting accuracy with five commonly used tourism forecasting techniques, we found that the ANN and single exponential smoothing forecasting models outperformed other models in terms of the chosen dimensions. Apart from its direct relevance to Hong Kong, this research provides the basis of an accurate forecasting technique that can be applied to any other travel destination.

INTRODUCTION

Planning has been widely recognized as one of the most important functions for industrial practitioners and government policy makers at all levels. In the tourism industry, planning is particularly important because of the rapid economic and political changes, increased operational complexity, and complicated tourism businesses. To a large extent, planning relies heavily on accurate forecasts. In other words, accurate forecasts of demand for tourism are crucial for effective planning by all providers of services and products in tourism.

Despite the consensus on the need for accurate forecasting, and a clear understanding of the advantages of accurate forecasts, there appears to be no standard supplier of tourism forecasts. Also, there does not exist a single tourism forecasting technique that outperforms all other techniques, in terms of forecasting accuracy, in every situation. Classical studies on tourism demand analysis and forecasting have demonstrated mixed results of forecasting quality in error magnitude accuracy.

The Asian financial crisis, which has drawn worldwide attention, started in mid-1997. Prior to the crisis, international currency speculators believed that the Asian national banking systems were becoming over-expanded. These speculators, therefore, invested in Asian currency futures, and hoped to make huge profits if the financial crash came. In mid-1997, the crash did come and the currencies of most countries in the Asia Pacific Region largely depreciated against the US and major European currencies (Prideaux, 1999; Leiper & Hing, 1998). The crisis caused many affected countries to lose national wealth and, therefore, their citizens' disposable income. Since travel is normally considered as a luxury commodity, overseas travel is greatly affected by national and personal wealth levels. An immediate outcome of the crisis was the substantial drop of tourist arrivals recorded in most Asian countries (Law, 2001a).

The tourism industry is one of the few key industries in Hong Kong, thus the demand for accurate tourism forecasting is particularly important due to the industry's significant contributions to the economy. However, in Hong Kong, the tourism industry has been facing many challenges since mid-1997. Data in Table 1 were obtained and reorganized from the official records of the Hong Kong Tourist Association (1967-2000) which show an overview of the tourist arrivals and tourism receipts in Hong Kong in the period 1970 to 1999. As revealed in Table 1, after the outbreak of the Asian financial crisis, the number of international tourist arrivals to Hong Kong and tourism receipts in 1997 dropped 11.1% and 14.7% compared to 1996. The corresponding figures in 1998 were a further drop of 8.0% and 23.4%. In 1999, although there was an 11.5% increase in the number of tourist arrivals, this figure is still less than that in 1996. In addition, income from tourism in 1999 was still 4.1% less than the previous year. This slump in demand for tourism, particularly in tourism receipts, together with the change in major market segments for inbound tourists — from North Asia to Mainland China and Taiwan, necessitate the urgent need to develop accurate techniques to forecast international demand for travel to Hong Kong. The application of accurate forecasting techniques in the context of tourism demand in Hong Kong positively contributes to meeting this challenge. The recent downturn in Hong Kong's tourism industry, with a nonlinear (and non-positive) growth in tourism demand, provides an excellent opportunity for tourism researchers to refocus their attentions on alternative forecasting techniques. Hence, ANNs are expected to provide the characteristics of forecasting that are difficult to simulate using traditional tourism demand forecasting techniques.

The primary objective of this study is to examine whether ANNs can accurately forecast international demand for travel, in this case to Hong Kong, in terms of error magnitude accuracy for the key tourist generating origins. The research also provides the basis of an ANN-based forecasting technique that could be applied to other destinations.

As stated, the countries/origins included in this study are China, Japan, UK, USA, and Taiwan. Official publications indicate that the number of tourist arrivals from these five countries and their expenditures have consistently contributed to more than 65% of total tourist arrivals and total tourism receipts in Hong Kong. To date, there exist no published articles in the tourism literature which attempts to apply ANNs to tourism demand forecasting. Tourism researchers have previously examined the relationship of tourist arrivals and several tourism forecasting techniques, including ANNs, but these studies either covered a single source market (Burger et al., 2001) or concentrated on

Table 1: An Overview of Tourist Arrivals and Tourism Receipts in Hong Kong

Year	Number of tourist arrivals	Total tourism receipts (HK$mn)	Annual increase/decrease of tourist arrivals	Annual increase/decrease of total tourism receipts
1970	927,256	2,309		
1971	907,295	2,119	-2.15%	-8.21%
1972	1,082,253	2,545	19.28%	20.12%
1973	1,291,950	2,619	19.38%	2.89%
1974	1,295,462	2,812	0.27%	7.36%
1975	1,300,836	2,976	0.41%	5.83%
1976	1,559,977	3,888	19.92%	30.66%
1977	1,755,669	4,055	12.54%	4.31%
1978	2,054,739	5,107	17.03%	25.92%
1979	2,213,209	6,339	7.71%	24.13%
1980	2,301,473	6,472	3.99%	2.10%
1981	2,523,250	8,103	9.64%	25.20%
1982	2,592,012	8,711	2.73%	7.50%
1983	2,753,549	11,283	6.23%	29.53%
1984	3,107,737	13,821	12.86%	22.49%
1985	3,370,308	14,471	8.45%	4.70%
1986	3,733,347	17,863	10.77%	23.44%
1987	4,501,889	25,437	20.59%	42.40%
1988	5,589,292	33,328	24.15%	31.02%
1989	5,361,170	36,905	-4.08%	10.73%
1990	5,932,854	39,251	10.66%	6.36%
1991	6,032,081	39,607	1.67%	0.91%
1992	6,986,163	48,390	15.82%	22.18%
1993	8,937,500	60,026	27.93%	24.05%
1994	9,331,156	64,263	4.40%	7.06%
1995	10,199,994	74,914	9.31%	16.57%
1996	11,702,735	84,520	14.73%	12.82%
1997	10,406,261	72,086	-11.08%	-14.71%
1998	9,574,711	55,251	-7.99%	-23.35%
1999	10,678,460	52,984	11.53%	-4.1%

Note: Monetary values are at current market prices

some regions which were not the major tourist generating origins (Law, 2001a). Hence, these prior studies are not as extensive, in both time span and geographical scope, as this present research. Being able to accurately forecast the demand for travel to Hong Kong from the key tourist generating origins will benefit Hong Kong's tourism managers and government officials in better planning and decision-making.

Having introduced the research motivation and significance, the remaining parts of this chapter are organized as follows. The next section discusses the background of the research, in which general tourism demand forecasting techniques and detailed ANNs in forecasting are discussed. Then there is a section to cover the methodology and data used in this research. After that, the experimental results are presented and findings are analyzed. The last section concludes the study and makes suggestions for future research possibilities.

BACKGROUND
Traditional Tourism Demand Forecasting Models

Unoccupied airline seats, unused hotel rooms and unsold event or festival entrance tickets cannot be stockpiled for future use. The perishable nature of the tourism industry's products and services requires an accurate forecast of future demand, in both the short and long terms (Lim, 1997, 1999). For this reason, tourism researchers have been, and shall be, making attempts to develop various kinds of prediction techniques relating to specific aspects of tourism demand.

In its broadest classification, tourism demand forecasting divides into qualitative and quantitative streams (Frechtling, 1996). A qualitative approach, such as a desk reviewing method or an expert-opinion technique stresses the qualitative insight, intuition, and non-quantifiable knowledge of a particular tourism event. However, these qualitative relationship-identification methods are slow and tedious. Walle (1997) criticized qualitative tourism demand forecasting techniques as "artistic in nature" where tourism researchers are unable to generalize their findings. As a result, qualitative forecasting methods have not been of major interest to tourism researchers. Moreover, formal scientific techniques that unambiguously represent the relationship between demand for travel and its underlying factors would certainly help tourism decision-makers more clearly understand the demand for travel to a destination.

Quantitative (formal) tourism demand forecasting models attempt to use mathematical functions to form the relationships of some phenomena using numeric data (Dalrymple & Greenidge, 1999; Makridakis, Wheelwright, & Hyndman, 1998). These quantitative models are then used to estimate the future values based on the models' past performance. Quantitative tourism forecasting approaches are comprised of causal-relationship (also known as regression) techniques and time series techniques. Time series forecasting techniques attempt to model a tourism relationship, using a mathematical function between the current and past values of a time series (Chu, 1998; Qu & Zhang, 1996, 1997). The advantages of time series forecasting approaches are that they are simple to apply, requiring only the past values of a data series, and no assumption about other variables. Although time series forecasting approaches have attained a certain degree of success, a fundamental problem for these approaches is their inability to predict changes that are associated with other determining factors.

A causal-relationship technique tries to quantify the relationship of a dependent variable and a set of independent variables using a multivariate mathematical function through statistical analysis (Clements & Hendry, 1998; Qu & Lam, 1997). This function can then be used to predict future values of the dependent variable. Causal-relationship techniques have the advantages of explicitly representing the relationships that are evident in reality, assisting decision-makers in assessment of alternative plans, and accommodating a wide range of relationships. Multivariate regression forecasting models generally have high explanatory power and prediction accuracy. However, these regression models also have some limitations. Examples of these limitations include the large amount of time and financial costs involved and the potential existence of multi-collinearity.

On the basis of multivariate regression analyses, researchers have also developed other tourism demand forecasting techniques such as gravity models that measure the degree of interaction between two geographical areas. Recently, the success of computer systems that simulate human nervous systems has drawn some tourism researchers' attention, and initial efforts have been made to investigate the feasibility of incorporating computerized neural systems into the area of tourism demand analyses (Law, 2000b; Uysal & Roubi, 1999).

Artificial Neural Networks in Tourism Demand Forecasting

The biological metaphors of the dense neural connections in a human neural (nervous) system have been the interest of researchers for many years. This biological resemblance in particular has guided researchers to believe that neural systems have great potential for applications where there is intense human sensory processing, such as pattern classification and vision. ANNs are generally referred to as the computer software that simulate biological neural systems. At present, much progress has been achieved in the application of

ANNs to scientific and engineering fields. In spite of their promising industrial applicability, ANNs have not been of major interest to tourism researchers. At present, the number of published articles on ANNs is very limited in the tourism literature. This dearth of published articles is particularly true in the context of tourism demand forecasting. In addition to tourism demand analyses, examples of recent ANNs research in hospitality and tourism include individual choice behavior modeling (Jeng & Fesenmaier, 1996), tourist behavior forecasting (Pattie & Snyder, 1996), hotel room occupancy rate forecasting (Law, 1998), tourism demand analysis for a single market (Law, 2000b; Law, 2001b; Law & Au, 1999), and hotel spending by visitors (Law, 2000a). However, the large-scale integration of ANNs into international demand for travel to a destination is virtually nonexistent. The research reported here attempts to bridge this gap. In other words, it aims to incorporate ANNs to model the international demand for travel to a particular destination (Hong Kong) from that destination's major inbound tourist generating countries. The following paragraphs overview the concepts and operations of a back-propagation ANN used in this study. Detailed technical descriptions and mathematical theories of ANNs can be found in other references (Mehrotra, Mohan, & Ranka, 1996; Van Hulle, 2000; Whittle, 1998).

In its simplest form, an ANN with an input layer I_i, which contains l input nodes, uses a function $f()$ such that an input vector X_{li} is associated with an output $O = f(X_{li})$. In other words, an ANN computes a mapping from the input space to the output space. In practical situations, connections between nodes in an ANN are on a sequential layer-to-layer basis with each node on one layer connecting to all nodes of the next layer. Each connection is associated with a numeric weight w that returns a mathematical value for the relative strength of connections to transfer data from one layer to another layer. Additionally, there is a summation function y which computes the weighted sum of all input elements entering a node. For a given pattern p, the weighted sum of inputs y_{pj} to a hidden node j for pattern p is computed as:

$$y_{pj} = \Sigma(I_i \times w_{ij}) + \Theta_j, \, i = 1, \, \ldots, \, l \ldots \ldots \ldots \ldots \quad (1)$$

where Θ_j is a bias weight associated with each node. This bias affects a translation of the activation function $f(y_{pj})$ of each unit i for p, and enables better fitting of the ANN to the training data. For a three-layer ANN with m hidden nodes, estimated output O at the output layer k is obtained by:

$$O = \Sigma \, (f(y_{pj}) \times w_{jk}), j = 1, \, \ldots, \, m \ldots \ldots \ldots \quad (2)$$

Theoretically, a multi-layer ANN can form arbitrarily complex decision regions in the input space X_{li} (Kartalopoulos, 1996). Different learning algorithms have been adopted for multi-layer ANNs, and back-propagation is the most commonly used one. Back-propagation training begins with random initial connection weights w_{ij} and w_{jk}. Each training observation is fed through the network. This produces an output in the final layer, and the estimated value is compared with a target value. The difference between the ANNs' classification and the targeted classification for every training pattern is represented by a discrepancy function. After that, all discrepancy functions will be combined into a total discrepancy function for the entire training set. This total discrepancy function is then minimized by back-propagation's variant of gradient descent. In theory, the values of w_{ij} and w_{jk} can take any value that minimizes the discrepancy, and they can start from any random point. Under certain conditions, according to Refenes et al. (1996), this procedure is able to produce a universal approximator. That is, when there are enough layers and weights, a composite solution can usually be found that minimizes the residual errors.

METHODOLOGY

Data and Variables

This research used data from secondary sources for forecasting model estimation and model validation. Having performed a wide scale database search, the final selection of data was based on data availability, measurability, and reliability. Data were obtained from the following sources of official publications for all of the included countries/origins:

- *Hong Kong Hotel Industry* (1971-1999) published by the Hong Kong Tourist Association.
- *Hong Kong Monthly Digest of Statistics* (1970-2000) published by the Census and Statistics Department, Hong Kong SAR Government.
- *Hong Kong Tourist Association Annual Report* (1970-1999) published by the Hong Kong Tourist Association.
- *Visitor Arrival Statistics* (1971-1999) published by the Hong Kong Tourist Association.

Additional information for some countries/origins was also available, as follows:

China (1984-1999)
- *China Statistical Yearbook* (2000) published by National Bureau of Statistics, People's Republic of China.

Japan (1970-1999)

- *Japan Statistical Yearbook* (2001) published by the Statistics Bureau Management and Coordination Agency Government of Japan.
- *Nippon a Charted Survey of Japan* (1973-1995) published by the Kokusei-Sha.
- *Statistical Handbook of Japan* (1995-2000) the Statistics Bureau Management and Coordination Agency Government of Japan.
- *Statistical Survey of Japan's Economy* (1976-1987) published by the Economic and Foreign Affairs Research Association of Japan.

UK (1970-1999)

- *Great Britain Central Statistical Office Monthly digest of statistics* (1984, 2001) published by London H.M.S.O.

USA (1970-1999)

- *Datastream* (2001) CD-ROM Database published by Datastream International Limited.

Taiwan (1970-1999)

- *Statistical Yearbook of the Republic of China* (1980-2000) published by Taiwan: Directorate-General of Budget, Accounting & Statistics.

Following previous studies on tourism demand forecasting, demand for travel to Hong Kong is represented by the following function f (Kim & Uysal, 1998; Lathiras & Siriopoulos, 1998; Lee, Var, & Blaine, 1996; Lim, 1997):

$$Q_{ijt} = f (Inc_{it}, RP_{ijt}, HR_{jt}, FER_{ijt}, Pop_{it}, Mkt_{jt}) \qquad \ldots\ldots\ldots\ldots\ldots \quad (3)$$

Where:

$i = 1, 2, \ldots, I$ (for I origins); I is set for five in this research.

$j = 1, 2, \ldots, J$ (for J destinations); in this research, J has the value of one, which covers Hong Kong.

$t = 1, 2, \ldots, K$ (for K time periods); K is set for 30 in this research for annual data (due to data unavailability, K equals 16 for China).

Q_{ijt} = origin i's demand for travel to destination j at time t;

Inc_{it} = income of origin i at time t;

RP_{ijt} = relative prices in destination j relative to origin i at time t;

HR_{it} = average hotel rate in origin i at time t;

FER_{ijt} = foreign exchange rate, measured as units of destination j's currency per unit of origin i's currency at time t;

Pop_{it} = population in origin i at time t;

Mkt$_{jt}$ = marketing expenses to promote destination j's tourism industry at time t.

In this research, all monetary figures are in real US dollars due to the currency peg between the US$ and HK$. Also, the monetary values are adjusted by the Hong Kong Consumer Price Index (CPI for Hong Kong in 1990 = 100). Following the mainstream of tourism forecasting, demand for travel is measured by the total number of visitor arrivals in Hong Kong (Goh & Law, 2002; Law & Au, 2001). Income of an origin country is represented by gross domestic expenditure per capita. Relative price is a proxy variable which is defined as the CPI ratio of Hong Kong to the origin country, with 1990 being the base year. In addition, average hotel rate is used as a proxy variable which measures the tourists' costs of living in Hong Kong. Foreign exchange rate and population are real variables that are widely used in tourism forecasting studies. Lastly, marketing expenses are used as a proxy variable for the former Hong Kong Tourist Association to promote Hong Kong's tourism industry. Hence, data in Tables 2a through 2e are relevant to measure demand for travel to Hong Kong from China, Japan, the UK, the US, and Taiwan.

Table 2a: An Overview of Chinese Tourist Arrivals in Hong Kong

Year	Service Price in Hong Kong Relative to China	Average Hotel Rate in Hong Kong (US$)	Foreign Exchange Rate (CNY/ US$)	Population in China (1,000)	Marketing (Promotional) Expenses in Hong Kong (US$)	Gross Domestic Expenditure Per Capita in China (US$)	No. of Chinese Visitors
1984	0.68	74.77	1.99	1,043,570	6,814,507.59	341.62	214,854
1985	0.70	87.09	2.80	1,058,510	6,356,883.49	293.34	308,978
1986	0.72	93.64	3.21	1,075,070	9,510,360.83	288.65	363,479
1987	0.74	99.11	3.73	1,093,000	11,783,751.59	279.19	484,592
1988	0.72	110.75	3.73	1,110,260	11,118,639.93	308.79	683,604
1989	0.79	106.21	3.73	1,127,040	10,792,868.68	339.79	730,408
1990	1.00	89.00	4.73	1,143,330	13,402,905.38	338.46	754,376
1991	1.11	75.52	5.24	1,158,230	11,318,582.56	349.27	875,062
1992	1.18	69.90	5.45	1,171,710	12,897,916.80	393.01	1,149,002
1993	1.19	72.31	5.77	1,185,170	13,243,262.54	454.20	1,732,978
1994	1.20	82.71	8.72	1,198,500	12,519,725.22	370.78	1,943,678
1995	1.39	87.23	8.47	1,211,210	14,474,121.67	502.37	2,243,245
1996	1.59	90.57	8.34	1,223,890	15,280,099.87	637.51	2,389,341
1997	1.78	87.46	8.33	1,236,260	15,366,824.88	729.53	2,364,223
1998	1.89	51.48	8.31	1,248,100	17,585,359.61	800.16	2,671,628
1999	1.83	47.94	8.28	1,259,090	23,098,089.62	823.05	3,206,452

Table 2b: An Overview of Japanese Tourist Arrivals in Hong Kong

Year	Service Price in Hong Kong Relative to Japan	Average Hotel Rate in Hong Kong (US$)	Foreign Exchange Rate (JPY/US$)	Population in Japan (1,000)	Marketing (Promotional) Expenses in Hong Kong (US$)	Gross Domestic Expenditure Per Capita in Japan (US$)	No. of Japanese Visitors
1970	0.58	72.57	358.03	104,665	4,021,360.84	5,910.57	171,990
1971	0.56	77.30	346.95	105,968	4,623,055.90	6,140.91	242,917
1972	0.57	75.33	302.71	107,332	5,480,636.78	7,815.00	356,501
1973	0.60	75.55	271.53	108,710	6,430,591.79	9,489.47	486,677
1974	0.56	71.88	291.75	110,049	6,759,144.14	8,331.56	423,098
1975	0.52	67.80	296.60	111,940	5,539,572.49	7,832.86	382,740
1976	0.49	73.02	296.44	113,089	6,935,647.31	7,917.57	437,931
1977	0.48	79.14	268.34	114,154	10,507,162.06	8,947.65	485,495
1978	0.49	87.08	210.40	115,174	7,445,780.83	11,907.55	487,250
1979	0.53	99.72	219.24	116,133	7,991,799.62	11,749.55	508,011
1980	0.56	108.22	226.36	117,060	7,399,959.55	11,632.07	472,182
1981	0.61	98.08	220.34	117,884	7,189,619.10	11,971.51	507,960
1982	0.66	88.90	248.90	118,693	6,580,337.63	10,679.57	515,697
1983	0.71	73.92	237.35	119,483	5,912,922.95	11,421.79	502,175
1984	0.75	74.77	237.47	120,235	6,814,507.59	11,924.31	584,013
1985	0.76	87.09	238.39	121,049	6,356,883.49	12,358.30	635,767
1986	0.78	93.64	168.45	121,672	9,510,360.83	17,872.07	727,219
1987	0.82	99.11	144.59	122,264	11,783,751.59	21,981.29	1,033,525
1988	0.87	110.75	128.15	122,783	11,118,639.93	26,162.99	1,240,470
1989	0.94	106.21	137.93	123,255	10,792,868.68	25,644.23	1,176,189
1990	1.00	89.00	144.76	123,611	13,402,905.38	25,296.37	1,331,677
1991	1.08	75.52	134.46	124,043	11,318,582.56	27,750.62	1,259,837
1992	1.16	69.90	126.68	124,452	12,897,916.80	29,186.11	1,324,399
1993	1.25	72.31	111.22	124,764	13,243,262.54	33,041.26	1,280,905
1994	1.34	82.71	102.19	125,034	12,519,725.22	36,028.84	1,440,632
1995	1.46	87.23	94.04	125,570	14,474,121.67	39,869.87	1,691,283
1996	1.54	90.57	108.77	125,864	15,280,099.87	35,098.36	2,758,483
1997	1.60	87.46	120.99	126,166	15,366,824.88	31,422.97	1,624,420
1998	1.64	51.48	130.81	126,486	17,585,359.61	28,279.65	1,100,579
1999	1.58	47.94	113.74	126,686	23,098,089.62	32,129.36	1,174,071

Forecasting Models

In this research, in addition to a back-propagation ANN, five traditional forecasting models were established to forecast demand for travel to Hong Kong. These five models included moving average (3), moving average (5), single exponential smoothing, Holt's exponential smoothing, and regression. Other than ANN, the included forecasting models are commonly used by tourism researchers (Frechtling, 1996, 2001). A regression model attempts to

Table 2c: An Overview of UK Tourist Arrivals in Hong Kong

Year	Service Price in Hong Kong Relative to UK (US$)	Average Hotel Rate in Hong Kong (US$)	Foreign Exchange Rate GBP/US$	Population in UK (1,000)	Marketing (Promotional) Expenses in Hong Kong (US$)	Gross Domestic Expenditure Per Capita in UK (US$)	No. of UK Visitors
1970	1.36	72.57	0.42	55,632	4,021,360.84	15,131.40	46,104
1971	1.27	77.30	0.41	55,907	4,623,055.90	15,607.35	42,036
1972	1.27	75.33	0.40	56,079	5,480,636.78	16,626.72	56,955
1973	1.38	75.55	0.41	56,210	6,430,591.79	17,141.61	44,430
1974	1.36	71.88	0.43	56,224	6,759,144.14	15,941.77	43,060
1975	1.14	67.80	0.45	56,215	5,539,572.49	15,380.77	47,477
1976	1.01	73.02	0.56	56,206	6,935,647.31	12,683.88	57,783
1977	0.92	79.14	0.57	56,179	10,507,162.06	12,345.00	71,097
1978	0.90	87.08	0.52	56,167	7,445,780.83	14,483.77	84,324
1979	0.89	99.72	0.47	56,240	7,991,799.62	16,551.39	95,344
1980	0.87	108.22	0.43	56,330	7,399,959.55	17,979.23	121,054
1981	0.88	98.08	0.50	56,357	7,189,619.10	15,206.63	167,117
1982	0.90	88.90	0.57	56,325	6,580,337.63	13,343.63	156,414
1983	0.94	73.92	0.66	56,384	5,912,922.95	12,068.14	164,597
1984	0.97	74.77	0.75	56,513	6,814,507.59	10,798.40	171,389
1985	0.95	87.09	0.78	56,693	6,356,883.49	10,726.19	187,906
1986	0.94	93.64	0.68	56,859	9,510,360.83	12,681.72	214,704
1987	0.95	99.11	0.61	57,015	11,783,751.59	14,903.97	251,791
1988	0.98	110.75	0.56	57,166	11,118,639.93	17,199.56	285,590
1989	1.00	106.21	0.61	57,365	10,792,868.68	16,052.47	269,716
1990	1.00	89.00	0.56	57,567	13,402,905.38	17,195.27	279,333
1991	1.05	75.52	0.57	57,814	11,318,582.56	16,886.22	275,626
1992	1.11	69.90	0.57	58,013	12,897,916.80	16,843.29	314,231
1993	1.19	72.31	0.67	58,198	13,243,262.54	14,852.23	339,162
1994	1.25	82.71	0.65	58,401	12,519,725.22	15,625.93	379,577
1995	1.32	87.23	0.63	58,612	14,474,121.67	16,381.29	360,545
1996	1.36	90.57	0.64	58,807	15,280,099.87	16,708.04	444,689
1997	1.40	87.46	0.61	59,014	15,366,824.88	18,012.51	369,572
1998	1.39	51.48	0.60	59,237	17,585,359.61	18,612.02	352,835
1999	1.31	47.94	0.62	59,501	23,098,089.62	18,676.83	333,973

represent the relationship between a set of dependent variables and an independent variable using a multivariate mathematical function. In this study, the regression model appears in the form of:

$$\text{Arrival} = a + b\text{Inc} + c\text{RP} + d\text{HR} + e\text{FER} + f\text{Pop} + g\text{Mkt} \dots\dots (4)$$

where a is the constant, and $b, c, d, e, f,$ and g are variable coefficients.

Table 2d: An Overview of US Tourist Arrivals in Hong Kong

Year	Service Price in Hong Kong Relative to USA	Average Hotel Rate in Hong Kong (US$)	Foreign Exchange Rate (US$/US$)	Population in USA (1,000)	Marketing (Promotional) Expenses in Hong Kong (US$)	Gross Domestic Expenditure Per Capita in USA (US$)	No. of US Visitors
1970	0.67	72.57	1.00	205,052	4,021,360.84	17,060.65	255,145
1971	0.66	77.30	1.00	207,661	4,623,055.90	17,531.70	220,754
1972	0.68	75.33	1.00	209,896	5,480,636.78	18,507.98	215,679
1973	0.76	75.55	1.00	211,909	6,430,591.79	19,213.01	227,921
1974	0.79	71.88	1.00	213,854	6,759,144.14	18,587.96	230,995
1975	0.75	67.80	1.00	215,973	5,539,572.49	18,403.78	183,635
1976	0.73	73.02	1.00	218,035	6,935,647.31	19,190.59	238,605
1977	0.73	79.14	1.00	220,239	10,507,162.06	19,882.76	254,186
1978	0.71	87.08	1.00	222,585	7,445,780.83	20,679.07	284,642
1979	0.72	99.72	1.00	225,056	7,991,799.62	20,554.04	303,583
1980	0.73	108.22	1.00	227,726	7,399,959.55	19,469.80	346,910
1981	0.75	98.08	1.00	229,966	7,189,619.10	19,569.37	372,133
1982	0.79	88.90	1.00	232,188	6,580,337.63	19,025.36	377,853
1983	0.83	73.92	1.00	234,307	5,912,922.95	19,793.52	451,566
1984	0.87	74.77	1.00	236,348	6,814,507.59	20,932.73	562,764
1985	0.86	87.09	1.00	238,466	6,356,883.49	21,471.91	638,168
1986	0.87	93.64	1.00	240,651	9,510,360.83	22,048.57	704,428
1987	0.89	99.11	1.00	242,804	11,783,751.59	22,463.72	793,341
1988	0.92	110.75	1.00	245,021	11,118,639.93	23,021.66	749,244
1989	0.96	106.21	1.00	247,342	10,792,868.68	23,391.94	624,400
1990	1.00	89.00	1.00	249,973	13,402,905.38	23,215.31	612,262
1991	1.07	75.52	1.00	252,665	11,318,582.56	22,737.26	619,685
1992	1.14	69.90	1.00	255,410	12,897,916.80	23,048.47	694,290
1993	1.20	72.31	1.00	258,119	13,243,262.54	23,265.04	755,666
1994	1.26	82.71	1.00	260,637	12,519,725.22	23,867.37	776,039
1995	1.33	87.23	1.00	263,082	14,474,121.67	24,110.73	748,911
1996	1.37	90.57	1.00	265,502	15,280,099.87	24,513.15	832,725
1997	1.42	87.46	1.00	268,048	15,366,824.88	25,209.40	861,217
1998	1.44	51.48	1.00	270,509	17,585,359.61	25,966.68	828,326
1999	1.35	47.94	1.00	272,945	23,098,089.62	26,719.08	858,925

For an order N moving average forecasting model, the forecast value of A' at time period $t+1$ is calculated as the average of the last N numbers.

A single exponential smoothing (α) model improves the moving average model by incorporating a portion of the error that the previous forecast produced. The model forecasts the value of A' at time t by:

$$F_t = F_{t-1}(\alpha) + A_{t-1}(1-\alpha) \ \ldots\ldots \tag{5}$$

Table 2e: An Overview of Taiwanese Tourist Arrivals in Hong Kong

Year	Service Price in Hong Kong Relative to Taiwan	Average Hotel Rate in Hong Kong (US$)	Foreign Exchange Rate (TW$/US$)	Population in Taiwan (1,000)	Marketing (Promotional) Expenses in Hong Kong (US$)	Gross Domestic Expenditure Per Capita in Taiwan (US$)	No. of Taiwanese Visitors
1970	0.72	72.57	40.10	14,582	4,021,360.84	5,877.95	21,158
1971	0.73	77.30	40.10	14,899	4,623,055.90	6,320.08	24,690
1972	0.75	75.33	40.10	15,191	5,480,636.78	6,821.30	31,122
1973	0.83	75.55	40.10	15,465	6,430,591.79	6,988.74	47,925
1974	0.64	71.88	38.10	15,750	6,759,144.14	4,953.00	54,832
1975	0.63	67.80	38.05	16,046	5,539,572.49	4,854.13	60,539
1976	0.64	73.02	38.05	16,402	6,935,647.31	5,275.02	77,794
1977	0.63	79.14	38.05	16,705	10,507,162.06	5,332.58	87,488
1978	0.63	87.08	36.05	16,974	7,445,780.83	5,947.92	128,924
1979	0.64	99.72	36.08	17,307	7,991,799.62	5,744.50	206,344
1980	0.62	108.22	36.06	17,642	7,399,959.55	5,083.89	123,644
1981	0.61	98.08	37.89	17,974	7,189,619.10	4,334.59	135,621
1982	0.65	88.90	39.96	18,293	6,580,337.63	4,061.66	153,133
1983	0.71	73.92	40.32	18,603	5,912,922.95	4,235.34	156,600
1984	0.77	74.77	39.52	18,865	6,814,507.59	4,713.49	166,762
1985	0.79	87.09	39.90	19,132	6,356,883.49	4,839.01	176,617
1986	0.81	93.64	35.55	19,363	9,510,360.83	5,949.49	220,469
1987	0.85	99.11	28.60	19,559	11,783,751.59	8,212.08	354,195
1988	0.90	110.75	28.22	19,781	11,118,639.93	8,761.44	1,094,004
1989	0.95	106.21	26.16	20,008	10,792,868.68	9,684.63	1,132,904
1990	1.00	89.00	27.11	20,233	13,402,905.38	9,355.01	1,344,641
1991	1.08	75.52	25.75	20,456	11,318,582.56	10,111.95	1,298,039
1992	1.13	69.90	25.40	20,652	12,897,916.80	10,446.45	1,640,032
1993	1.19	72.31	26.63	20,841	13,243,262.54	10,264.38	1,777,310
1994	1.24	82.71	26.24	21,037	12,519,725.22	10,618.91	1,665,330
1995	1.29	87.23	27.27	21,217	14,474,121.67	10,399.21	1,761,111
1996	1.33	90.57	27.49	21,382	15,280,099.87	10,537.84	2,023,977
1997	1.39	87.46	27.49	21,567	15,366,824.88	11,044.65	1,920,014
1998	1.41	51.48	32.64	21,784	17,585,359.61	9,472.09	1,885,550
1999	1.35	47.94	32.22	21,957	23,098,089.62	10,019.13	2,063,027

where α is a smoothing constant and F_{t-1} is the forecast value of A at time $t-1$.

As an extension of the single exponential smoothing approach by assuming the existence of a trend, a Holt's exponential smoothing model generates an estimate of the base level (L_t) and the per-period trend (T_t) of the series. The value of A' at period $t + 1$ then is calculated as:

$$L_t = \alpha \times A_t + (1 - \alpha) \times (L_{t-1} + T_{t-1})$$
$$T_t = \beta \times (L_t - L_{t-1}) + (1 - \beta) \times T_{t-1}$$
$$A'_t = L_t + T_t \ldots \ldots \ldots \qquad (6)$$

where α and β are smoothing constants, such that $0 < \alpha, \beta < 1$.

The next section will discuss the computer implementation of the forecasting models and forecasting results of the included models.

FINDINGS AND ANALYSIS

In this research, SPSS 10.0 was used to build and test the traditional forecasting models. The ANNs for modeling the demand for travel to Hong Kong from the selected countries/regions were developed using Qnet v97, a commercially available generic ANN system running on Windows 98 on a Pentium IV PC (www.simtel.net/pub/pd/36835.html for updated information), and following the algorithm analyzed in the background section. Presented in Figure 1, the tourism demand forecasting ANN consisted of six input nodes (independent variables) and one output node (dependent variable) was developed. A sigmoid function transfer function and two stopping criteria for the training stage were used for each of the ANNs for the selected countries/regions. The first criterion stopped the training process if the total number of iterations was 20,000. The second stopping criterion was based on the tolerance level of 500. That is, whenever the total output error term fell below a minimum tolerance bounding level (500 in this case), the training process was terminated. The learning rate, which determines how fast the ANN learns the pattern in the training data, was initially set to 0.2. The auto mode was then turned on to let the program adjust its value automatically. Additionally, since the selected entries did not show smooth data, a value of 0.3 was chosen as the momentum rate to control the fraction of previous error to be used for weight adjustments.

This study builds different forecasting techniques to model the recent demand for the key tourist generating countries/regions to Hong Kong. As previously mentioned, there exists no published article that makes such an attempt. Among the sample entries, the first two-thirds (11 for China, and 20 for other origins) were selected for model establishment (calibration or training in ANNs) and the remaining entries were used for model testing (validation). It should be noted that there was a drastic decrease in total tourist arrivals in Hong Kong since 1997 due to the Asian financial crisis (Table 1). In order to

Figure 1: A Demand Artificial Neural Network Model for Travel by Overseas Travelers to Hong Kong

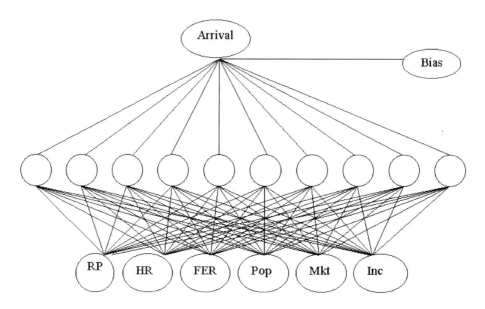

preserve the information about this drastic structural change, the last one-third of entries were included in the validation set.

The forecasting quality was measured in terms of mean absolute deviation (MAD), mean absolute percentage error (MAPE), and root mean square percentage error (RMSPE). According to Law (2000b), MAD measures the overall accuracy, and provides an indication of the overall spread, where all errors are given equal weights. MAPE is a relative measurement that corresponds to MAD. Finally, RMSPE is a relative measurement, corresponding to the overall accuracy of the spreading level. Table 3 shows the empirical findings of the six forecasting techniques.

In general, the selected models were not very accurate in most of the measuring dimensions. Frechtling (2001) classified forecasts with MAPE values of less than 10% as highly accurate forecasting, between 10% and 20% as good forecasting, between 20% and 50% as reasonable forecasting, and larger than 50% as inaccurate forecasting. As indicated in Table 3, the only models which did not attain any inaccurate forecasting result were ANN, moving average (3), and single exponential smoothing. Among these three

Table 3: Comparisons of Forecasting Accuracy Measurements

	ANN	Moving Average (3)	Moving Average (5)	Single Exponential Smoothing	Holt's Exponential Smoothing	Regression
China						
MAD	415,000	854,086	1,461,630	631,300	151,893	1,404,488
MAPE	15.40%	32.19%	15.10%	23.28%	5.55%	54.87%
RMSPE	16.50%	33.08%	15.82%	25.04%	6.68%	61.69%
Japan						
MAD	264,740	340,627	1,058,000	337,985	275,956	342,471
MAPE	15.26%	18.02%	24.86%	17.85%	17.11%	22.53%
RMSPE	26.84%	24.11%	29.52%	23.95%	25.99%	27.83%
United Kingdom						
MAD	68,852	73,046	256,060	75,238	29,712	39,687
MAPE	19.92%	19.71%	24.51%	20.35%	8.06%	11.94%
RMSPE	17.77%	22.52%	26.23%	23.05%	10.19%	13.06%
United States						
MAD	147,760	99,860	704,558	151,735	899,751	285,924
MAPE	20.37%	12.92%	12.41%	17.08%	102.84%	37.07%
RMSPE	15.83%	14.11%	13.40%	20.54%	119.81%	38.10%
Taiwan						
MAD	753,803	756,656	758,164	604,999	283,178	825,571
MAPE	42.11%	42.37%	55.87%	33.33%	15.77%	45.58%
RMSPE	50.22%	43.28%	56.05%	34.96%	16.75%	48.43%

models, both ANN and moving average (3) were able to achieve three good forecasts and two reasonable forecasts; whereas single exponential smoothing attained two good forecasts and three reasonable forecasts. As revealed in Tables 2a to 2e, the number of Japanese and British tourist arrivals had largely dropped after 1996. In other words, the ANN and single exponential smoothing models could attain good forecasts for both the Japanese and British tourist arrivals. The values of MAD and RMSPE further supported such forecasting quality. The findings are in accordance with previous studies on tourism demand forecasting which state that ANNs can perform well in forecasting accuracy (Law, 2000b; Law, 2001b; Law & Au, 1999).

CONCLUSION

This research has attempted to investigate the forecasting quality of artificial neural networks and five other commonly used tourism forecasting techniques in terms of error magnitude accuracy. Empirical results indicate that most of the models did not forecast very accurately, and that ANN and single exponential smoothing models outperformed other selected models.

Despite the limited scope of this research, both in number of origins and time frame, the findings should be of use to tourism practitioners in Hong Kong, and very likely in other tourist receiving destinations, as well as researchers who are interested both in forecasting techniques and the application of ANNs. Tourism as an industry is of particular importance to Hong Kong, being both a very significant source of foreign exchange as well as a provider of direct and indirect employment. The need for accurate tourism forecasting is thus particularly important due to the industry's significant contribution to the economy. In the tourism industry of any country, planning is particularly important because of the rapid economic and political changes, augmented operational complexity, and complicated tourism businesses. To a large extent, planning relies heavily on accurate forecasts. In other words, accurate forecasts of demand for tourism are crucial for effective planning by all providers of services and products in tourism. Tourism practitioners can take advantage of the research findings to plan for future development of tourist attractions, accommodations, transportation and infrastructure for the major tourist generating regions/countries. Likewise, tourism researchers can apply the forecasting techniques which produced the best results for their future investigations of tourism demand forecasting, especially in situations where there are unexpected drastic environmental or economical changes, such as the Asian Financial Crisis.

Some areas are open for future research. First, a qualitative approach can be adopted to collect primary data from tourism industry practitioners through personal interviews and/or questionnaires. This is to seek opinions from industrial professionals in order to maintain the quality of research findings. More importantly, this qualitative approach ensures that any findings have a direct applicability to the local tourism industry. Similarly, views from overseas tourism professionals can be collected to verify the research findings. It would be valuable to gain practitioners' acceptance by explaining how ANNs arrive at the forecasts. Another future research possibility is to extend the number of the countries/origins which have consistently generated the leading number of inbound tourists to Hong Kong. Lastly, it would be beneficial to compare and contrast forecasting accuracy with other forecasting techniques, and in other accuracy measuring dimensions. The techniques for future research can include the more advanced time series forecasting models such as ARIMA and SARIMA, and the sophisticated causal models like general-to-specific and vector autoregression models.

ACKNOWLEDGMENT

This research is partly supported by a Hong Kong Polytechnic University research grant under contract number: G-T456.

REFERENCES

Burger, C., Dohnal, M., Kathrada, M., & Law, R. (2001). A practitioners guide to time-series methods for tourism demand forecasting – A case study of Durban, South   Africa. *Tourism Management*, 22(4), 403-409.

Chu, F. L. (1998). Forecasting tourism demand in Asian-Pacific countries. *Annals of Tourism Research,* 25(3), 597-615.

Clements, M. P. & Hendry, D. F. (1998). *Forecasting Economic Time Series.* Cambridge: Cambridge University Press.

Dalrymple, K. & Greenidge, K. (1999). Forecasting arrivals to Barbados. *Annals of Tourism Research,* 26(1), 188-191.

Frechtling, D. C. (1996). *Practical Tourism Forecasting.* Oxford: Butterworth-Heinemann.

Frechtling, D. C. (2001). *Forecasting Tourism Demand: Methods and Strategies.* Oxford: Butterworth-Heinemann.

Goh, C. & Law, R. (2002). Modeling and forecasting tourism demand for arrivals with stochastic nonstationary seasonality and intervention. *Tourism Management*, 23(5), 499-510.

Hong Kong Tourist Association (1967-2000). *A Statistical Review of Tourism.* Hong Kong: HKTA.

Jeng, J. M. & Fesenmaier, D. R. (1996). A neural network approach to discrete choice modeling. *Journal of Travel & Tourism Marketing,* 5(1/2), 119-144.

Kartalopoulos, S. V. (1996). *Understanding Neural Networks and Fuzzy Logic.* New York: IEEE Press.

Kim, Y. & Uysal, M. (1998). Time-dependent analysis for international hotel demand   in Seoul. *Tourism Economics,* 4(3), 253-263.

Lathiras, P. & Siriopoulos, C. (1998). The demand for tourism to Greece: A cointegration approach. *Tourism Economics,* 4(2), 171-185.

Law, R. (1998). Room occupancy rate forecasting: A neural network approach. *International Journal of Contemporary Hospitality Management,* 10(6), 234-239.

Law, R. (2000a). Demand for hotel spending by visitors to Hong Kong: A study of various forecasting techniques. *Journal of Hospitality & Leisure Marketing,* 6(4), 17-29.

Law, R. (2000b). Back-propagation learning in improving the accuracy of neural network-based tourism demand forecasting. *Tourism Management,* 21(3), 331-340.

Law, R. (2001a). The impact of the Asian financial crisis on the accuracy of tourist arrival forecasts. *Journal of Hospitality & Leisure Marketing,* 8(1/2), 5-17.

Law, R. (2001b). The impact of the Asian Financial Crisis on Japanese demand for travel to Hong Kong: A study of various forecasting techniques. *Journal of Travel & Tourism Marketing,* 10(2/3), 47-65.

Law, R. & Au, N. (1999). A neural network model to forecast Japanese demand for travel to Hong Kong. *Tourism Management,* 20(1), 89-97.

Law, R. & Au, N. (2001). Marketing Hong Kong to the Taiwanese visitors. *Journal of Travel & Tourism Marketing,* 10(1), 51-67.

Lee, C. K., Var, T., & Blaine, T. W. (1996). Determinants of inbound tourist expenditures. *Annals of Tourism Research,* 23(3), 527-542.

Leiper, N. & Hing, N. (1998). Trends in Asia-Pacific tourism in 1997-1998: From optimism to uncertainty. *International Journal of Contemporary Hospitality Management,* 10(7), 245-251.

Lim, C. (1997). Review of international tourism demand models. *Annals of Tourism Research,* 24(4), 835-849.

Lim, C. (1999). A meta-analytic review of international tourism demand. *Journal of Travel Research,* 37, 273-284.

Makridakis, S., Wheelwright, S. C., & Hyndman, R. J. (1998). *Forecasting Methods and Applications.* New York: John Wiley & Sons.

Mehrotra, K., Mohan, C. K., & Ranka, S. (1996). *Elements of Artificial Neural Networks.* Boston, MA: The MIT Press.

Pattie, D. C. & Snyder, J. (1996). Using a neural network to forecast visitor behavior. *Annals of Tourism Research,* 23(1), 151-164.

Prideaux, B. (1999). The Asian Financial Crisis causes and implications for Australia's tourism industry. *Australian Journal of Hospitality Management,* 6(2), 35-44.

Qu, H. & Lam, S. (1997). A travel demand model for Mainland Chinese tourists to Hong Kong. *Tourism Management,* 18(8), 593-597.

Qu, H. & Zhang, H. Q. (1996). The projection of international tourist arrivals in East Asia and the Pacific to the year 2005. *Journal of Travel Research,* 35(1), 27-34.

Qu, H. & Zhang, H. Q. (1997). The projected inbound market trends of 12 tourist destinations in South East Asia and the Pacific, 1997-2001. *Journal of Vacation Marketing,* 3(3), 247-263.

Refenes, A. N., Zapranis, A. D., Connor, J. T., & Bunn, D. W. (1996). Neural networks in investment management. In S. Goonatilake & P. Treleaven (Eds.), *Intelligent Systems for Finance and Business* (pp. 177-208). Chichester, UK: John Wiley & Sons.

Van Hulle, M. C. (2000). *Faithful Representations and Topographic Maps: From Distortion- to Information-Based Self-Organization.* New York: John Wiley & Sons.

Walle, A. H. (1997). Quantitative versus qualitative tourism research. *Annals of Tourism Research*, 24(3), 524-536.

Whittle, P. (1998). *Neural Nets and Chaotic Carriers.* Chichester, UK: John Wiley & Sons.

Uysal, M. & Roubi, M. S. E. (1999). Artificial neural networks versus multiple regression in tourism demand analysis. *Journal of Travel Research,* 38, 111-118.

Chapter VII

Using an Extended Self-Organizing Map Network to Forecast Market Segment Membership

Melody Y. Kiang, California State University, Long Beach, USA

Dorothy M. Fisher, California State University,
Dominguez Hills, USA

Michael Y. Hu, Kent State University, USA

Robert T. Chi, California State University, Long Beach, USA

ABSTRACT

This chapter presents an extended Self-Organizing Map (SOM) network and demonstrates how it can be used to forecast market segment membership. The Kohonen's SOM network is an unsupervised learning neural network that maps n-dimensional input data to a lower dimensional (usually one- or two-dimensional) output map while maintaining the original topological relations. We apply an extended version of SOM networks that further groups the nodes on the output map into a user-specified number of clusters to a residential market data set from AT&T. Specifically, the extended SOM is used to group survey respondents using their attitudes towards modes of communication. We then compare the extended SOM network solutions with a two-step procedure that uses the factor scores from factor analysis as inputs to K-means cluster analysis. Results using AT&T data indicate that the extended SOM network performs better than the two-step procedure.

INTRODUCTION

Market segmentation refers to the formation of distinct subsets of customers where any subset may conceivably be selected as a market target to be reached with a distinct marketing mix (Kotler, 1980). Consumers are put into relatively homogeneous groups so that the marketing manager can select and effectively execute segment-specific marketing mixes. The identification of consumer segments is of critical importance for key strategic issues in marketing involving the assessment of a firm's opportunities and threats. The value of performing marketing segmentation analysis includes better understanding of the market to properly position a product in the marketplace, identifying the appropriate segment/s for target marketing, finding opportunities in existing markets, and gaining competitive advantage through product differentiation (Kotler, 1980). The bottom line is to increase profitability by enabling firms to more effectively target consumers. Although it was introduced into the academic marketing literature in the fifties, market segmentation continues to be an important focal point of ongoing research and marketing practices (e.g., Chaturvedi et al., 1997). Most of the academic research in market segmentation has been in the development of new techniques and methodologies for segmenting markets. The common thread running through these diverse streams of research is the attempt to segment consumers, deterministically or probabilistically, into a finite number of segments such that consumers within a segment are relatively homogeneous with respect to the variables used in the segmentation.

It should be noted that the usefulness of market segmentation hinges upon accurate forecasts of segment memberships. Relatively low accuracy in forecasting segment memberships indicates a high portion of unintended members in each segment. Misplacements will result in less efficient implementation of the marketing program designed to stimulate sales and potential negative impact on revenue generation from the unintended segment members.

From a methodological point of view, a key component in market segmentation is the formation of groups or segments of consumers. Oftentimes a clustering procedure will be employed to form segments of consumers with similar preferences. When the number of dimensions underlying preferences is large, a researcher may first use a dimension reduction technique such as principal component or factor analysis to reduce the dimensions to a manageable set before subjecting the output factors to a clustering routine. Thus, a two-step approach typically is used (Wedel & Kamakura, 1999).

Statistical dimension reduction routines such as factor analysis evolve around the Pearson's product moment correlation coefficient. Multivariate normality and linearity among the variables are the key assumptions underlying the use of correlation coefficient. Clustering algorithms in general are heuristics that assign objects into clusters based on some distance measures between the object and the centroid of the cluster. Clustering algorithms are not statistical in the sense that they do not rely on any distributional assumptions. Violation of statistical assumptions in this two-step procedure will likely come about in the data reduction stage. In commercial market research applications, measures such as consumer product ratings and customer satisfaction assessments tend to be markedly skewed (Sharma et al., 1989). Violations of the normality assumption may lead to bias and incorrect assignment of consumers to the resulting segments and eventually lead to ineffective marketing strategies.

The Kohonen's Self-Organizing Map (SOM) network, a variation of neural computing networks, is a nonparametric approach that makes no assumptions about the underlying population distribution and is independent of prior information (1984, 1989, 1995). Similar to principal component and factor analysis, the main function of a SOM network is dimension reduction, i.e., it maps an n-dimensional input space to a lower dimensional (usually one- or two-dimensional) output map while maintaining the original topological relations and, thus, enables decision makers to visualize the relationships among inputs. While Kohonen's self-organizing networks have been successfully applied as a classification tool to various problem domains, including speech recognition (Zhao & Rowden, 1992; Leinonen et al., 1993), image data compression (Manikopoulos, 1993), image or character recognition (Bimbo et al., 1993; Sabourin & Mitiche, 1993), robot control (Walter & Schulen, 1993; Ritter et al., 1989), and medical diagnosis (Vercauteren et al., 1990), its potential as a robust substitute for clustering tools remains relatively unexplored. Given the nonparametric feature of SOM, it can be anticipated that SOM for market segmentation will yield superior results to the factor/cluster procedure.

Balakrishnan et al. (1994) compared several unsupervised neural networks with K-means analysis. Due to the lack of an extended grouping function, such as the one implemented in our extended SOM network, the two-layer Kohonen network implemented in their study is designed so that the number of nodes in the output layer (Kohonen layer) corresponds to the number of desired clusters. This is a different kind of Kohonen network that does not provide a two-dimensional map that allows users to visualize the relationships among data points. Most of the studies we have found that apply Kohonen network to clustering have implemented this type of network. The performance of these neural networks is examined with respect to changes in the number of attributes, the number of clusters, and the amount of error in the data. The results show that the K-means procedure almost always outperforms the neural networks, especially when the number of clusters increases from two to five. Unlike Balakrishnan's compromising approach, our extended SOM method preserves the dimension reduction function of the original SOM and further groups the nodes in the output map into the number of clusters specified by the user. The extended SOM will be discussed and presented in detail in a later section. Key features specific to the extended SOM will be pointed out. How these added features serve to enhance the performance of SOM in dimension reduction and clustering will also be examined.

The balance of the chapter is organized as follows: the next section presents the basic concepts of SOM network and illustrates its use as a data-reduction tool (analogous to factor analysis). This is followed by a discussion of the extended grouping capability integrated into the original SOM networks. The section that follows describes the experimental procedures and results from an AT&T data set. Then we compare the performance of the extended SOM with that of the factor score-based approach both qualitatively and quantitatively. This chapter concludes with a summary of our findings.

SELF-ORGANIZING MAP (SOM) NETWORKS

The Self-Organizing Map (SOM) network is a neural-networks-based method for dimension reduction. SOM can learn from complex, multi-dimensional data and transform them into a map of fewer dimensions, such as a two-dimensional plot. The two-dimensional plot provides an easy-to-use graphical user interface to help the decision-maker visualize the similarities between consumer preference patterns. In the AT&T data set there are 68 customer attitude variables. It would be difficult to visually classify individuals based on all of these attributes because the grouping must be done in a 68 dimensional space. By using the information contained in the 68-variable set, but mapping the information into a two-dimensional plot, one can visually group customers with similar attitudinal dimensions into clusters. These relationships can then be translated into an appropriate type of structure that genuinely represents the underlying relationships between market segments. Hence, SOM networks can be used to build a decision support system for marketing management.

Teuve Kohonen (1984) developed the SOM network between 1979 and 1982 based on the earlier work of Willshaw and von der Malsburg (1979). It is designed to capture topological and hierarchical structures of higher dimensional input spaces. Unlike most neural networks applications, the SOM performs unsupervised training, i.e., during the learning (training) stage, SOM processes the input units in the networks and adjusts their weights primarily based on the lateral feedback connections. The nodes in the network converge to form clusters to represent groups of consumers with similar properties. A two-dimensional map of the input data is created in such a way that the orders of the interrelationships among objects are preserved (Kohonen, 1989). The number and composition of clusters can be visually determined based on the output distribution generated by the training process.

The SOM network typically has two layers of nodes, the input layer and the Kohonen layer. The input layer is fully connected to a two-dimensional Kohonen layer. During the training process, input data are fed to the network through the processing elements (nodes) in the input layer. An input pattern x_v ($v = 1, \ldots, V$) is denoted by a vector of order m as: $x_v = (x_{v1}, x_{v2}, \ldots, x_{vm})$, where x_{vi} is the ith input signal in the pattern and m is the number of input signals in each pattern. An input pattern is simultaneously incident on the nodes of a two-dimensional Kohonen layer. Associated with each of the N nodes in the $n \times n$ ($N = n \times n$) Kohonen layer, is a weight vector, also of order m, denoted by: $w_i = (w_{i1}, w_{i2}, \ldots, w_{im})$, where w_{ij} is the weight value associated with node i corresponding to the jth signal of an input vector. As the training process proceeds, the nodes adjust their weight values according to the topological relations in the input data. The node with the minimum distance is the winner and adjusts its weights to be closer to the value of the input pattern.

The network undergoes a self-organization process through a number of training cycles, starting with randomly chosen weights (w_i's). During each training cycle, every input vector is considered in turn and the winner node is determined such that:

$$\| x_v - w_i \| = \min \| x_v - w_i \|, \ (i = 1, \dots, N)$$

where $\| . \|$ indicates Euclidean distance which is the most common way of measuring distance between vectors. The weight vectors of the winning node and the nodes in the neighborhood are updated using a weight adaptation function based on the following Kohonen rule:

$$\Delta w_i = \alpha \left(x_v - w_i^{old} \right), \text{ for } i \in N_r,$$

where α is the learning coefficient, x_v is the input vector, and N_r is the collection of all nodes in the neighborhood of radial distance r. For a two dimensional Kohonen layer, there could be up to a total of eight neighboring nodes when $r=1$ (see Figure 1). The process will adjust the weights of the winning node along with its neighbor nodes closer to the value of the input pattern. The neighborhood size (r) can change and is usually reduced as training progresses.

A Gaussian type of neighborhood adaptation function, which decreases both in the spatial domain and the time domain, has been proposed (Cottrell & Fort, 1986; Ritter & Schulten, 1986; Lo & Bavarian, 1991). Lo and Bavarian (1991) have shown that an algorithm that uses the Gaussian type function will enforce ordering in the neighborhood set for every training iteration, yielding faster convergence. We use a Gaussian type neighborhood adaptation function $h(t, r)$, similar to the one used by Mitra and Pal (1994):

$$h(t,r) = \frac{\alpha(1 - r * f)}{\left[1 + \left(\frac{t}{cdenom} \right)^2 \right]}$$

Figure 1: A 4x4 *Kohonen Layer and Definition of Neighboring Nodes with Radial Distance (r = 1)*

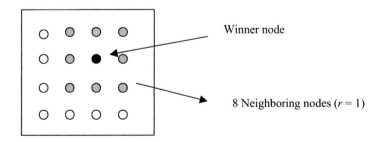

This function decreases in both spatial and time domains. In the spatial domain, its value is the largest when node i is the winner node and it gradually decreases with increasing distance from i. Parameter α determines the initial value of $|h|$ while the parameter f $(0 < f < 1/r)$ determines the rate of decrease of $|h|$ in the spatial domain. In the time domain, t controls the value of $|h|$ whereas the parameter $cdenom$ determines the rate of its decay.

The training is conducted in many stages; at each stage, we reduce r by one. Note that r affects the number of nodes in the set N_i. To determine the number of training cycles to be run at each stage, we use the index of disorder D proposed by Mitra and Pal (1994). Essentially, D measures the "improvement" in the "state" of the network at discrete time intervals. When this index falls below a certain threshold (D < convergence coefficient δ), the next stage of training begins with a reduced r value. The reader may refer to Mitra and Pal (1994) for the detailed algorithm.

To avoid a few nodes representing too much of the input data due to the effect of the initial random weight values assigned to them, we incorporate a "conscience" mechanism that prevents the nodes with higher winning frequency from winning repeatedly and makes the nodes with lower winning frequency more likely to win. The purpose of this mechanism is to give each node in the Kohonen layer an opportunity to represent approximately equal information about the input data.

The conscience mechanism that we use is proposed by DeSieno (1988). It adjusts the Euclidean distance between a node's weight vector and the input vector $\|x_v - w_i\|$ by a bias B_i. B_i is proportional to the difference between the node's winning frequency and the average winning frequency:

$$B_i = \gamma\left(\frac{1}{N} - F_i\right).$$

F_i is the winning frequency of node i and is updated at every iteration of the training process. Initially, F_i is assigned the average value $1/N$; thus $B_i = 0$. In this study, we start the g (gamma) coefficient at a larger value, 4 (a number in the range of appropriate values suggested in NeuralWare (1990)), and gradually decrease the value of γ to 0 (when no conscience mechanism is implemented) toward the end of training process.

The winning frequencies are updated as:

for the winning node: $F_{i,t+1} = F_{i,t} + \beta (1.0 - F_{i,t})$,
for all other nodes: $F_{i,t+1} = F_{i,t} + \beta (0.0 - F_{i,t})$,

where β is a small positive fraction (see NeuralWare, 1990). In this study, we set the value of β fixed at 0.1, a number in the range of appropriate values suggested in NeuralWare (1990).

The Extended Clustering Function

Sometimes it is hard to visually group the output from SOM, especially when the map is highly populated. Hence, a more scientific approach that can help the user to group the output from SOM network based on certain objective criteria is needed. To automate the segmentation process to complement the usage of the Kohonen SOM networks, Murtagh (1995) proposed an agglomerative contiguity-constrained clustering method. The method groups the output from SOM based on a minimal distance criterion to merge the neighboring nodes together. The rationale is that the SOM networks will maintain the original topological relations; therefore, the nodes that are closely located on the representational grid should have similar cluster centers. Murtagh also stated that a minimal variance criterion might be used in place of the minimal distance criterion. To test our cases, we have implemented both approaches. After a few preliminary runs, we found that the minimal variance criterion we implemented consistently outperformed the minimal distance approach using our sample cases. Hence, we decided to use the minimal variance criterion for our contiguity-constrained clustering method. The criterion we implemented is modified from Murtagh's (1985) and tries to minimize the overall within cluster variance at each step of the process. We start with each node in the map representing one group, and calculate the centroid of each group. Then we try to merge two neighboring groups so the result of the merge will maintain the global minimal variance for that number of clusters. The merge process is repeated until a user-specified number of clusters is derived or when only one cluster remains. The detailed process for implementing the contiguity-constrained clustering method is described in the following:

Step 1. For each $node_i$, calculate the centroid ($\bar{c}_i$) of $node_i$ as:

$$\bar{c}_i = \frac{1}{|node_i|} \sum_{\bar{x} \in node_i} \bar{x}.$$

where $|node_i|$ is the number of input vectors associated with the node.

Step 2. Assign a group number (G_k) to each $node_i$ if $|node_i| > 0$, and update the corresponding centroid value.

Step 3. Calculate the overall variance of the map:
(a)   Sum the square distance between input vector x and the group centroid $\bar{c}_k$ for all $\bar{x}$ in G_k. Calculate for every group k.

$$V_k = \sum \| \bar{x} - \bar{c}_k \|, \ \bar{x} \in G_k.$$

(b)   Total the variances from all groups. This will give us the global variance of the map:

$$V_{Total} = \sum V_k.$$

Step 4. For each pair of neighboring groups, calculate the total variance of the map if the two groups were merged. Merge the two groups that result in the minimum global variance.
(a)   Calculate the new centroid for G_{pq} if G_p and G_q were merged:

$$\bar{c}_{pq} = (| node_p | * \bar{c}_p + | node_q | * \bar{c}_q) / (| node_p | + | node_q |).$$

(b)   Calculate the new variance if G_p and G_q were merged (modified from Murtagh, 1985):

$$V_{pq} = \sum \| \bar{x} - \bar{c}_{pq} \|, \text{ for all } \bar{x}, \ \bar{x} \in G_p \text{ or } \bar{x} \in G_q.$$

(c)   Calculate the new global variance for merging G_p and G_q:

$$V_{pqTotal} = V_{Total} + V_{pq} - V_p - V_q.$$

(d)   Calculate the $V_{pqTotal}$ for every pair of p and q on the map. For each iteration, groups p and q must be within a fixed radius distance on the grid. We start with radius distance $= 1$, hence, for each node there are eight neighboring nodes within that distance. We increase the radius distance by one each time if there is no neighboring group within current radius distance for all groups k. Finally, we merge the two groups that result in global minimal variance.

(e) Update V_{Total} and the group number and group centroid of the two newly merged groups.

Step 5. Repeat Step 4 until only one cluster or the pre-specified number of clusters has been reached.

AN EMPIRICAL ILLUSTRATION

Data Set

Data were obtained from a panel study that the American Telephone and Telegraph Company (AT&T) undertook for the purpose of market segmentation and strategy development. The company maintained a demographically proportional, national panel of 3,602 heads of households who participated in a 12-month diary. The AT&T sample was demographically balanced in terms of income, marital status, age, gender, population density, and geographic region. In a pre-diary survey, each panel member was asked to respond to a series of 68 attitude questions related to long distance communications. The items were derived from a series of focus group interviews and had been tested for reliability and validity. Examples of the items are: "Sometimes I make a long distance call simply to save the hassle of writing a letter," "some people expect long distance calls from me at fairly regular intervals," and "it bothers me that I have lost touch with many friends that I was close to at one time." A six-point Likert scale ranging from 'agree completely' (coded as '6') to 'disagree completely' (coded as '1') was used for each of these 68 items.

The Method of Factor Analysis and K-Means

In this chapter we used Version 11.0 for Windows of the SPSS Statistical package to perform the two-step procedure that uses the factor scores from factor analysis as inputs to K-means cluster analysis. The first step was to factor analyze the data set and reduce the 68 attitude variables to a smaller and more interpretable set of factors. Specifically, principal factor analysis with varimax rotation was used to condense the customers' responses to the 68 questions into 14 attitude factor scores. The resulting factor scores represent the following major attitudinal dimensions uncovered in the AT&T study:

- Personal emotional satisfaction with long distance calling
- Lack of expressive skills on long distance calls
- Long distance calling is better than writing
- Long distance calling is seen as obligatory
- Cost-consciousness about long distance usage
- Long distance seen as a medium for exchange function information
- Compulsive planning
- Insensitivity to communication situations
- Long distance calls seen as disturbing
- Demonstrative personality
- Emotionally reserved life style
- Long distance seen as a luxury for special occasions
- Long distance calls show others you care
- Long distance rates are reasonable

The second step was to use the K-means clustering algorithm to group the 3,602 respondents into six segments with the 14 factor scores. Respondents grouped into a segment using K-means cluster analysis had a unique pattern of responses to the attitude items that were different from the patterns of all other segments. Based on respondents' responses to the attitude factors, the AT&T study labeled the six segments as: routine communicators, emotional communicators, anxious worriers, budgeters, detached communicators, and functionalists.

The Extended SOM Clustering Method

First, we used the SPSS Statistical package to perform a normality test on each of the 68 attitude items in the AT&T data set. All 68 variables exhibit significant deviations from normality as indicated by the Shapiro-Wilk statistic (Royston, 1992; Wilk & Shapiro, 1968). This strongly suggests that SOM as a nonparametric approach that makes no assumptions about the underlying population distribution may be more appropriate than parametric models to describe this data set.

An implementation of the extended SOM in C++ was used to reduce the 68 attribute variables to a two-dimensional plot. After some preliminary runs, it shows that the network size has no significant effect on the performance of the network. We fixed the Kohonen layer to a 7x7 network. Since the AT&T study has identified six market segments, we grouped the respondents into six clusters. Then we examined the average scores of attitude items within each segment. Based on the average attitude scores, segments were labeled as routine communicators, emotional communicators, anxious worriers, budgeters, detached communicators, and functionalists. For example, routine communicators "see long distance communications as an everyday necessary tool for frequent communication"; emotional communicators "derive great personal emotional gratification from long distance usage"; anxious worriers "associate long distance communications with disturbing experiences"; budgeters "are very cost-conscious"; detached communicators "do not have strong need to communicate caring to others"; and functionalists "do not relate to long distance communications emotionally." Since there are 68 attitude variables and six segments, the resulting average attitude scores were too numerous to list here. Instead we present the resulting two-dimensional plot depicting the six market segments as shown in Figure 2. The segment boundaries are delineated in Figure 2. Emotional communicators constitute the segment with the largest market potential and budgeters, the smallest potential.

Figure 2: The 7x7 SOM with Six Labeled Clusters

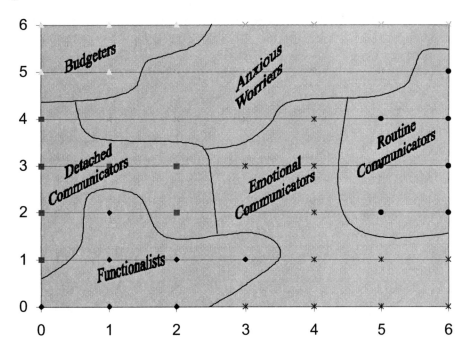

THE COMPARATIVE STUDY

In market segmentation studies, the accurate assignments of respondents to clusters/segments are critical. Kiang and Kumar (2001) used simulated data where true cluster memberships are known and found that SOM networks provide more accurate recovery of underlying cluster structures when the input data are skewed. Since true cluster memberships are unknown for the real-world data set, it is difficult to determine which clustering method is best for the real-life problem.

The accuracy of membership assignments can be measured using the pooled within cluster variance or the sum of squares (SSE). Given the fact that only two output dimensions are used in the extended SOM and 14 factor scores are used for clustering, in order to establish a more valid basis for comparison, all 68 items are used in the calculation of total within group variance. The extended SOM has a variance of 562241.1 as compared to 584196.5 for the two-step approach, yielding a difference of 21955.4 (roughly a 4% reduction).

The salient feature of the extended SOM network is its ability to reduce the input space to a one- or two- dimensional output map while maintaining the original topological relations. In other words, the data points that were close in the higher dimensional space should remain close in the reduced lower dimensional map. The two-dimensional plot provides an easy-to-use graphical interface and helps the decision maker visualize the relationships among inputs. On the other hand, by using factor scores we are able to interpret and label the six segments.

CONCLUSION

In this chapter we first identify the importance of market segmentation in market management and strategy development. The first and primary component in market segmentation is the formation of groups. Accurate forecast of segment membership is the key to successful market segmentation programs. The traditional approach relies heavily on factor analysis for dimension reduction and cluster analysis for grouping. The imposition of linearity and normality assumptions may lead to less desirable segment memberships. This chapter examines the viability of using the extended SOM method for dimension reduction and grouping.

The extended SOM network is a contiguity-constraint based clustering method integrated with the original SOM networks. The extended SOM network is applied to perform clustering analysis on a real world data set.

Based on the total within cluster variance, the extended SOM method outperformed the two-step factor/cluster procedure. Moreover, the extended SOM network provides the user with a visual rendering of the market segments. Our procedure is a robust substitute for the current approach of market segmentation with K-means analysis and also for other problem domains that require clustering.

REFERENCES

Balakrishnan, P. V., Cooper, M. C., Jacob, V. S., & Lewis, P. A. (1994). A study of the classification capabilities of neural networks using unsupervised learning: A comparison with K-means clustering. *Psychometrika*, 59(4), 509-525.

Bimbo, A. D., Landi, L., & Santini, S. (1993). Three-dimensional planar-faced object classification with Kohonen maps. *Optical Engineering*, 32(6), 1222-1234.

Chaturvedi, A., Carroll, J. D., Green, P. E., & Rotondo, J. A. (1997). A feature-based approach to market segmentation via overlapping k-centroids clustering. *Journal of Marketing Research*, 34, 370-377.

Cottrell, M. & Fort, J. C. (1986). A stochastic model of retinotopy: A self-organizing process. *Biol. Cybern.*, 53, 405-411.

DeSieno, D. (1988). Adding a conscience to competitive learning. *Proceedings of the International Conference on Neural Networks* (Vol. 1, pp. 117-124). New York: IEEE Press.

Kiang, M. Y. & Kumar, A. (2001). An evaluation of self-organizing map networks as a robust alternative to factor analysis in data mining applications. *Information Systems Research*, 12(2), 177-194.

Kohonen, T. (1984). *Cybernetic Systems: Recognition, Learning, Self-Organization.* E.R. Caianiello, G. Musso (Eds.). Letchworth, Herfordshire, UK: Research Studies Press, Ltd.

Kohonen, T. (1989). *Self-Organization and Associative Memory* (2nd edition). Springer-Verlag.

Kohonen, T. (1995). *Self-Organizing Maps.* Springer.

Kotler, P. (1980). *Marketing Management – Analysis, Planning, and Control* (4th edition). Prentice-Hall.

Leinonen, L., Hiltunen, T., Torkkola, K., & Kangas, J. (1993). Self-organized acoustic feature map in detection of fricative-vowel co-articulation. *Journal of Acoustical Society of America*, 93(6), 3468-3474.

Lo, Z. P. & Bavarian, B. (1991). On the rate of convergence in topology preserving neural networks. *Biol. Cybern.*, 65, 55-63.

Manikopoulos, C. N. (1993). Finite state vector quantisation with neural network classification of states. *IEEE Proceedings-F*, 140(3), 153-161.

Mitra, S. & Pal, S. K. (1994). Self-organizing neural network as a fuzzy classifier. *IEEE Transactions on Systems, Man, and Cybernetics*, 24(3), 385-399.

Murtagh, F. (1985). *Multidimensional Clustering Algorithms*. Physica-Verlag, Wurzburg.

Murtagh, F. (1995). Interpreting the Kohonen self-organizing feature map using contiguity-constrained clustering. *Pattern Recognition Letters*, 16, 399-408.

NeuralWare Reference Guide. (1990). Pittsburgh, PA: NeuralWare, Inc.

Ritter, H. & Schulten, K. (1986). On the stationary state of Kohonen's self-organizing sensory mapping. *Biol. Cybern.*, 54, 99-106.

Ritter, H., Martinetz, T., & Schulten, K. (1989). Topology-conserving maps for learning visuo-motor-coordination. *Neural Networks*, 2, 159-168.

Royston, J. P. (1992). Approximating the Shapiro-Wilk's W test for non-normality. *Statistics and Computing*, 2, 117-119.

Sabourin, M. & Mitiche, A. (1993). Modeling and classification of shape using a Kohonen associative memory with selective multi-resolution. *Neural Networks*, 6, 275-283.

Sharma, S., Durvasula, S., & Dillon, W. R. (1989). Some results on the behavior of alternate covariance structure estimation procedures in the presence of non-normal data. *Journal of Marketing Research*, 26, 214-221.

Vercauteren, L., Sieben, G., Praet, M., Otte, G., Vingerhoeds, R., Boullart, L., Calliauw, L., & Roels, H. (1990). The classification of brain tumors by a topological map. *Proceedings of the International Neural Networks Conference,* Paris (pp. 387-391).

Walter, J. A. & Schulten, K. J. (1993). Implementation of self-organizing neural networks for visuo-motor control of an industrial robot. *IEEE Transactions on Neural Networks*, 4(1), 86-95.

Wedel, M. & Kamakura, W. (1999). *Market Segmentation: Conceptual and Methodological Foundations*. Kluwer Academic Publisher.

Wilk, M. B. & Shapiro, S. S. (1968). The joint assessment of normality of several independent samples. *Technometrics*, 10, 825-839.

Willshaw, D. J. & Malsburg, C. v.d. (1979). *Philos. Trans. Roy. Soc.* London Ser. B287, 203.

Zhao, Z. & Rowden, C. G. (1992). Use of Kohonen self-organizing feature maps for HMM   parameter smoothing in speech recognition. *IEEE Proceedings-F*, 139(6), 385-390.

Chapter VIII

Backpropagation and Kohonen Self-Organizing Feature Map in Bankruptcy Prediction

Kidong Lee, University of Incheon, South Korea

David Booth, Kent State University, USA

Pervaiz Alam, Kent State University, USA

ABSTRACT

The back-propagation (BP) network and the Kohonen self-organizing feature map, selected as the representative types for the supervised and unsupervised artificial neural networks (ANN) respectively, are compared in terms of prediction accuracy in the area of bankruptcy prediction. Discriminant analysis and logistic regression are also performed to provide performance benchmarks. The findings suggest that the BP network is a better choice when a target vector is available. Advantages as well as limitations of the studied methods are also identified and discussed.

INTRODUCTION

Artificial neural networks are often classified into two distinctive training types, supervised and unsupervised. Supervised training requires training pairs, that is, input vectors as well as corresponding target vectors. A BP network is a good example of the supervised training type and is the most popular training method in the ANN literature. The reason for the success of the multilayer perceptron (MLP) and its learning algorithm, BP, is that the outputs of the BP network are the estimates of posterior probabilities that have a central role in statistical pattern classification theory (Berardi, 1998).

However, to train supervised networks such as the BP network, we must provide a target vector. In the case of bankruptcy prediction tasks, the target vector is *"whether or not a firm has failed"* which must be embedded in the supervised training process. But in some situations, especially in today's fast-changing, real-time-based business environment that demands prompt responses, such extra target information may not be readily available for training. In such circumstances, unsupervised neural networks might be more appropriate technologies to be applied. Unlike supervised networks, unsupervised neural networks need only input vectors for training. Developed by Kohonen (1997, 1982) and many others, the training algorithms for the unsupervised networks modify the algorithm weights to process input vectors into similar output classes (or clusters).

The BP supervised network has been the most widely used network type for bankruptcy prediction. These two different approaches, supervised and unsupervised, should be compared so that the feasibility and effectiveness of diverse neural network algorithms may be better understood. Note that it is somewhat difficult to compare these supervised and unsupervised networks directly because of their radically different orientations. Thus, in this study, we confine ourselves to comparing the BP network and the Kohonen self-organizing feature map, selected as the representative types for the supervised and unsupervised neural networks respectively, in the context of bankruptcy prediction. Quadratic discriminant analysis (QDA) and logistic regression are also performed to provide performance benchmarks. QDA was used because the group covariance matrices failed to pass an equality of variance test (SAS Proc Discrim).

Since the BP network (supervised) utilizes one more critical variable, the target vector, in the training process, it might be expected that the BP network would be more accurate than the Kohonen self-organizing feature map (unsupervised). However, the focus of this study is to compare prediction accuracy between the two neural networks (and the two other statistical techniques). In doing so, we may observe different characteristics and behaviors of a Kohonen network versus a BP network.

The rest of the chapter is organized as follows: the next section illustrates the brief introduction of BP and the Kohonen network algorithms followed by prior research in the area of bankruptcy prediction. This is followed with a section that provides the research design and methodologies in terms of data, variables, cross-validation scheme, and classification technologies used for the study. Next, experimental results are shown and discussed where the results of each of the four individual classification techniques are compared. The limitations, future research directions, and conclusions are given at the end of the chapter.

PRIOR LITERATURE
Back Propagation (BP) Network

The BP algorithm, a systematic training method for a Multi-Layer Perceptron (MLP), has been most widely used in bankruptcy prediction tasks. The BP algorithm is well explained throughout the literature such as Zhang (1998), Refenes (1995), and Wasserman (1989). In BP, the differences (or errors) between the target values and the actual network outputs are first computed. The main idea of the BP network is to reduce this error measure to some desirable level by means of adjusting a weight vector (Wasserman, 1989; O'Leary, 1998; Zhang, 1998). To do so, researchers must first search for an optimal architecture for the BP network, along with its associated parameters. This task involves determining a number of design variables for a BP network (e.g., activation functions, error measure functions, MLP architecture, and a particular training method). Determining an appropriate architecture and parameters for a BP network is not a simple, but an exhaustive and time-consuming task (Zhang, 1998; Refenes, 1995).

Kohonen Self-Organizing Neural Network

Another popular neural network model is the unsupervised Kohonen self-organizing feature map (Kohonen, 1997, 1982). The Kohonen self-organizing neural networks have appeared in many fields, for example, classification (Corridoni et al., 1996; Deschenes & Noonan, 1995), pattern recognition (Xin-Hua & Hopke, 1996), clustering (Martin-del-Brio & Serrano-Cinca, 1995; Kiviluoto, 1998), and forecasting (Der Voort et al., 1996). The Kohonen training process is explained in Kohonen (1997, 1982) and succinctly summarized by Nour (1994). Many researchers propose that the unsupervised training type is more plausible in an ever-changing business environment, as occurs today, than is the supervised training method (Waldrop, 1992; Kelly, 1994; Hinton & Sejnowski, 1999).

In Table 1, we summarize the marked differences of these two learning styles of neural networks. A supervised learning network needs input/output pairs, retrieves a target, does not self-organize, needs error functions, and is computationally heavy. On the other hand, an unsupervised learning network needs only inputs, produces an output as the reconstruction form of the input, does self-organize, does not need error functions, and is computationally simple.

Bankruptcy Prediction

Bankruptcy prediction, a binary decision-making process, has long been a popular subject for business researchers. The improvement of the bankruptcy prediction process has come from the incessant effort of past researchers to use techniques such as ratio analyses, linear models, or nonlinear models, including neural networks.

Beaver (1966) was one of the first researchers to study bankruptcy prediction by testing the efficacy of several financial ratios in their classification and prediction capabilities. Altman (1968) introduced a class of models based on discriminant analysis for classifying potential bankruptcy using the following five variables: working capital/total assets, retained earnings/total assets, earnings before interest and taxes/total assets, market value of equity/total debt, and sales/total assets. Ohlson (1980), with the use of a logistic regression to estimate the probabilities of a bankruptcy, reported a more successful approach to corporate failure.

Table 1: Characteristics of the Supervised vs. Unsupervised Learning Types

Learning Type	SUPERVISED	UNSUPERVISED
Example	BP	Kohonen self-organizing feature map
Characteristics	Input/Output needed Retrieves a target Error function needed Derivatives needed Does not self-organize Computationally heavy	Only input needed Reconstructs an input Error function not needed Derivatives not needed Self-organizes Computationally light

Neural networks were not used as a bankruptcy classification method until the early 1990s. Odom and Sharda (1990) were the first researchers to investigate the feasibility of neural networks in firm failure prediction. They found that BP networks are at least as accurate as discriminant analysis. After this first neural experiment, a significant volume of neural network research followed (Tam & Kiang, 1992; Salchenberger et al., 1992; Udo, 1993; Tsukuda & Baba, 1994; Wilson & Sharda, 1994; Sharda & Wilson, 1996; Martin-del-Brio & Serrano-Cinca, 1995; Jo, Han, & Lee, 1997; O'Leary, 1998; Kiviluoto, 1998; Zhang et al., 1999; Alam et al., 2000). As it is seen, many ANN researchers heavily relied on the BP network. Also, O'Leary's study (1998) summarized these early ANN studies, almost all of them using BP networks.

Recently many studies have tried to experiment with the Kohonen self-organizing feature maps (e.g., Martin-del-Brio & Serrano-Cinca, 1995; Kiviluoto, 1998; Alam et al., 2000). The popularity of using unsupervised networks, i.e., Kohonen, stems from the notion that business events themselves are showing self-organizing behaviors of each business event. Once again, direct comparison between these two different learning styles is somewhat difficult, but we try to contrast supervised and unsupervised neural networks using their most widely used models, hoping that the advantages and disadvantages of the Kohonen self-organizing feature map to the BP network become apparent.

RESEARCH DESIGN AND METHODOLOGY
Data and Variables
The data sample for this bankruptcy prediction study consists of Korean listed companies that have filed for bankruptcy during the 1995-1998 period. An initial search of bankrupt firms is made through the Security and Exchange Commission (SEC) filings stored in an on-line database (commercially available in an electronic format) of the Korea Investors Service (KIS), Inc., a strategic partner with Moody's Investors Service in the Korean security market. Financial institutions such as commercial banks or investment banks are excluded from this data set because in the Korean market the fate of such financial intermediaries seems to be much more affected by government policies, rather than by their financial position.

Searching for failed firms resulted in 113 nonfinancial failed firms among the listed companies on the Korean stock market. Then, the availability of the financial ratios for the failed firms further reduced the final bankrupt sample size to 84, since some of them seemed not to report their financial status in their bankruptcy filings. Each failed firm is matched with a non-failed firm in terms of (1) asset size and (2) a two-digit Standard Industrial Classification (SIC) code as control measures. The asset size of a non-failed firm is matched with that of a failed firm using the three-year period prior to the bankruptcy filing. As a result, we have a matched sample of 168 firms; 84 failed firms and 84 non-failed firms. Two time-framed financial data sets, the two-year and the three-year prior to bankruptcy filing, are prepared for this experiment in order to see if any of these tested classification methods can detect any problem financial condition of a firm prior to bankruptcy.

Each firm is described by Altman's five variables because the prediction capabilities of these ratios are well documented in the previous literature (Zhang et al., 1999; Boritz & Kennedy, 1995; Odom & Sharda, 1990; Altman, 1968). The variables are:

1. WCTA = working capital/total assets, a measure of the net liquid assets of the firm to the total capitalization.
2. RETA = retained earnings/total assets, a measure of cumulative profitability.
3. EBITTA = earnings before interest and taxes/total assets, a measure of true productivity of the firm's assets.
4. MEDEBT = market value of equity/book value of total debt, a measure of how much the firm's assets can decline in value before the liabilities exceed the assets and the firm becomes insolvent.
5. SALETA = sales/total assets, a measure of the sales generating ability of the firm's assets.

Cross-Validation Scheme

Any bias due to changing data set composition could have a detrimental impact on determining neural network architecture and its parameters. A cross-validation technique is introduced to investigate the classification performance of neural networks in terms of sampling variation. The cross-validation technique enables us to use a whole data set in a systematic way so that, it is hoped, any bias effect would be minimized (Zhang et al., 1999; Tam & Kiang, 1992).

In this study, a four-fold cross-validation technique is used. The total data set that contains 84 matched firms (84 failed firms and 84 non-failed firms) is divided into four equal and mutually exclusive subsets, each of which contains 21 matched objects (21 failed firms and 21 non-failed firms). Table 2 shows the details of this four-fold cross-validation scheme.

Table 2: Four-Fold Cross-Validation Technique

	Entire set of data			
	First (One-fourth)	Second (One-fourth)	Third (One-fourth)	Fourth (One-fourth)
Subset1*	Training set		Validation set	Testing set
Subset2	Testing set	Training set		Validation set
Subset3	Validation set	Testing set	Training set	
Subset4	Training set	Validation set	Testing set	Training set

* Note that each subset contains 21 matched objects.

Training is conducted on any two of the four subsets while the remaining two sets are used for validation and testing purposes, respectively. The validation set is introduced as an early stopping technique, to improve generalization (MathWorks, 1997). Using this early stopping technique, the validation process is embedded into the training results, which would prevent a possible upward bias of the classification accuracy of a training set.

Pattern Classification Methodologies

Two groups of pattern classification methods used here are neural network and statistical modeling techniques. Two statistical modeling techniques, discriminant analysis and logistic regression, are employed to provide benchmarks for the neural network classifiers. From the two groups of neural network classification techniques, supervised and unsupervised, the BP and the Kohonen self-organizing feature map were selected as the most representative type for each group and were used to test their prediction accuracy in bankruptcy prediction. For the BP experiment, the Matlab Neural Network Toolbox is used. A BP network with a three-layer model (also called a one-hidden layer model) is considered in this study. The previous studies show that as long as there are sufficient numbers of hidden nodes provided, this architectural BP network is able to approximate any arbitrary function well (Funahashi, 1989; Hornik et al., 1989). A two-dimensional Kohonen output layer is used to help provide a visual presentation. The Viscovery Som 3.0 system (http://www.eudaptics.com) software is used for the Kohonen experiment. Full details of the architectural structures are available from the authors.

Figure 1: A Result of the Kohonen Self-Organizing Feature Map Applied to a Subset 3

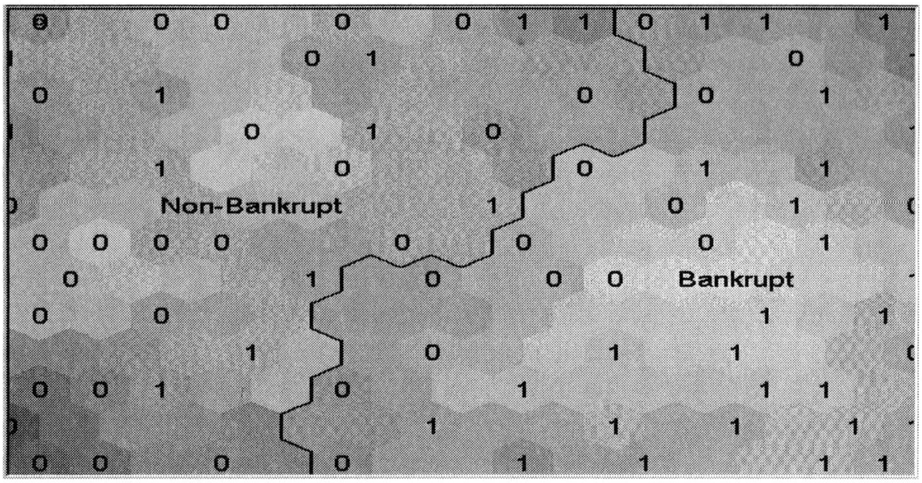

EXPERIMENTAL RESULTS

Figure 1 is a result of the Kohonen self-organizing feature map that applies to one subset, produced by the four-fold cross-validation scheme. In Figure 1, 0s indicate non-failed firms, and 1s indicate bankrupt firms. Two regions, non-bankrupt and bankrupt, are separated by the Kohonen self-organizing feature map. Further, we can see some misclassified objects in the two regions.

Table 3 provides a summary performance comparison among the four methodological choices used in this bankruptcy prediction study: the two neural networks, the BP networks and the Kohonen self-organizing feature maps, and of the two statistical classifiers, QDA and logistic regression. In Table 3, note that the # column shows the number of objects correctly classified while the % column shows the % of objects correctly classified, and that the best *classification* model (for training) for each subset is identified by underlining the model classification rate.

As expected, the BP networks show the highest classification accuracy. Among the total eight sets, seven from the BP network, one from the Kohonen network, and another from discriminant analysis are selected as the best classification models. Note that there is a tie in the classification result between the BP and the Kohonen in Subset 3 in the three-year data set being used.

Again, the best *prediction* model (for test) for each subset is identified by typing the prediction rate in **bold**-face. The BP networks show the best prediction capabilities across the sample variability. Among the total eight sets, six from the BP network, two from the logistic regression, and one from the Kohonen network are recognized as the best prediction models. Note again that there is a tie between the BP network and the logistic model in one subset being used.

Effectiveness of each individual technique should also be tested, which is shown in Table 4. It gives the SAS ANOVA results with the Duncan Option for training as well as test sets. Letters in the Duncan grouping columns show the group to which the mean of each group belongs. Different letters in the Duncan Option indicate that groups are significantly different at a 5% level.

In Table 4, the BP network seems to be the most accurate model. Duncan grouping shows that BP method gives A's for both training and test sets. The runner-up is logistic regression as shown in the test section of the Duncan grouping. The results of the Kohonen network are third and QDA shows the least accuracy among the classification methods compared. Their prediction rates are, however, comparable to the logistic regression.

In Table 4, discriminant analysis does not seem to show a comparable performance to the remaining three techniques, and thus its presence might obscure some statistical tests. For this reason, we drop the discriminant

Table 3: Summary of Prediction Accuracy Results of the Datasets

Year	Subset	Type	BP		Kohonen		QDA		Logistic	
			#	%	#	%	#	%	#	%
2	Subset 1	Training	66	78.57%	58	69.05%	59	70.24%	64	76.19%
		Test	31	73.81%	28	66.67%	25	59.52%	24	57.14%
	Subset 2	Training	64	76.19%	54	64.29%	56	66.67%	56	66.67%
		Test	30	71.43%	27	64.29%	28	66.67%	29	69.05%
	Subset 3	Training	59	70.24%	56	66.67%	54	64.29%	56	66.67%
		Test	33	78.57%	28	66.67%	28	66.67%	33	78.57%
	Subset 4	Training	69	82.14%	62	73.81%	56	66.67%	62	73.81%
		Test	25	59.52%	23	54.76%	23	54.87%	27	64.29%
3	Subset 1	Training	61	72.62%	59	70.24%	62	73.81%	59	70.24%
		Test	30	71.43%	32	76.19%	26	61.90%	26	61.90%
	Subset 2	Training	59	70.24%	58	69.05%	51	60.71%	52	61.90%
		Test	30	71.43%	25	59.52%	27	64.29%	26	61.90%
	Subset 3	Training	56	66.67%	56	66.67%	51	60.71%	52	61.90%
		Test	30	71.43%	28	66.67%	27	64.29%	28	66.67%
	Subset 4	Training	62	73.81%	59	70.24%	54	64.29%	56	66.67%
		Test	28	66.67%	22	52.38%	26	61.90%	26	61.90%

Table 4: Results of Duncan's Multiple Range Tests for Training and Test Sets

Set	Technique	Means	Duncan Grouping	
Training	BP	62.000	A	
	Logistic Regression	57.125		B
	Kohonen	57.750		B
	Discriminant Analysis	55.375		B
Test	BP	29.625	A	
	Logistic Regression	27.375	A	B
	Kohonen	26.625		B
	Discriminant Analysis	26.250		B

analysis method in the following ANOVA test, which focuses on the prediction (test) performance of the remaining three individual classification techniques. A one-way ANOVA with one repeated-measure design is used to compare the possible performance (test) rate differences among the three classification techniques. The null hypothesis is that there is no difference in the prediction rates of the three classification techniques. Since the p value is .0434 ($F_{2,14} = 3.96$) for the one-way ANOVA with one repeated-measure design, our test result rejects the null hypothesis of no differences in the mean levels of prediction rates among the three classification techniques. Thus, we give a paired multiple comparisons among the three methods as: (1) the BP versus the Kohonen, (2) the Kohonen versus the logistic regression, and finally (3) the logistic regression versus the BP networks in Table 5.

Table 5 shows that there is a prediction rate difference between the BP network and the Kohonen network at about a 1% level. Also, the performance rates between the BP network and the logistic regression differ nearly at a 5% significance level. That means that the BP networks show the best performance results among the three classification methods. It is reassuring that the results of this study confirm the findings of the previous literature that the BP networks provide a good mapping function for bankruptcy indication (Zhang et al., 1999; Berardi, 1998; Tam & Kiang, 1992).

Table 5: Paired Comparison Among the Three Classifiers, BP, Kohonen, and Logistic

	BP vs. Kohonen	Kohonen vs. Logistic	Logistic vs.BP
F-value	11.45	0.29	5.30
p-value	0.0117	0.6083	0.0548

The performance results of the Kohonen self-organizing feature maps are not as good as the BP networks, but they are comparable to logistic regression in this study. Considering that supervised networks, like the BP network, need target vector information such as bankruptcy-filing statements to make training possible, an unsupervised network may provide a new way of investigating data sets when such critical information is not available. However, some bankruptcy information is needed to identify the clusters.

CONCLUSION

The main purpose of this study is to investigate two different training (or learning) types of neural networks using their representative networks — the BP network (supervised) versus the Kohonen self-organizing feature map (unsupervised) — in terms of their performance accuracy in the area of bankruptcy prediction. Discriminant analysis and logistic regression have also been introduced to give some performance benchmarks for the neural network classifiers.

The testbed for this study is the Korean listed companies. It should be noted that training data sets (84 objects) used in this study is, indeed, a small one. Usually, BP networks provide a good posterior probability when they have enough objects to be learned. That is because the neural network paradigm is, in essence, a data driven non-parametric approach. However, we show that even with the small sample size, the BP networks consistently outperform logistic regression as well as the other classification techniques.

REFERENCES

Alam, P., Booth, D., Lee, K., & Thordarson, T. (2000). The use of fuzzy clustering algorithm and self-organizing neural networks for identifying potentially failing banks: An experimental study. *Expert Systems with Applications,* 18, 185-199.

Altman, E. L. (1968). Financial ratios, discriminate analysis and the prediction of corporate bankruptcy. *Journal of Finance,* 23(3), 589-609.

Beaver, W. (1966). Financial ratios as predictors of failure, empirical research in accounting, selected studies 1966. *Journal of Accounting Research,* 4, 71-111.

Berardi, V. (1998). *An Investigation of neural network ensemble methods for posterior probability estimation.* Unpublished Ph.D. dissertation, Kent State University, USA.

Boritz, J. E. & Kennedy, D. B. (1995). Effectiveness of neural network types for Prediction of Business Failure. *Expert Systems with Applications,* 9(4), 503-512.

Corridoni, J. M., Del Bimbo, A., & Landi, L. (1996). 3D object classification using multi-object Kohonen networks. *Pattern Recognition,* 29(6), 919-935.

Der Voort, M., Dougherty, M., & Watson, S. (1996). Combining Kohonen maps with arima time series models to forecast traffic flow. *Transportation Research Part C: Emerging Technologies,* 4(5), 307-318.

Deschenes, C. J. & Noonan, J. (1995). Fuzzy Kohonen network for the classification of transients using the wavelet transform for feature extraction. *Information Sciences,* 87(4), 247-266.

Funahashi, K. (1989). On the approximate realization of continuous mappings by neural networks. *Neural Networks,* 2, 189-192.

Hinton, G. & Sejnowski, T. (eds.) (1999). *Unsupervised Learning: Foundations of Neural Computation.* Cambridge, MA: The MIT Press.

Hornik, K., Stinchcombe, M., & White, H. (1989). Multi-layer feedforward networks are universal approximators. *Neural Networks,* 2, 359-366.

Jo, H. Y., Han, I. G., & Lee, H. Y. (1997). Bankruptcy prediction using case-based reasoning, neural networks, and discriminant analysis. *Expert Systems with Applications,* 13(2), 97-108.

Kelly, K. (1994). *Out of Control, The New Biology of Machines, Social Systems, and the Economic World.* Reading, MA: Perseus Books.

Kiviluoto, K. (1998). Predicting bankruptcies with the self-organizing map. *Neurocomputing,* 21, 191-201.

Kohonen, T. (1982). Self-organized formation of topologically correct feature maps. *Biological Cybernetics,* 43, 59-69.

Kohonen, T. (1997). *Self-organizing Maps* (2nd edition). Berlin: Springer-Verlag.

Martin-del-Brio, B. & Serrano-Cinca, C. (1995). Self-organizing neural networks: The financial state of Spanish companies. Refenes (Ed.), *Neural Network in the Capital Markets.* Refenes (pp. 341-357).

MathWorks. (1997). *Matlab: Neural Network Toolbox, User's Guide.* Natick, MA: The MathWorks, Inc.

Nour, M. A. (1994). *Improved clustering and classification algorithms for the Kohonen self-organizing neural network.* Unpublished Ph.D. dissertation, Kent State University, USA.

Odom, M. & Sharda, R. (1990). A neural network model for bankruptcy prediction. *Proceedings of the IEEE International Conference on Neural Networks* (pp. 163-168).

Ohlson, J. (1980). Financial ratios and the probabilistic prediction of bankruptcy. *Journal of Accounting Research,* 18(1), 109-131.

O'Leary, D. E. (1998). Using neural networks to predict corporate failure. *International Journal of Intelligent Systems in Accounting, Finance & Management,* 7, 187-197.

Refenes, A.-P. (1995). *Neural Networks in the Capital Market.* New York: John Wiley & Sons (Chapters 1-6, 3-98).

Salchenberger, L. M., Cinar, E. M., & Lash, N. A. (1992). Neural networks: A new tool for predicting thrift failures. *Decision Sciences,* 23, 899-916.

Sharda, R. & Wilson, R. L. (1996). Neural network experiments in business-failure forecasting: Predictive performance measurement issues. *International Journal of Computational Intelligence and Organization,* 1(2), 107-117

Tam, K. Y. & Kiang, M. Y. (1992). Managerial applications of neural networks: The case of bank failure predictions. *Management Science,* 38(7), 926-947.

Tsukuda, J. & Baba, S. I. (1994). Predicting Japanese corporate bankruptcy in terms of financial data using neural network. *Computers and Industrial Engineering, 26,* 445-448.

Udo, G. (1993). Neural network performance on the bankruptcy classification problem. *Computers and Industrial Engineering,* 25, 377-380.

Waldrop, M. M. (1992). *Complexity.* New York: Simon & Schuster, Inc.

Wasserman, P. D. (1989). *Neural Computing: Theory and Practice.* New York: Van Nostrand Reinhold.

Wilson, R. L. & Sharda, R. (1994). Bankruptcy prediction using neural networks. *Decision Support Systems,* 11, 545-557.

Xin-Hua, S. & Hopke, P. K. (1996). Kohonen neural network as a pattern recognition method based on the weight interpretation. *Analytica Chimica Acta,* 336, 57-66.

Zhang, G. (1998). *Linear and nonlinear times series forecasting with artificial neural networks,* Unpublished Ph.D. dissertation, Kent State University, USA.

Zhang, G., Hu, M.Y., Patuwo, B. E., & Indro, D. C. (1999). Artificial neural networks in bankruptcy prediction: General framework and cross-validation analysis. *European Journal of Operational Research,* 116, 16-32.

ELECTRONIC REFERENCES

Viscovery Som 3.0 System neural network web site: http://www.eudaptics.com.

Chapter IX

Predicting Consumer Situational Choice with Neural Networks

Michael Y. Hu, Kent State University, USA

Murali Shanker, Kent State University, USA

Ming S. Hung, Optimal Solutions Technologies, Inc., USA

ABSTRACT

This study shows how neural networks can be used to model posterior probabilities of consumer choice and a backward elimination procedure can be implemented for feature selection in neural networks. Two separate samples of consumer choice situations were selected from a large consumer panel maintained by AT&T. Our findings support the appropriateness of using neural networks for these two purposes.

INTRODUCTION

In recent years, there has been an upsurge in the business applications of artificial neural networks (ANNs) to forecasting and classification. Examples include prediction of bank bankruptcies (Tam & Kiang, 1992), success in joint ventures (Hu et al., 1996, 1999a), consumer choices (Kumar et al., 1995; West et al., 1997), derivative/option, stock prices (Lo, 1996; Refenes et al., 1996), and forecasting of currency exchange rates (Hu et al., 1999b), to name a few. An extensive review of forecasting models using ANNs is provided in Zhang et al. (1998). Despite this upsurge, many market researchers still treat ANNs as black boxes. However, just like any statistical model, neural networks must be carefully modeled for the application to be successful. In this study, we consider the various aspects of building neural network models for forecasting consumer choice. Specifically, a situational consumer choice model is constructed, and neural networks are used to predict what product or service a consumer will choose. Our approach relies on the estimation of *posterior probabilities* for consumer choice. The posterior probability, being a continuous variable, allows more interesting analysis of the relationships between consumer choice and the predictor variables.

The type of ANNs that we consider are multi-layer feedforward networks. Probably the most popular training method for such networks is back-propagation (Rumelhart et al., 1986). In this study, we use the algorithm developed by Ahn (1996) for training. As feedforward networks are now well established and discussions can be found in most textbooks on neural networks, they will not be presented here. But, one frequent and valid criticism of neural networks is that they can not explain the relationships among variables. Indeed, since neural networks usually use nonlinear functions, it is very difficult, if possible at all, to write out the algebraic relationship between a dependent and independent variable. Therefore, traditional statistical relationship tests — on regression parameters, for example — are either impossible or meaningless. A typical approach in neural network modeling is to consider the entire network as a function and just investigate the predicted value of a dependent variable against the independent variables. In this chapter, such analysis is reported. In addition, we highlight two modeling issues when using neural networks:

- *Model selection.* Selection of an appropriate model is a nontrivial task. One must balance *model bias* (accuracy) and *model variance* (consistency). A more complex model tends to offer smaller bias (greater accuracy), but also greater variance (less consistency). Among neural networks, a larger network tends to fit a training data set better, but perform more poorly when it is applied to new data.

- *Feature selection.* A modeler strives to achieve parsimony. So the goal here is to build a model with the least number of independent variables, yet producing equal or comparable predictive power. For neural networks, as mentioned above, parameter testing does not apply and, therefore, more computational intensive methods must be employed to determine the variables that should be included in a model. We offer and validate a heuristic that has worked well for the test data set.

The organization of this chapter is as follows. The next section briefly discusses the use of posterior probabilities for consumer choice. The entire approach to model situational choice prediction is then illustrated. The data came from a large-scale study conducted by the American Telephone and Telegraph Company (AT&T). As can be expected, one of the objectives of the study was to find out how consumers choose between various modes of communication. The results are then presented, which is followed by a section describing an experiment that evaluates and validates our feature selection heuristic. The final section contains the conclusion.

ESTIMATION OF
POSTERIOR PROBABILITIES

Definitions

A classification problem deals with assigning an object, based on its attributes, to one of several groups. Let $\mathbf{x}$ be the attribute vector of an object and ω_j denote the fact that the object is a member of group j. Then the probability $P(\omega_j \mid \mathbf{x})$ is called the posterior probability and it measures the probability that an object with attributes $\mathbf{x}$ belongs to group j. Traditional classification theory computes the posterior probability with the Bayes formula, which uses the prior probability and conditional density function (see, for example, Duda & Hart, 1973).

Posterior probabilities correspond to the likelihood of a consumer making a purchase in a consumer choice problem. Armed with the estimates of these probabilities, a marketer would know how likely a consumer is to alter his choice decision. For instance, a consumer with a probability of 0.498 is more likely to change one's choice than another with a probability of 0.20. Under this scenario, the marketer can more effectively target his product or messages to those consumers whose probabilities are closer to 0.5; and design strategies to increase these posterior probabilities for his product.

Typically, the posterior probability is a nonlinear function of **x** and cannot be derived directly. Hung et al. (1996) showed that the least squares estimators produce unbiased estimates of this probability. Neural networks provide a convenient way to perform this computation. For a prediction problem with **d** features and **m** groups, the neural network structure will have **d** input nodes and **m** output nodes. If we define the target values for the output nodes as in (1), and use the *least-square* objective function, it turns out the predicted value of the jth output variable is an unbiased estimator of the posterior probability that **x** belongs to group j (Hu et al., 2000). For a two group prediction, only one output node is sufficient and the target values will be 1 for group 1 and 0 for group 2.

$$T_j^p = \begin{cases} 1 \text{ if object } x \text{ belongs to group } j \\ 0 \text{ otherwise} \end{cases} \qquad (1)$$

Two critical conditions must be met for the estimates of posterior probabilities to be accurate. One is sample size. In a previous study with simulated data sets (Hung et al., 1996), we found that the larger the training sample is, the greater the accuracy. The second is the network size. Theoretically speaking, the larger the network is (with more hidden nodes), the greater the accuracy of function approximation. However, for a given training sample, too large a network may lead to overfitting the sample, at the expense of generalization to the entire population.

Model Selection

Model selection addresses the issue of what is the appropriate model (in our case, the neural network) for a given sample. Theoretically, model selection should be based on the trade-off between *model bias* and *model variance* (Geman et al., 1992). The bias of a model relates to the predictive accuracy of the model, whereas variance refers to the variability of the predictions. A model with low bias — by having many hidden nodes, for example — tends to have high variance. On the other hand, a model with low variance tends to have high bias. For a more detailed explanation of this issue, see Bishop (1995).

Empirically, we wish to select the smallest (in terms of hidden nodes) network with the best generalizability. A typical method to determine the generalizability of a model is to use a data set separate from the training set. In this project, the data set is divided into three subsets: *training*, *validation*, and *test sets*. For a given network architecture (here, it refers to the network with a specific number of hidden and input nodes), the training set was used to determine the network parameters. The resultant network is then used to predict the outcome of the validation set. The architecture with the best generalizability is then chosen. The test set is used to measure how well the chosen model can predict new, unseen observations.

EMPIRICAL EXAMINATION OF SITUATIONAL INFLUENCES ON CHOICE

The American Telephone and Telegraph Company maintained a consumer diary panel to study the consumer choice behavior in selecting long distance communication modes over time (Lee et al., 2000). The company embarked on a major research effort to understand the effect of situational influences on consumer choices of communication modes. It is envisioned that the usage of long distance phone calling is largely situational, since the service is readily available within a household and is relatively inexpensive. A demographically proportional national sample of 3,990 heads of households participated over a 12-month period. The sample was balanced with respect to income, marital status, age, gender, population density and geographic region. Each participant has to record the specifics on a weekly basis of one long distance (50 miles or more) communication situation. As a result, the company has compiled information on a total of roughly 250,000 communication situations.

Choice Modeling

The communication modes being reported are of three types, long distance telephone calling (LD), letter or card writing. Since long distance telephone calling is verbal and the other two are nonverbal, letter and card in this study are combined into one category. The dependent variable, COMMTYPE, is coded as '1' for LD and '0' for 'letter and card.'

For a communication initiated by the consumer, information on five situation-related factors is also reported. These factors are:

- the nature (TYCALL) of the communication decision, whether it is 'impulse' (coded as '0') or 'planned' (coded as '1');
- reasons (REASON) for communication, 'ordinary' (coded as '1') or 'emergency' (coded as '0');
- receivers (RECEIVER) of the communication, 'relatives' (coded as '1') or 'friends' (coded as '0');

- total number of communications made and received (TOTALCOM) during the diary week; and
- total number of LD calls made and received (NUMCALLS) during the diary week.

Information gathered on TYCALL, REASON, and RECEIVER has marketing implications for how the long distance call services can be positioned in an advertising campaign. Also, based on past studies, the company has found that as TOTALCOM increases for a consumer, the frequency of using LD increases. Thus, a viable strategy is to remind a consumer to keep in touch with friends/relatives. Information on NUMCALLS also has implication for advertising positioning. Consumers, in general, tend to reciprocate in their communication behavior. When a phone call is received, a consumer is likely to respond by calling. The company can encourage consumers to respond when a call is received.

In addition, information on six consumer demographic and socioeconomic variables is also reported at the start of the diary keeping activities. These variables include number of times the consumer has moved his/her place of residence in the past five years (MOVES); number of relatives (RELATIVE) and friends (FRIENDS) that live over 50 miles or more away; age (AGE), average number of cards and letters sent in a typical month (NUMCLET) and average number of long distance telephone calls made in a typical month (MEANCALL).

In this study, we use all five situation-based and the six demographic variables to predict choice of modes. These demographic variables are potential candidates for segmentation while allowing the differences in situational and demographic influences to be captured.

A sample of 1,480 communication situations is used from the weekly diary database, 705 (47.64%) are LD calls made and the remaining 775 (52.46%) written communications. The entire sample of situations is from a total of 707 diarists. The maximum number of situations reported is three per diarist.

For neural network modeling, the data set, as mentioned before, is randomly partitioned into training, validation, and test sets. The distribution is 60%, 20%, 20% — exactly the same as in West et al. (1997). The specific composition is shown in Table 1.

Design of Neural Network Models

As previously mentioned, the networks used in this study are feedforward networks with one hidden layer. There are direct connections from the input

Table 1: Number of Situations by Choice and Partition

	Training	Validation	Test
Long Distance Call	440	134	131
Letter/Card	448	162	165
Total	888	296	296

layer to the output layer. There is one output node and only it has a scalar. The activation function of the hidden nodes and the output node is logistic. An issue in neural network modeling is the scaling of input variables before training. Previous research (Shanker et al., 1996) indicates that data transformation is not very helpful for such problems and, hence, it is not performed here.

Given the choices made above, model selection is now reduced to the determination of the number of hidden nodes. Several practical guidelines have been proposed: *d* (Tang & Fishwick, 1993), *2d* (Wong, 1991), and *2d+1* (Lippmann, 1987), for a one-hidden-layer of *d* input nodes. However, none of these heuristics works well for all problems. Here we start with a network of 0 hidden nodes. It is trained on the training set and then applied to the validation set. Next we train a network of 1 hidden node and calculate the validation set *sums of square error* (SSE) similarly. This is repeated until a reasonably large number of hidden nodes has been investigated. (This number cannot be predetermined because the validation set SSE may go up and down for some time until a pattern develops.) Figure 1 shows the plot of SSE for the validation set as the number of hidden nodes varies from 0 to 6, with all the eleven feature variables as inputs.

Since the SSE in the validation sample takes on the smallest value at 1 hidden node, this architecture is selected for subsequent runs.

Selection of Input Variables

As discussed earlier, feature selection is an important and difficult topic in neural network modeling. Since hypothesis tests on parameters are not applicable here, we resort to a backward elimination method. Train a network with all *d* features included. Then delete one variable and train a new network. Delete a different variable from the original set and train another new network. We end up with *d* networks, each having *d-1* features. Select the network with the smallest validation set SSE. Now consider the selected set of features as the

Figure 1: Validation Set SSE vs. Number of Hidden Nodes

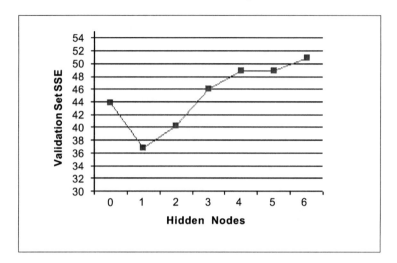

original set and repeat the process. This process continues until the validation set SSE increases drastically. This heuristic is admittedly "brute force," but the resultant network has been shown to classify better than the full-featured network in previous studies (Hu et al., 1996; Hung et al., 2001; Shanker, 1996). In addition, the following sections present an experiment that shows the backward-elimination approach for this dataset indeed selects the best of all possible network models.

As indicated in Figure 2, the validation set SSE for the 11-variable model is around 37. It drops to around 34 for the 10-, nine- and eight-variable models. It increases to about 36 and remains there for seven- to four-variable models. The next variable removal brings about a sharp increase in SSE. Although the eight-variable model has the smallest SSE, the four-variable is more attractive, because with only half of the variables its SSE is only slightly higher. So we decided on that model for further analysis.

The variables selected are REASON, RECEIVER, TOTALCOM and NUMCALLS. It is interesting to note that all the demographic variables are excluded from the final model. Researchers have found that situational and contextual factors have a major impact on situation-based choices (Hui & Bateson, 1991; Simonson & Winer, 1992). Conceptually, one can expect situation-specific factors to exercise a greater impact on these choices, since the consumer demographic factors are more enduring in nature and thus their influences may or may not enter into a particular purchase situation.

Figure 2: SSE vs. Number of Features

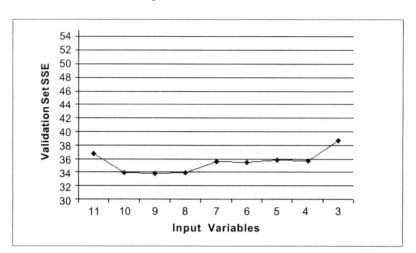

The appropriateness of the architecture being used is verified again by experimenting with the number of hidden nodes from 0 to 6. Once again the architecture with one hidden node is selected.

RESULTS

Investigation of Relationships

Suppose we knew that the four features — REASON, RECEIVER, TOTALCOM and NUMCALLS — would be useful to predict the type of communication. We can carry out some preliminary analyses before the models are built. Two of the variables, REASON and RECEIVER, are zero-one variables, so contingency tables such as Table 2 can be used.

Each ratio is the proportion of long distance calls with respect to the total number of communications. The observations are those in the training and validation sets. For example, there are 83 communications for REASON = 0 (emergency) and RECEIVER = 0 (friends), among them 59 are telephone calls. In general, the likelihood of placing a LD call is substantially higher in emergency situations and when the call is placed with relatives.

The other two variables are continuous and their relationships with the dependent variable can be explored with scatter plots. It was difficult to see any

Table 2: Frequency Table for COMMTYPE

| | REASON | | |
RECEIVER	0	1	Total
0	59/83 = .711	191/545 = .350	250/628 = .398
1	84/103 = .816	240/453 = .530	324/556 = .583
Total	143/186 = .769	431/998 = .432	574/1184 = .485

relationship between the dependent variable and either of the continuous variables in the scatter plots. In the interest of brevity, the plots are not shown here.

A neural network with one hidden node and four input nodes was trained on the combined training and validation sets, using the four features selected. The posterior probability is the probability that a consumer will choose long distance call for communication. So the first question a marketer may ask is, what is the relationship between each situational variable and such a choice? Table 3 shows the mean posterior probability for each combination of REASON and RECEIVER. The same pattern observed in the contingency table is clearly visible again — the probability to use long distance is highest under emergency situations to relatives. The fact that the average posterior probabilities are reasonably close to the raw relative frequencies in Table 2 confirms the validity of our neural network estimations.

With posterior probability as the dependent variable, and TOTALCOM and NUMCALLS as the two continuous independent variables, Figure 3 shows a clear pattern when REASON = 0 and RECEIVER = 0. First, the

Table 3: Mean Posterior Probability

| | REASON | | |
RECEIVER	0	1	Total
0	.744	.323	.379
1	.781	.514	.564
Total	.764	.410	.466

posterior probability functions are all nonlinear functions of TOTALCOM and NUMCALLS. Second, the function suggests a positive relationship with respect to NUMCALLS. With respect to TOTALCOM, the relationship is not clear when the variable is small, but seems positive when it is high. Similar patterns were observed in the other three plots and will not be presented here.

Some marketing implications can be drawn from the results of these graphs. The positive relationship between the posterior probability and NUMCALLS suggests that when a phone call is received, it is more likely for a consumer to respond with the same mode of communication. Notice that the process of reciprocity being generated can potentially lead to a multiplicative effect on the total volume of calls being made. A long distance phone company is well advised to remind consumers to reciprocate any long distance communication with the same mode.

Our results imply that as the total number of communication situations made and received (TOTALCOM) is small, the probability of making an LD call is widely scattered from 0 to 1; hence, it is difficult to predict the choice. However, when TOTALCOM is large (roughly more than 30), then the

Figure 3: Posterior Probability Function

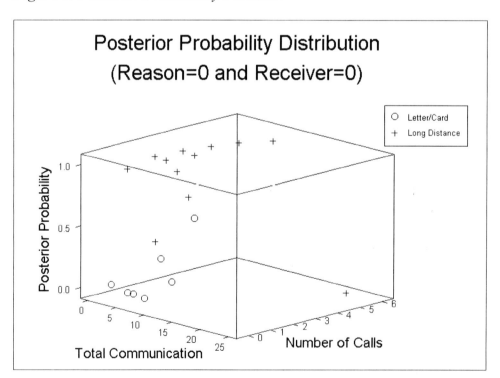

probability of placing an LD call is very high, close to 1. In addition, as TOTALCOM goes up, the number of LD calls made should go up also. Therefore, it would benefit a long distance telephone company to encourage consumers to communicate more.

Predictive Accuracy

To evaluate the ability of neural network models to generalize to previously unseen objects, a total of three models are constructed. The first includes all 11 original features. The second includes seven features selected by the backward elimination procedure in logistic regression (SAS, 1998). And the third uses only the four features selected by our own backward elimination procedure. For ease of reference, the lists of features are provided below.

- All 11 features: MOVES, RELATIVE, FRIENDS, AGE, NUMCLET, MEANCALL, TYCALL, REASON, RECEIVER, TOTALCOM, NUMCALLS.
- The seven features selected by logistic regression: NUMCLET, MEANCALL, TYCALL, REASON, RECEIVER, TOTALCOM, NUMCALLS.
- The four features selected by neural network: REASON, RECEIVER, TOTALCOM, NUMCALLS.

A neural network was built for each feature set and data used were the combined training and validation sets. The optimal number of hidden nodes for the seven-feature model was again one. Each feature set was also used to build a logistic regression model. All six models were then asked to predict the observations in the test set. Their performance is summarized in Table 4. The classification rate is based on the fact that there are a total of 296 observations in the test set, of which 131 involve long distance calls and the remaining 165 involve letters/cards.

Several important observations can be made. First, the neural network models are superior to logistic regression models in all cases except one (seven features, long distance). Second, the four-feature model outperforms every other model. This speaks voluminously for the merit of feature reduction used in this study. It also validates our own feature selection procedure. Third, the feature selection scheme for both neural networks and logistic regression seems able to find the optimal model: four-variable model for the former and seven-variable model for the latter.

The next section discusses model selection in greater detail, and presents experiments to validate our backward elimination feature-selection method.

MODEL SELECTION

In all nonlinear models, including ANNs, model selection consists of specifying the nonlinearity component and feature selection. Architecture selection in ANN corresponds to specifying the nonlinear structure.

Architecture Selection

Typically, the size of a neural network refers to its number of parameters (i.e., the number of arc weights and node biases). Given that we are concentrating on networks of one layer, the size of a network is directly related to the number of hidden nodes.

The methods to determine the appropriate network architecture can be summarized as follows:

1. Eliminate arcs whose weights are small or zero. Cottrell et al. (1995) construct an approximate confidence interval for each weight and if it contains zero, then the arc is eliminated.

2. Eliminate arcs whose *saliency* — a measure of relative importance — is small. Saliency is typically based on the partial derivative of the SSE with respect to the arc. Methods differ in the approximation of this derivative. The *optimal brain damage* of Le Cun et al. (1990) defines saliency of arc i as $H_{ii}w_i^2/2$ where H_{ii} is the i-th diagonal element of the *Hessian* matrix,

Table 4: Classification Rates (Correct Classifications) for the Test Set

Model	Group	Neural Network	Logistic Regression
11 Features	Total	.818 (242)	.787 (233)
	Long Distance	.870 (114)	.817 (107)
	Letter/Card	.776 (128)	.764 (126)
7 Features	Total	.818 (242)	.804 (238)
	Long Distance	.763 (100)	.817 (107)
	Letter/Card	.861 (142)	.794 (131)
4 Features	Total	.831 (246)	.794 (235)
	Long Distance	.840 (110)	.779 (102)
	Letter/Card	.824 (136)	.806 (133)

the matrix of second derivatives (of SSE with respect to arc weights), and w_i is the weight of arc i. The *optimal brain surgeon* (Hassibi & Stork, 1993), on the other hand, uses the diagonal element of the inverse of the Hessian matrix.

3. Build networks with different numbers of hidden nodes and then select one using some performance measure. The measure used by Moody and Joachim (1992) is called the *prediction risk* and it is the mean squared error on the validation set, adjusted by the number of weights. They also compute the prediction risk by using cross-validation, which first divides a data set into k subsets and uses $k-1$ subsets for training and the kth subset for validation. The validation set then rotates to the first subset, and then to the second, etc., in a round-robin fashion.

As discussed in the next section, our paper uses a measure similar to that of Moody and Joachim (1992). For other methods, please see Bishop (1995, section 9.5).

Feature Selection

In modeling, the principle of parsimony is important. Feature selection refers to the process of determining which subset of input variables is to be retained. It is a standard procedure in conventional pattern recognition (see, e.g., Fukunaga, 1990). Clearly one can use the methods mentioned above to eliminate one arc at a time until an input node is disconnected from the network and is thus eliminated by default. However, more efficient methods can be developed for this purpose.

There are two general approaches used in feature selection: *forward addition* and *backward elimination*. The former successively adds one variable at a time, starting with no variables, until no attractive candidate remains. The latter starts with all variables in the model and successively eliminates one at a time until only the "good"' ones are left. Whether a variable is attractive or not depends on its contribution to the model. For linear regression, well known measures for identifying good subsets of variables include (degree of freedom-adjusted) mean square error and prediction sum of squares (PRESS). For detailed discussions, see Neter et al. (1996) and Draper and Smith (1981).

In general, since backward elimination starts with the entire set of input variables, it is less likely to overlook any one variable's contribution in explaining the variability in the dependent variable, thus it is more likely for the procedure to arrive at the smallest subset of desirable variables.

For neural networks, several measures have also been proposed. Belue and Bauer (1995) calculate the (absolute) derivative of the *SSE* over each variable (called *saliency metric*) and drop the variables whose saliency is small. Moody and Joachim (1992) develop a sensitivity analysis (of a variable on *SSE*) based on their prediction risk and eliminate variables whose sensitivity is low. For other methods, please see Bishop (1995, section 8.5).

The next section presents our proposed method, which uses the backward elimination method for feature selection.

Proposed Feature Selection Method

Our proposed method for feature selection is a backward elimination method based on our measure of prediction risk, which is very similar to that of Moody and Joachim (1992). Given a trained network of n features and h hidden nodes, denoted as M_n^h, the prediction risk is the mean sum of squared errors of a validation set V. That is:

$$MSE\left(M_n^h\right)=\frac{1}{|V|}SSE\left(M_n^h\right)=\frac{1}{|V|}\sum_{p=1}^{|V|}\sum_{j=1}^{l}\left(Y_j^p - T_j^p\right)^2$$

where $|V|$ is the number of patterns in the validation set $V=(Y, T)$ and l is the number of output nodes of the neural network M_n^h. As the validation sets in our study are all of the same size, we use the sums of square error $SSE(M_n^h)$ as a measure of prediction risk in our method below.

1.   Start with all n features and train a network over a range of hidden nodes; i.e., $h = 0, 1, 2, \ldots$
2.   Select the optimal hidden nodes h^* which yields the smallest sums of square error $SSE(M_n^h)$.
3.   Reduce the number of features by one, and train every possible $(n-1)$ feature network with h^* hidden nodes. Let $SSE^*(M_{(n-1)}^{h^*})$ indicate the network with the smallest SSE of the $(n-1)$ networks.
4.   If $(SSE^*(M_{(n-1)}^{h^*}) - SSE^*(M_n^{h^*})) < D$, where D is a predetermined positive quantity, then $n = (n-1)$, and go to Step 3. Otherwise, go to Step 5.
5.   Use the features selected in Step 3, train networks over the range of hidden nodes used in Step 1 and select the optimal hidden nodes h^* again.

Experiment

An experiment was conducted to evaluate the backward elimination procedure. The experiment consists of training neural networks with all possible combinations of the features of a data set and computes the prediction risks of each trained network. Results from the backward elimination procedure will then be compared with those from all possible combinations. The initial set of variables was the seven variables chosen by logistic regression.

A second random sample of 3,377 communication situations is drawn from the weekly diary database, where 1,594 (47.20%) entail LD calls and the remaining 1,783 (52.80%) involve written communications. The entire sample of situations is from a total of 2,111 diarists. The maximum number of situations is three per diarist. Since the primary objective is model selection, only training and validation samples will be needed. Of these 3,377 observations, 1,535 are used as training and the remaining 1,842 as validation. To measure the robustness of the backward elimination procedure, the validation sample is subdivided into three sets of equal size with Set 1 composed of 286 LDs and 328 written; Set 2 of 278 LDs and 336 written, and Set 3 of 298 LDs and 316 written. This cross validation scheme will show how sensitive model selection is with respect to validation samples.

Network Architecture

All networks used have one output node, since there is one target variable COMMTYPE, and one hidden layer with h hidden nodes. There are arcs connecting each input node to both the output node and the hidden nodes. The activation function at each hidden node and the output node is logistic. In addition, each hidden node has a scalar. For the purpose of model selection, the number of hidden nodes h varies from 0 to 7.

Results

A neural network was set up for each of the 127 possible combinations of the seven input variables. Each network was then trained using eight different architectures (zero to seven hidden nodes). These correspond to a total of 1,016 networks. Table 5 shows the minimum SSEs across all hidden nodes and sets of input variables for each validation sample. In Sample 1, among the seven one-variable networks, variable six (not shown) with four hidden nodes is tied with variable six with three hidden nodes with *SSE* equal to 103.87. Among the six-variable networks, the network with two hidden nodes has the minimum *SSE* of 68.62. The network with the smallest *SSE* among all combination of variables and hidden nodes is shown in bold.

Results from validation Set 2 are similar to those from Set 1. Both indicate that the six-variable network with variables 2, 3, 4, 5, 6 and 7, and two hidden nodes has the smallest *SSE*. Validation Set 3 shows a slight difference from the other two samples. The four-variable (variable 4, 5, 6, 7) with two hidden nodes has the smallest *SSE*.

Next, we experiment with the backward elimination procedure. The seven input variables were trained in eight network architectures, hidden nodes from zero to seven. With validation sample 1, Table 5 shows that the network with two hidden nodes has the smallest SSE of 73.73 for seven variables. With the number of hidden nodes fixed at two, we then proceeded to examine the *SSE*s from the seven six-variable networks. As shown in Table 6, the network with variables 2, 3, 4, 5, 6, 7 has the smallest *SSE*, 68.62. Further elimination of variables resulted in an increase in *SSE*. The set of variables 2, 3, 4, 5, 6, 7 is then used to train networks of 0 to 7 hidden nodes, and the minimum *SSE* corresponds to the network with two hidden nodes (see Table 7). So the recommended feature set, based on validation sample 1, is (2, 3, 4, 5, 6, 7) and the network architecture is the one with two hidden nodes. This is the "best"' selection indicated by the all-combination experiment (Table 5).

With validation sample 2, the backward elimination method ends with the same "best" selection. The minimum *SSE* is 61.80. For validation sample 3, the backward elimination method starts with three hidden nodes for all seven variables and ends with four variables — 4, 5, 6, 7. Table 6 shows the *SSE* for this combination is 72.48. The set of four variables is then used to train networks of zero to seven hidden nodes and the minimum *SSE* corresponds to the network with two hidden nodes (see Table 7). This is the same as the best selection in the all-combination experiment (Table 5).

Overall results indicate that the backward elimination procedure identifies the same "best" models as the all-possible-combinations approach in each of the three validation samples. Neural networks are quite robust with respect to architecture and feature selection. Networks with two or three hidden nodes seem to be appropriate for this data set.

From a practical perspective, there seems to be little difference between models of six features and those of four features. In validation samples 1 and 2, the four-variable models end up with only a slight increase in *SSE* over the six-variable models. For example, in validation sample 1, the four variable model 4, 5, 6, 7 leads to an *SSE* of 70.82 compared to the smallest *SSE* of 68.62 for the six-variable model. However, a four-variable network with two hidden nodes has only 14 arcs, whereas a six-variable network with two hidden nodes has 20 arcs. A researcher can easily justify the selection of the four-variable model because of the greater reduction in the size of the network (which translates into greater degree of freedom for statistical analysis).

Table 5: Minimum SSE Across Hidden Nodes and Number of Variables

# of Variables	Number of Hidden Nodes							
	0	1	2	3	4	5	6	7
Validation Sample 1								
1	114.68	106.13	106.13	103.87	103.87	115.04	114.74	115.24
2	101.40	84.45	77.78	78.81	79.54	80.27	81.80	80.83
3	98.74	79.82	73.72	74.70	76.30	77.31	77.48	76.72
4	95.45	76.91	70.82	71.54	73.03	73.18	73.74	73.97
5	92.88	74.38	68.68	70.23	69.95	73.18	74.66	75.45
6	92.24	75.37	**68.62**	70.73	72.37	72.88	73.32	75.29
7	92.29	75.51	73.73	74.38	77.65	78.31	80.84	82.72
Validation Sample 2								
1	115.19	103.11	103.11	98.27	98.27	110.73	109.94	110.01
2	87.17	80.58	69.54	70.37	70.17	70.86	71.76	72.37
3	86.21	79.44	67.70	68.09	68.66	70.25	70.47	70.85
4	83.27	75.63	64.50	65.06	66.24	67.17	67.31	68.06
5	82.74	74.29	63.19	64.78	64.98	66.51	69.43	70.18
6	82.88	73.63	**61.80**	63.87	64.25	64.63	65.93	66.79
7	83.14	73.67	66.46	67.73	71.31	74.24	74.65	75.46
Validation Sample 3								
1	118.07	108.24	108.24	108.17	108.17	111.93	111.89	112.19
2	96.29	84.18	75.00	75.19	75.74	76.64	76.51	76.97
3	94.76	83.90	75.08	74.04	75.62	74.89	75.04	77.15
4	91.91	79.41	**72.06**	72.48	72.74	73.20	74.67	75.80
5	91.26	78.85	73.11	73.23	72.66	75.55	76.11	78.29
6	91.52	79.74	74.03	75.55	76.09	75.21	77.68	77.04
7	91.73	80.57	76.80	76.13	78.08	78.10	78.66	80.14

CONCLUSION

Applications of neural networks in marketing research are just now emerging. The few marketing studies we have identified all focused on using the technique for classification problems in particular choice decisions. Marketers are obviously interested in consumer choices. Prior researchers have shown the classification rates attained by neural networks to be superior to those by the traditional statistical procedures, such as logistic regression and discriminant analysis. Yet, marketers are also more interested in the likelihood of a choice outcome than the simple aggregate percentage of consumers choosing a product over the other.

Our study has shown that the posterior probabilities of choice can be estimated with neural networks via the least squares principle and that neural network in fact provides a direct estimate of these probabilities. Thus, the focus of this study is on the estimation of these posterior probabilities and the

Table 6: Backward Elimination Procedure for All Validation Samples

Validation Sample 1		Validation Sample 2		Validation Sample 3	
Variables Selected	SSE	Variables Selected	SSE	Variables Selected	SSE
1234567	73.73	1234567	66.46	1234567	76.13
Start with the above 7 variable model.					
123456	89.44	123456	84.45	123456	95.78
123457	97.65	123457	89.43	123457	98.32
123467	71.71	123467	68.89	123467	80.13
123567	75.71	123567	68.16	123567	79.51
124567	77.02	124567	67.89	124567	76.97
134567	72.87	134567	64.91	134567	76.12
234567	**68.62**	**234567**	**61.80**	234567	75.55
Use the best 6 variable model (shown in **bold** above).					
23456	90.30	23456	91.57	23456	98.27
23457	97.53	23457	90.08	23457	97.47
23467	71.31	23467	67.68	23467	76.57
23567	71.51	23567	64.73	23567	76.45
24567	75.40	24567	65.36	24567	78.70
34567	**68.68**	**34567**	**63.19**	34567	73.23
Use the best 5 variable model.					
3456	91.50	3456	93.14	3456	97.27
3457	98.14	3457	93.40	3457	100.21
3467	70.98	3467	66.28	3467	75.30
3567	70.87	**3567**	**64.50**	3567	74.90
4567	**70.82**	4567	65.31	**4567**	**72.48**
Use the best 4 variable model.					
456	93.66	356	99.02	456	96.93
457	103.02	357	99.02	457	100.36
467	**79.65**	**367**	**67.70**	**467**	**74.04**
567	132.21	567	106.76	567	116.07
Use the best 3 variable model.					
46	97.94	36	100.87	46	100.72
47	108.73	37	105.91	47	107.14
67	**77.78**	**67**	**69.54**	67	75.19
Use the best 2 variable model.					
6	**106.13**	**6**	**103.11**	**6**	**108.17**
7	119.37	7	112.39	7	113.74

nonlinear functional relationships between these probabilities and the predictor variables.

Most market researchers treat neural networks as a black box. They leave the decision on model selection to computer software packages (if the packages have such capabilities) and typically rely on logistic regression for feature selection. Our study encompasses a rather comprehensive approach to neural network modeling. It provides guidelines for sample selection and shows how model selection should be carried out experimentally. A backward

Table 7: SSE Across Hidden Nodes

Hidden Nodes	Validation Sample 1 Variables: 234567	Validation Sample 2 Variables: 234567	Validation Sample 3 Variables: 4567
0	92.24	82.88	91.91
1	75.37	73.63	79.41
2	**68.62**	**61.80**	**72.06**
3	70.73	63.87	72.48
4	72.37	64.25	72.74
5	72.88	64.63	73.20
6	73.32	65.93	76.39
7	75.29	66.79	76.28

elimination procedure adapted in this study actually identified a parsimonious model with even better classification rate. These results truly attest to the nonlinear modeling capabilities of neural networks.

The situational choice data set from AT&T contains variability over time and across consumers. Dasguta et al. (1994) report that most neural network applications have been with aggregate consumer data. There are only a handful of applications with disaggregate consumer survey response data. Data at a lower level of disaggregation typically contains more noise. Results reported in this study illustrate the potential for superior performance of neural networks for this domain of applications.

The variables retained by our feature selection procedure are all situation-based. As indicated in previous research in situational influences, situation-based factors should have a stronger bearing on situational choices as compared to the more enduring, consumer factors. This finding provides some validation for our suggested procedure. The nonlinear relationship between the posterior probabilities and the input variables was clearly captured graphically in our study. It is shown that these probabilities are more informative and useful for marketers in planning their strategies.

Practical managerial implications can be drawn from the results of this study. The benefits of long distance phone calling, particularly in emergency situations, are to be reinforced. Also, consumers are to be reminded that when communicating with relatives, long distance phone calling is the preferred choice. In addition, consumers are to be reminded to reciprocate in terms of modes of communications. When a consumer receives a long distance phone call, the consumer should be encouraged to use the same mode of communication in his/her response. Lastly, a long distance phone company should continuously remind its consumers to keep in touch with one's friends and relatives. As the total frequency of communications increases, the likelihood of using long distance phone calling also goes up.

Major advances have been made in the past decade in neural networks. This study intends to introduce some of these major breakthroughs for researchers in the field of marketing. It is our hope that market researchers will be able to gain a better appreciation of the technique. Of course, these advances are available at a cost. Neural networks are much more computationally intensive than classical statistical methods such as logistic regression. The model selection and feature selection procedures require customized programs. However, as computation cost is getting cheaper each day, these problems are becoming less of an obstacle for modelers.

REFERENCES

Ahn, B. –H. (1996). Forward additive neural network models. *Ph.D. dissertation*, Kent State University, Kent, Ohio, USA.

Belue, L. & Bauer, K. J. (1995). Determining input features for multilayer perceptrons. *Neurocomputing*, 7, 111-121.

Bishop, C. M. (1995). *Neural Networks for Pattern Recognition*. Oxford, UK: Oxford University Press.

Cottrell, M., Girard, B., Mangeas, M., & Muller, C. (1995). Neural modeling for time series: A statistical stepwise method for weight elimination. *IEEE Transactions on Neural Networks*, 6, 1355-1364.

Dasgupta, C. G., Dispensa, G. S., & Ghose, S. (1994). Comparing the predictive performance of a neural network model with some traditional market response models. *International Journal of Forecasting*, 10(2), 235-244.

Draper, N. & Smith, H. (1981). *Applied Regression Analysis*. New York: John Wiley & Sons.

Duda, R. O. & Hart, P. E. (1973). *Pattern Classification and Scene Analysis*. New York: John Wiley & Sons.

Fukunaga, K. (1990). *Introduction to Statistical Pattern Recognition (2nd edition)*. San Diego, CA: Academic Press.

Geman, S., Bienenstock, E., & Doursat, R. (1992). Neural networks and the bias/variance dilemma. *Neural Computation,* 4, 1-58.

Hassibi, B. & Stork, D. (1993). Second order derivatives for network pruning: Optimal   brain surgeon. In S. Hanson, J. Cown & C. Giles (Eds.), *Advances in Neural Information Processing Systems* (Vol. 5, pp. 164-171). San Mateo, CA: Morgan Kaufmann.

Hu, M., Hung, M. S., & Shanker, M. (2000). Estimating posterior probabilities of consumer situational choices with neural networks. *International Journal of Research in Marketing*, 16(4), 307-317.

Hu, M., Hung, M. S., Shanker, M., & Chen, H. (1996). Using neural networks to predict the performance of Sino-foreign joint ventures. *International Journal of Computational Intelligence and Organizations*, 1(3), 134-143.

Hu, M., Patuwo, E., Hung, M. S., & Shanker, M. (1999a). Neural network analysis of performance of sino-Hong Kong joint ventures. *Annals of Operations Research*, 87, 213-232.

Hu, M., Zhang, G., Jiang, C., & Patuwo, E. (1999b). A cross-validation analysis of neural network out-of-sample performance in exchange rate forecasting. *Decision Sciences*, 30(1), 197-216.

Hui, M. K. & Bateson, J. E. G. (1991, September). Perceived control and the effects of crowding and consumer choice on the service experience. *Journal of Consumer Research*, 18, 174-184.

Hung, M. S., Hu, M., Shanker, M., & Patuwo, E. (1996). Estimating posterior probabilities in classification problems with neural networks. *International Journal of Computational Intelligence and Organizations*, 1(1), 49-60.

Hung, M. S., Shanker, M., & Hu, M. Y. (2001). Estimating breast cancer risks using neural networks. *Journal of the Operational Research Society*, 52, 1-10.

Kumar, A., Rao, V. R., & Soni, H. (1995). An empirical comparison of neural network and logistic regression models. *Marketing Letters*, 6(4), 251-263.

Le Cun, Y., Denker, J., & Solla, S. (1990). Optimal brain damage. In D. Touretzky (Ed.), *Advances in Neural Information Processing Systems* (Vol. 2, pp. 598-605). San Mateo, CA: Morgan Kaufmann.

Lee, E., Hu, M. Y., & Toh, R. S. (2000). Are consumer survey results distorted? Systematic impact of behavioral frequency and duration on survey response errors. *Journal of Marketing Research*, 37(1), 125-134.

Lippmann, R. P. (1997, April). An introduction to computing with neural networks. *IEEE ASSP Magazine*, 4-22.

Lo, A. (1996). Recent advances in derivative securities: Neural networks and other nonparametric pricing models. *International Workshop on State of the Art in Risk Management and Investments*, NUS, Singapore.

Moody, J. & Joachim, U. (1992). Principled architecture selection for neural networks: Application to corporate bond rating prediction. In D. Touretzky (Ed.), *Advances in Neural Information Processing Systems* (Vol. 4, pp. 683-690). San Mateo, CA: Morgan Kaufmann.

Neter, J., Kutner, M., Nachtsheim, C., & Wasserman, W. (1996). *Applied Linear Statistical Models.* Chicago, IL: Irwin.

Refenes, A. P. N., Abu-Mostafa, Y., Moody, J., & Weigend, A. (1996). *Neural Networks in Financial Engineering.* Singapore: World Scientific.

Rumelhart, D. E., Hinton, G. E., & Williams, R. J. (1986). Learning internal representation by error propagation. In D. E. Rumelhart & J. L. Williams (Eds), *Parallel Distributed Explorations in the Microstructure of Cognition.* Cambridge, MA: MIT Press.

SAS User's Guide: Statistics (1998). NC: SAS Institute.

Shanker, M., Hu, M., & Hung, M. S. (1996). Effect of data standardization on neural network training. *Omega*, 24(4), 385-397.

Shanker, M. S. (1996). Using neural networks to predict the onset of diabetes mellitus. *Journal of Chemical Information and Computer Sciences*, 36(1), 35-41.

Simonson, I. & Winer, R. S. (1992, June). The influence of purchase quantity and display format on consumer preference for variety. *Journal of Consumer Research*, 19, 133-138.

Tam, K. Y. & Kiang, M. Y. (1992). Managerial applications of neural networks: The case of bank failure predictions. *Management Science*, 38(7), 926-947.

Tang, Z. & Fishwick, P. A. (1993). Feedforward neural nets as models for time series forecasting. *INFORMS Journal on Computing*, 5(4), 374-385.

West, P. M., Brockett, P. L., & Golden, L. L. (1997). A comparative analysis of neural networks and statistical methods for predicting consumer choice. *Marketing Science*, 16(4), 370-391.

Wong, F. S. (1991). Time series forecasting using backpropagation neural networks. *Neurocomputing*, 2, 147-159.

Zhang, G., Patuwo, E., & Hu, M. (1998). Forecasting with artificial neural networks: The state of art. *International Journal of Forecasting*, 14(1), 35-62.

Chapter X

Forecasting Short-Term Exchange Rates: A Recurrent Neural Network Approach

Leong-Kwan Li, The Hong Kong Polytechnic University, Hong Kong

Wan-Kai Pang, The Hong Kong Polytechnic University, Hong Kong

Wing-Tong Yu, The Hong Kong Polytechnic University, Hong Kong

Marvin D. Troutt, Kent State University, USA

ABSTRACT

Movements in foreign exchange rates are the results of collective human decisions, which are the results of the dynamics of their neurons. In this chapter, we demonstrate how to model these types of market behaviors by recurrent neural networks (RNN). The RNN approach can help us to forecast the short-term trend of foreign exchange rates. The application of forecasting techniques in the foreign exchange markets has become an important task in financial strategy. Our empirical results show that a discrete-time RNN performs better than the traditional methods in forecasting short-term foreign exchange rates.

INTRODUCTION

Exchange rates are important variables in virtually every international financial market decision. Most countries are adopting the floating exchange rate system, under which the exchange rate is free to adjust in response to changing relative macroeconomic conditions. The volatility of exchange rates becomes one of the most important concerns for all types of participants involved in international financial activities. Foreign exchange risk is one of the many business risks faced by multinational companies and its successful management has become one of the key factors in overall financial management. Recently, Marshall (2000) has done a survey on the foreign exchange risk practices of large UK, USA and Asian Pacific multinational companies. The results showed that although multinational companies from different regions might use different techniques in managing foreign exchange risks, all of them emphasized the importance of foreign exchange risk management. Traders in the foreign exchange markets are always actively seeking profit opportunities by trying to forecast exchange rate movements. Some banks are actively trading in the foreign exchange markets. Levich (2001) showed that there was a dramatic growth in income derived from foreign exchange trading for some international banks over the last 20 years.

The needs for foreign exchange risk management and profit opportunities from foreign exchange trading provide a great incentive for participants in the foreign exchange markets to develop a reliable forecasting model of exchange rate movements. Economists have studied exchange rates intensively for the last 25 years. The international parity conditions that are built on purchasing power, interest rates and market expectations have become the fundamental theories in explaining the determination of exchange rates and can be found in all textbooks on international finance nowadays. There appears to be consensus that the long-term trend of exchange rate movements is mainly determined by the structural macroeconomic variables such as the balance of payments, inflation rate, interest rate and money supply. Yet, to many economists exchange rate models built around a set of structural macroeconomic variables seem to have little power to explain the patterns of short-term exchange rate behavior. One extreme view advocated by the market efficiency theorists is that if the foreign exchange markets were efficient, the exchange rates should follow a simple random walk and evolve strictly according to the new information arriving in the markets. If markets are efficient and prices fully reflect all available information, including structural economic information, then unanticipated exchange rate movements are only the results of unanticipated events — and, by definition, these cannot be forecast. However, the view that exchange rates follow a simple random walk and evolve without regard to macroeconomic fundamentals is an extreme characterization. Mussa (1990) argued that the random walk behavior of exchange rates is only approximate. Klein, Mizrach and Murphy (1991) and Almeida, Goodhart and Payne (1998) demonstrated a significant association between exchange rate movements and traditional macroeconomic fundamentals during certain periods. Their results show evidence that some structural models appear capable of outperforming random walk in out-of-sample tests, and that short-run exchange rate changes were not dissociated with economic events. Rather, foreign exchange rate changes appear closely connected with news about key fundamental economic variables.

It is also clear that exchange rate movements are not determined by only a single variable, but by a variety of monetary and other variables, affecting the demand for a currency or for financial assets denominated in that currency. The "character" of the economic news and the context in which it occurs help formulate the scenario that traders extrapolate from a particular news story. It is this scenario for the future that determines how the exchange rate reacts to news. If it were possible to describe how the exchange rate would respond to each news report, then we would have an economic model of exchange rate determination. The presence of nonrandom-walk behavior offers market economists an opportunity to add value.

An important element in selecting a forecasting approach is the forecast horizon. It seems reasonable to assume that some techniques would be more suitable for very short-run forecasts while others are more effective at longer-run horizons. For example, many macroeconomic fundamentals (such as inflation, national income, and the trade balance) are reported on a monthly or quarterly basis and sometimes after a long time lag, which makes it difficult to forecast daily exchange rates using fundamentals. On the other hand, using a random-walk model to forecast exchange rates five or 10 years in the future essentially places no weight on economic fundamentals, which could have a dramatic effect on rates over such a long period. In practice, the majority of the foreign exchange market participants place great reliance on technical models for their very short-run (intraday to one-week) forecasts. In this chapter, we show that a neural network model can help us to predict short-term foreign exchange rates. By feeding the time series data and technical indicators, such as moving averages, to our neural network model, we can capture the underlying trend of the movements in currency exchange rates. We perform the foreign exchange rates forecasting between the US dollar and four other major currencies, Japanese Yen, Euro, Sterling and Swiss France. Our results show that this neural network can produce useful predictions of the exchange rates and paper profits can possibly be made.

This chapter is organized as follows: next, we briefly review the different short-term foreign exchange forecasting methods; then, we discuss the nature of the neural network model; this is followed with a discussion on the approximation theorems and the applications of neural networks. Next, we present and discuss the forecasting results using our neural network model, and in the final section, we conclude our chapter.

AN OVERVIEW OF SHORT TERM FOREIGN EXCHANGE FORECASTING METHODS

Theories of exchange rate determination as econometric models have been studied by many others, such as Meese and Rogoff (1983), Alexander and Thomas (1987), Schinasi and Swamy (1989), Meese and Rose (1991) and Baillie and McMahon (1989). In the finance literature, Fama (1970) suggested that there are three schools of thought in terms of the ability to profit from the financial markets. The efficient market school believes that no investor can achieve above average trading advantages based on historical and present information. Any attempts trying to outperform the market by studying the information will be fruitless. The second school's view is that of fundamental analysis. It believes that the market is not always efficient in reflecting the information and by studying the fundamental variables determining security prices, profitable trading opportunities can be found. The third school of thought is that of technical analysis, which proposes that security prices move in trends. The technical analysts study the technical indicators and develop the charting patterns in order to capture the trends of price movement and use it for profitable forecasting. The technical techniques are popularly used in the foreign exchange markets for short-term forecasting. Heuristic methods, such as moving averages advocated by Brown (1963) and exponential smoothing and adaptive exponential smoothing advocated by Triggs (1967), were the most popular methods for short-term forecasting in the foreign exchange markets. These methods did not possess solid backgrounds in statistical theory. In the 1970s, practitioners started to use the more sophisticated Box-Jenkins (1970) ARIMA forecasting methods. This methodology was statistically more appealing and has been used widely in the financial markets right up to the early 1980s.

Later, in the mid 1980s, the volatility of foreign exchange rates became a great concern in the foreign exchange markets. Engle (1982) proposed the Autoregressive Conditional Heteroskedasticity (ARCH) model for short-term volatility. Details about the ARCH model can be found in the monograph by Talyor (1986). This method attracted much attention and became very popular in the late 1980s and the early 1990s. Bollerslev, Chou and Kroner (1992) presented a comprehensive review article about the applications of the ARCH model in various financial markets. Subsequently, the general ARCH (GARCH) model was developed and became the most popular method amongst practitioners in short-term forecasting in the foreign exchange markets (e.g., see Meade, 2002). The GARCH model, which is linear in the mean and nonlinear in variance, has been used to capture the heteroskedasticity of daily exchange rates by a number of researchers, such as Baillie and Bollerslev (1989), Milhoj (1987), Hsieh (1988, 1989), and Baillie and Bollerslev (1991). Another type of forecasting method used in forecasting foreign exchange rates is vector autoregression (VAR), such as Liu, Gerlow and Irwin (1994), and Sarantis and Stewart (1995). Chien and Leung (2003) developed a Bayesian vector error correction model for forecasting exchange rates.

However, the traditional statistical techniques for forecasting have reached their limitation in applications. Yao and Tan (2000) argued that classical time series analysis, based on the theory of stationary stochastic processes, does not perform satisfactorily on economic time series. Economic data are not simple autoregressive-integrated-moving-average (ARIMA) processes; they are not described by simple linear structural models; they are not simple white noise or even random walks. The high volatility, complexity, and noisy market environment lead to the suggestion of using neural network techniques for forecasting purposes. Neural network technology is a new option in many application areas in business, especially when the problem largely involves classification, recognition and prediction. In fact, White (1989) pointed out that neural networks are complementary to the conventional statistical approaches for time series forecasting. This chapter describes the application of neural networks in learning the dynamics of, as well as forecasting, foreign exchange rates.

RECURRENT NEURAL NETWORKS

The most common types of neural network used by practitioners are the feedforward neural network (FNN) and the recurrent neural network (RNN). In FNN, the neurons are laid out in layers labeled 1, 2, 3, …, etc. Activity feeds through from the input at layer 1 to layer 2, then to layer 3, and so on. While in RNN, the output of any layer may be fed back to itself and to earlier or later layers. The most well-known RNN is the single layer Hopfield net. In a recurrent neural network system, the activity is relaxed to settle to a stable or fixed point called an attractor. For example, the Hopfield net has a symmetric connection matrix W_{ij} and for all neurons i and j, the elements of W_{ij} are greater than zero. But, in general, a RNN has a connection matrix, W_{ij}, which is not necessarily symmetric, and for all i and j, the elements of the connection matrices are real valued. For more details about feedforward neural networks and RNN, one may refer to the two monographs by Taylor (1995, 1996).

AN RNN MODEL FOR FORECASTING FOREIGN EXCHANGE RATES

Data Collection

Daily quotes of foreign exchange rates are displayed as time series. The problem of prediction in time series has captured a lot of attention in the foreign exchange rate markets (see Mead, 2002, and the references therein). As opposed to the traditional trading methods by human decisions, neural networks offer a simple but automatic system in the trading of foreign exchange. In the present study, we collected 802 days of data consisting of the daily quotations of (1) Euro/US, (2) Yen/US, (3) Sterling/US and (4) CHF/US starting from January 1999 to May 2002. These data are displayed in Figures 1 through 4.

It is worth noting that Yao and Tan (2000) used the empirical Hurst exponent (Hurst, 1951) to show that statistically the foreign exchange series do not support the random walk hypothesis. The Hurst exponent, which is a measure of the bias in fractional Brownian motion, can be used to test the random walk hypothesis in economic and financial time series. Based on the results of Yao and Tan (2000), we assume also here that there exist short-term trends in our foreign exchange series and we could use other techniques, not necessarily statistical techniques, to model the short-term trend movement of the foreign exchange rates and further to make predictions. The neural network forecasting model is a good alternative. We will discuss our neural network methodology in the following section.

Figure 1

Euro-US Exchange Rate

Figure 2

Yen-US Exchange Rate

Figure 3

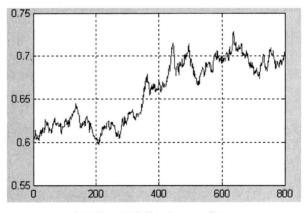

Sterling-US Exchange Rate

Figure 4

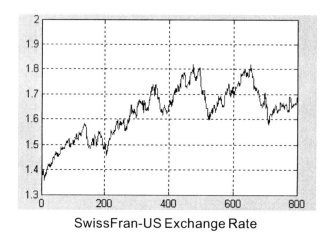

SwissFran-US Exchange Rate

The Neural Network Forecasting Model

In our study, we use the first 702 days observations to train and validate the neural network. After the training and validation stages, we then use the resulting neural network parameters to make the out-of-sample forecasts for the last 100 observations. Out-of-sample forecast errors are measured in order to judge how good our model is in terms of its prediction abilities. The learning dynamics used for the neural network is a first order differential equation. That is, we express the dynamical system for our neural network as:

$$y(t+1) = y(t) + h\frac{dy}{dt} \tag{1}$$

where h is a constant and $h > 0$. Yao and Tan (2000) used a purely time delayed model as their neural network structure to capture the relationship between next week's exchange rate and the historical exchange rates. While Yao and Tan (2000) pointed out that a purely time delayed model is one of the simplest technical analysis methods, our method is more sophisticated and has not yet been explored by others.

The corresponding discrete-time recurrent neural network for the dynamical system in (1) is defined by:

$$y(t+1) = y(t) + h[-y(t) + \sigma(Wy(t) + \theta) + J], \tag{2}$$

where J is the external input vector to the system and θ is the bias or threshold vector. $\sigma(\cdot)$ is a neuronal activation function of its variable. $\sigma(\cdot)$ is a bounded, differentiable and monotonic increasing function. It is in the range of -1 to +1. In fact, if we have $h = 0$, then the equation becomes:

$$y(t+1) = y(t) \qquad (3)$$

which represents the last-value forecast of $y(t+1)$. This is the usual *naive* model in forecasting. On the other hand, if $h = 1$ and $J = \mathbf{0}$, then:

$$y(t+1) = \sigma(Wy(t)+\theta) \qquad (4)$$

is the nonlinear time series model. W is the square connection matrix and the dimension of W depends on the dimension of $y(t)$. In particular, if we let σ be the identity mapping, it becomes the vector linear time series model. These models are used to capture the behavior of the linear internal mechanism of the financial market. Thus, we may regard the RNN as a nonlinear time series model as σ is nonlinear. Hence, for $0 < h < 1$, we may consider equation (2) as the convex combination of two forecasting models. From an optimization point of view, the discrete-time RNN should be at least as good as any time series model for a suitable choice of h.

Before the training process, we employ a normalization for each component series in y_t. This normalization is given by:

$$x_{ti} = \left(\frac{y_{ti} - \min\{y_{ti}\}}{\text{Range of } y_{ti}} - 0.5 \right) \times 1.90, \ t = 1, 2, \ldots, 802, \ i = 1, 2, 3, 4. \qquad (5)$$

This normalization will generally smooth out the extreme outliers. The values of x_{ti} will lie between -0.95 and +0.95, which means that x_{ti} is inside the range of the neuronal activation function, $\sigma(\cdot)$, defined in equation 1. The learning process involves the computation of numerical derivatives. Thus, if the x_{ti} are close to the limits of the range of $\sigma(\cdot)$ then the derivatives will be very close to zero. This will lead to no improvement in the learning process. Therefore, our normalization process will facilitate the computation work in the learning process.

Instead of using the normalized raw vector time series $\mathbf{x}_t$ to feed the system for training, we use the moving average series $\mathbf{z}_t$ of orders 5, 10, 20, 50, 100 and 250, respectively, obtained from $\mathbf{x}_t$. The advantage of using moving averages to model the short-term trend in foreign exchange rates can be found in Yao and Tan (2000).

To train the network, we fed $\mathbf{z}_t$ to the system. The training algorithm uses the gradient descent approach to minimize the errors between the target trajectory and the system output. This task is performed for each moving average series. Let $\mathbf{z}^o(0)$ be the initial state of the training process and $\mathbf{z}(0)$ is the first moving average value in each experiment. Then we approximate $\mathbf{z}(1)$, $\mathbf{z}(2), ..., \mathbf{z}(T)$ recurrently by feeding $\mathbf{z}(t)$ to the RNN and the number T depends on the order of the moving averages. The scheme operates diagrammatically as follows:

$$\mathbf{z}^o(0) \to W \to \mathbf{z}^o(1) \to W \to \mathbf{z}^o(2) ... \mathbf{z}^o(T\text{-}1) \to W \to \mathbf{z}^o(T) \qquad (6)$$

For each moving average series, we use the same dynamical learning system and find the optimal network parameters. In other words, we wish to find the optimal connection matrix W_{ij} for each of the six moving average series. From these six connection matrices, we select the optimal W^* to be the final estimate of the connection matrix in the training process.

In the training process, we need to find the optimal values of W, θ and h. This is done by using the gradient descent method to minimize the nonlinear L_2-norm error function:

$$E(\beta) = \left\| z_{ti}(t+1) - z_{ti}^0(t+1) \right\|^2$$

with respect to the parameter vector β, where the parameter vector β is a function of the elements in the connection matrix W, the elements in the vector θ and h. For technical details of this gradient descent method, one may refer to the articles by Williams and Zipser (1989) and Li (1994).

EMPIRICAL RESULTS

Results on In-Sample Training

From our empirical studies, we found that in the in-sample training process the optimal W^* is given by that for the 50 term moving average; namely:

$$\mathbf{W}^*_{50} = \begin{bmatrix} 0.3095 & -4.2290 & 1.5052 & -2.3421 \\ -0.0321 & 0.8357 & 0.1359 & -0.1309 \\ 0.2418 & 2.1019 & 0.2582 & 0.9632 \\ 0.4933 & 1.9452 & -0.4573 & 2.3083 \end{bmatrix}$$

and $h^* = 0.0623$. These two optimal values are obtained by using the moving average series of order 50. This is measured by calculating the L_2-norm error function which is defined by:

$$E(\mathbf{W}, h, \theta) = \mid \mathbf{z}^o(t) - \mathbf{z}(t) \mid^2$$

The results for all the L_2-norm error function values for given $h^* = 0.0623$ obtained from the RNN models are presented in Table 1.

As we can see from Table 1, the MA(50) series has the least $E(\mathbf{W}, h, \theta)$ value. For each currency, we show the $\mathbf{z}(t)$ series (solid line) where $\mathbf{z}(t)$ is the MA(50) series and the values of $\mathbf{z}^o(t)$ are generated by the best RNN approximation (black line) in Figures 5 through 8. Figures 5 through 8 show that $\mathbf{z}^o(t)$ follows $\mathbf{z}(t)$ closely in each case.

Out-of-Sample Forecasts

For the last 100 days' out-of-sample forecasts, we use equation (2) with given W^* and h^*. For each predicted value, $\mathbf{z}^o(t+1)$, we calculate the corresponding $\mathbf{y}^o(t+1)$ by using the inverse relation of equation (5). Here, $\mathbf{y}^o(t+1)$ is the forecast value for the moving average of the original time series. That is:

Table 1: The L_2-Norm Error Function Values Given h*

Model	MA(k)	$E(\mathbf{W}, h, \theta)$
1	MA(5)	2.82189×10^{-4}
2	MA(10)	2.06360×10^{-4}
3	MA(20)	1.44786×10^{-4}
4	MA(50)*	9.76841×10^{-5}
5	MA(100)	8.86660×10^{-4}
6	MA(250)	5.01534×10^{-4}

Figure 5

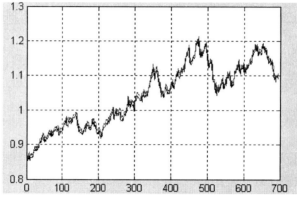

700 Daily Exchange Rate for Euro/US

Figure 6

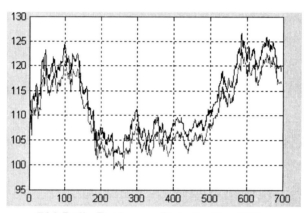

700 Daily Exchange Rate for Yen/US

Figure 7

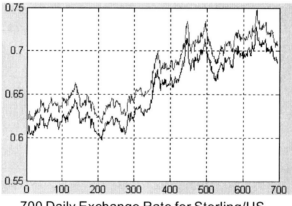

700 Daily Exchange Rate for Sterling/US

Figure 8

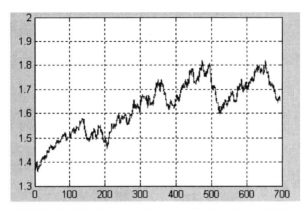

700 Daily Exchange Rate for Swiss Franc/US

$$y_i^o(t+1) = (1.90)^{-1} z_i^o(t+1) \times \text{Range of } \{y_{ti}\} + \min\{y_{ti}\}$$

The values of range of $\{y_{ti}\}$ and $\{\min y_{ti}\}$ are the same values used in the normalization process given in equation (5). We then calculate the root mean square error (RMSE) between the actual moving averages and the predicted moving average values. Here we also conduct the 100 days out-of-sample forecasts by two other traditional methods, namely, (1) moving averages, and (2) exponential smoothing. Table 2 lists the RMSE values after rescaling back to the original values obtained from (1) RNN, (2) moving averages, and (3) exponential smoothing with $\lambda = 0.6$.

We note that the RNN method produces the smallest RMSE value. In Figures 9 through 12, we also show the actual moving average series and the forecast moving average values generated by RNN for each currency for the last 100 days' out-of sample forecasts.

In Figures 9 to 12, the blue lines indicate the best RNN approximations while the red lines indicate the original data. From these figures, we see that the

Table 2: The RMSE Values

Currency	RNN	MA (50 days)	Exp. Smoothing
DM	0.061286	0.069162	0.064647
Yen	5.753643	6.230094	6.018765
CHF	0.028964	0.032995	0.029359
Sterling	0.099079	0.119516	0.101979

Figure 9

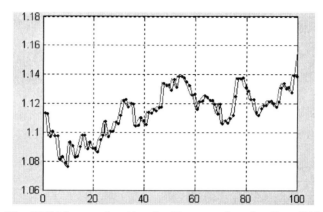

The RNN Approximation for Forecasting the Euro/US

Figure 10

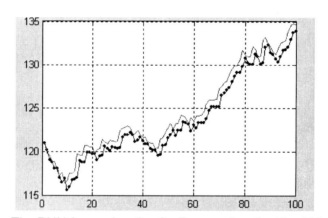

The RNN Approximation for Forecasting the Yen/US

Figure 11

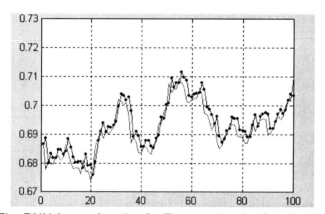

The RNN Approximation for Forecasting the Sterling/US

Figure 12

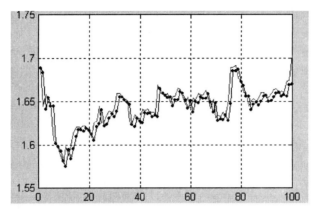

The RNN Approximation for Forecasting the Swiss Franc/US

forecast values generated by the RNN model follow closely with the actual observations for each currency.

CONCLUDING REMARKS

In this chapter, we have demonstrated that the dynamics between exchange rates can be captured by an RNN, which can help us to forecast the short-term trend of foreign exchange rates. The application of forecasting techniques in foreign exchange markets has become a key part in financial strategic planning. The RNN forecasting technique that we have demonstrated in this chapter might be further extended to the foreign exchange futures market in which futures trading can provide a means of hedging unforeseen events and, thereby, provide stability.

REFERENCES

Alexander, D. & Thomas, L. R. (1987). Monetary/asset models of exchange rate determination: How well have they performed in the 1980s. *International Journal of Forecasting, 3,* 53-64.

Almeida, A., Goodhart, C., & Payne, R. (1998). The effects of macroeconomic news on high frequency exchange rate behavior. *Journal of Financial and Quantitative Analysis*, 3, 383-408.

Baillie, R. T. & Bollerslev, T. (1989). The message in daily exchange rates: A conditional variance tale. *Journal of Business and Economic Statistics, 7,* 297-306.

Baillie, R. T. & Bollerslev, T. (1991). Intra day and inter market volatility in foreign exchange rates. *Review of Economic Studies, 58*, 565-585.

Baillie, R. T. & McMahon, P. (1989). *The Foreign Exchange Market: Theory and Econometric Evidence.* Cambridge: Cambridge University Press.

Blum, E. & Li, L. K. (1991). Approximation theory and feedforward networks. *Neural Networks*, 4(4), 511-515.

Bollerslev, T., Chou R. Y., & Kroner K. F. (1992). ARCH modeling in finance. *Journal of Econometrics, 52*, 5-59.

Box, G. E. P & Jenkins, G. M. (1970). *Time Series Analysis, Forecasting and Control.* San-Francisco, CA: Holden-Day.

Brown, R. G. (1963). *Smoothing, Forecasting and Prediction.* Englewood Cliffs, NJ: Prentice Hall.

Chien, A. J. & Leung, M. T. (2003). A Bayesian vector error correction model for forecasting exchange rates. *Computers & Operation Research*, 30, 887-900.

Engle, R. F. (1982). Autoregressive conditional heteroscedasticity with estimates of the variance of United Kingdom inflation. *Econometrica*, 50, 987-1007.

Fama, E. F. (1970). Efficient capital markets: A review of theory and empirical work. *Journal of Finance*, 25, 383-417.

Hornik, K., Stinchcombe, M., & White, H. (1989). Multi-layer feedforward networks are universal approximators. *Neural Networks*, 2, 359-366.

Hsieh, D. A. (1988). Statistical properties of daily exchange rates: 1974-1983. *Journal of International Economics, 24*, 129-145.

Hsieh, D. A. (1989). Modeling heteroskedasticity in daily foreign exchange rates. *Journal of Business and Economic Statistics, 7*, 307-317.

Hurst, H. E. (1951). Long term storage capacity of reservoirs. *Trans. Am. Soc. Civil Eng.*, 116, 770-808.

Klein, M., Mizarch, B., & Murphy, R. G. (1991). Managing the dollar: Has the plaza agreement mattered? *Journal of Money Credit and Banking*, 23, 742-751.

Levich, R. M. (2001). *International Financial Markets – Prices and Policies.* New York: McGraw-Hill International.

Li, L. K. (1992). Approximation theory and recurrent networks. *Proceedings of International Joint Conference on Neural Networks-Baltimore-92*, 2, 266-271.

Li, L. K. (1994). Learning fixed point patterns by recurrent networks. *Journal of Computer and System Sciences*, 48(2), 203-213.

Liu, T. R., Gerlow, M. E., & Irwin, S. H. (1994). The performance of alternative VAR models in forecasting exchange rates. *International Journal of Forecasting*, 10, 419-433.

Marshall, A. P. (2000). Foreign exchange risk management in UK, USA and Asia Pacific multinational companies. *Journal of Multinational Financial Management*, 10, 185-211.

Meade, N. (2002). A comparison of the accuracy of short term foreign exchange forecasting methods. *International Journal of Forecasting*, 18, 67-83.

Meese, R. A. & Rogoff, K. (1983). Empirical exchange rate models for the seventies: Do they fit out of sample. *Journal of International Economics*, 14, 3-24.

Meese, R. A. & Rose, A. K. (1991). An empirical assessment on nonlinearities in models of exchange rate determination. *Review of Economic Studies*, 58, 603-619.

Milhoj, A. (1987). A conditional variance model for daily deviations of an exchange rate. *Journal of American Statistical Association*, 5, 99-103.

Mussa, M. (1990). Exchange rates in theory and reality. *Princeton Essays in International Finance*, 179, December, Princeton, NJ: Princeton University.

Pearlmutter, B. A. (1989). Learning state space trajectories in recurrent networks. *Neural Computation*, 1, 263-269.

Rumelhalt, D. E., Hinton, G. E., & Williams (eds.) (1986). Learning internal representation by error propagation. In *Parallel Distributed Processing* (pp. 318-362). Cambridge, MA: MIT Press.

Sarantis, N. & Stewart, C. (1995). Structural, VAR and BVAR models of exchange rate determination: A comparison of their forecasting performance. *Journal of Forecasting*, 14, 201-215.

Schinasi, G. J. & Swamy, P. A. (1989). The out-of-sample forecasting performance of exchange rate determination rate models when coefficients are allowed to change. *Journal of International Money and Finance*, 8, 375-390.

Taylor, J. G. (1995). *Neural Networks*. London: Unicom Limited.

Taylor, J. G. (1996). *Neural Networks and Their Applications*. London: John Wiley & Sons.

Taylor, S. (1986). *Modeling Financial Time Series.* New York: John Wiley & Sons.

Triggs, D. W. (1967). Exponential smoothing with adaptive response rate. *Operations Research Quarterly,* 18, 53-59.

Trippi, R. R. & Turban, E. (eds.) (1993). *Neural Networks in Finance and Investment.* New York: Probus Publishing.

White, H. (1989). Learning in artificial neural networks: A statistical perspective. *Neural Computing,* 1, 425-464.

Williams, R. J. & Zipser, D. (1989). A learning algorithm for continually running fully recurrent neural networks. *Neural Computation,* 1, 270-280.

Yao, J. & Tan, C. L. (2000). A case study on using neural networks to perform technical forecasting of forex. *Neurocomputing,* 34, 79-98.

Chapter XI

A Combined ARIMA and Neural Network Approach for Time Series Forecasting

G. Peter Zhang, Georgia State University, USA

ABSTRACT

This chapter presents a combined ARIMA and neural network approach for time series forecasting. The model contains three steps: (1) fitting a linear ARIMA model to the time series under study, (2) building a neural network model based on the residuals from the ARIMA model, and (3) combine the ARIMA prediction and the neural network result to form the final forecast. By combining different models, we aim to take advantage of the unique modeling capability of each individual model and improve forecasting performance dramatically. The effectiveness of the combining approach is demonstrated and discussed with three applications.

INTRODUCTION

Forecasting plays a critical role in business planning. The ability to accurately predict the future is fundamental to many decision activities in retail, marketing, production, inventory control, personnel, and many other business functional areas. Increasing forecasting accuracy can facilitate the savings of millions of dollars to a company and is a major motivation for using formal systematic forecasting methods and for investigating new, better forecasting methods. Time series modeling approach is one of the major techniques widely used in practice. Compared to another major forecasting approach — causal method where a number of explanatory or causal variables have to be identified and predicted — time series approach has the benefit of easier data collection and modeling preparation. In time series forecasting, historical data of the prediction variable are collected and analyzed to develop a model that captures the underlying relationship among time series observations. The model is then used to extrapolate the time series into the future for forecasting.

Numerous efforts have been devoted to developing and improving time series forecasting methods. Broadly speaking, there are two approaches to time series modeling and forecasting: linear approach and nonlinear approach. The linear approach assumes a linear underlying data generating process. There are a large number of linear forecasting models such as moving average, exponential smoothing, time series regression, and time series decomposition. One of the most important and popular linear models is the autoregressive integrated moving average (ARIMA) that was popularized by Box and Jenkins (1976) in the 1970s. Often times, ARIMA is also called the Box-Jenkins model. Although ARIMA models are quite flexible in modeling a wide range of time series patterns, their major limitation is the presumed *linear* form of the model. That is, a linear autocorrelation structure is assumed before the model is fitted to the data. Therefore, an ARIMA model is not able to capture *nonlinear* patterns that are commonly seen in many business and economic time series. The approximation of linear models to complex real-world problems is not always satisfactory as evidenced by the well-known M-competition in the early 1980s (Makridakis et al., 1982).

Linear models have been used for a long time and are still very useful, but the linear assumption underlying these models may be too restrictive. The nonlinear approach to time series modeling is perhaps more appropriate for most real world problems. But, the nonlinear world is much more complex than the linear world since there are so many possible nonlinear relationships or structures. Most nonlinear models developed during the last two decades are parametric in nature. To use these models, the model forms have to be specified first. Therefore, these models may not be useful if the data characteristics do not match model assumptions.

A more flexible nonlinear model is the artificial neural networks (ANNs) which have received more attentions recently (Zhang et al., 1998). The major advantage of neural networks is that they are data driven and do not require restrictive assumptions about the form of the underlying model. This flexible nonparametric approach is fairly appropriate for many problems with complex nonlinear structures, but there is a lack of theory to suggest a specific form of the structure.

This study uses a combined approach of linear ARIMA and nonlinear ANN models for time series forecasting (Zhang, 2003). The idea is based on the fact that no single model is the best for any situation. Therefore, if we can use each model's unique features and strengths, we are able to better capture the patterns in the data. There are many contrasting features in ARIMA and ANNs. First, ARIMA is linear and ANNs are inherently nonlinear. ARIMA is a very comprehensive linear model and can represent many types of linear relationships, such as autoregressive (AR), moving average (MA), and mixed AR and MA time series structures. In addition, some exponential smoothing models can be represented by ARIMA models (Mckenzie, 1984). On the other hand, ANNs are universal functional approximators and can model any type of nonlinear relationship. Second, ARIMA is essentially parametric while ANN is non-parametric in nature. Thus, in using ARIMA, the general model form is known while in using ANNs, we don't need to specify a particular model form. Of course, linear ARIMA is relatively simple to understand and implement compared to ANNs. Finally, ARIMA models are developed based on formal statistical theory and statistical techniques are often used for model development and adequacy checking. But, there is no systematic method in neural network model building and ANNs are often treated as black boxes.

The motivations for the combined method are three-fold. First, in many forecasting situations, it is often difficult to determine whether a time series under study is generated from a linear or nonlinear underlying process or whether one particular method is more effective than the other in out-of-sample forecasting. Thus, it is difficult for forecasters to choose the right technique for their unique situation at the beginning. Typically, a number of different models are tried and the one with the most accurate result is selected. However, the final selected model is not necessarily the best for future uses due to many potential factors, such as sampling variation, model uncertainty, and structural change. By combining different methods, the problem of model selection can be eased with little extra effort. Second, real world time series are rarely pure linear or nonlinear. They often contain both linear and nonlinear patterns. If this is the case, then neither ARIMA nor ANNs can be adequate in modeling and forecasting time series since the ARIMA model can not deal with nonlinear relationships while the ANN model alone may not be able to handle both linear and nonlinear patterns equally well. Hence, by combining ARIMA with ANN models, complex autocorrelation structures in the data can be modeled more accurately. Third, it is almost universally agreed in the forecasting literature that no single method is the best in every situation. This is largely due to the fact that a real world problem is often complex in nature and any single model may not be able to capture different patterns equally well. Therefore, combining different models can increase the chance to capture different patterns in the data and improve forecasting performance. Several empirical studies have already suggested that by combining several different models, forecasting accuracy can often be improved over the individual model. In addition, the combined or hybrid model is typically more robust and is less likely to get dramatically worse results than each single model used in isolation.

The rest of the chapter is organized as follows. The next section will provide a concise review of the literature on neural network combination approach to time series forecasting. Then the hybrid model is presented, followed by a discussion of the results. The summary and conclusion are provided in the last section.

PREVIOUS RESEARCH

Combining several models to improve forecasting accuracy has been widely studied in the traditional forecasting literature. The literature is vast and growing. Clemen (1989) provides a comprehensive review and annotated bibliography for this area. The idea of model combination lies in the basic assumption that the true underlying structure of data is difficult or impossible to model by one model exactly and different models may play a complementary role in capturing different patterns in the data. The efficacy of forecast combination has been established both theoretically and empirically. In the first M-competition (Makridakis et al., 1982), most conventional forecasting models are tested using more than 1000 real time series and the combination of forecasts from more than one model often leads to improved forecasting performance. The conclusion that the accuracy of combining various methods outperformed, on average, the individual methods used has also been confirmed by two recent forecasting competitions, i.e., M2- and M3-competitions (Makridakis et al., 1993; Makridakis & Hibon, 2000).

Much research has been done in forecasting combination in the last two decades. Most of the research, however, focused on the linear model combination. Recently, several studies have proposed to combine multiple neural networks or combine neural networks with statistical methods. For example, Pelikan et al. (1992) demonstrate the improved forecasting accuracy by combining several ANN models with decorrelated residuals. Ginzburg and Horn (1994) show good results with multiple neural network models. Wedding and Cio (1996) propose a hybrid model of radial basis function (RBF) networks and ARMA models. Luxhoj et al. (1996) present a methodology that combines ANN models with econometric models to better forecast sales. Donaldson and Kamstra (1996) and Shi et al. (1999) suggest different approaches for forecasting by combining ANNs. Khotanzad et al. (2000) propose a two-stage approach to combine several neural networks for natural gas consumption prediction. Medeiros and Veiga (2000) use a hybrid linear-neural model for time series forecasting. Zhang and Berardi (2001) develop two ANN-based combining methods for time series forecasting.

It is important to note that although various forecasting combining methods have been proposed in the literature, most of them are designed to combine similar methods. For example, combining similar linear models is a focus in the traditional forecasting literature. In neural network forecasting research, neural network ensembles are often used to describe the combination of several neural networks. Although this type of combining has improved forecasting accuracy, the benefit of combining is reduced if similar or same types of models are combined, as each of the models in the combination provides similar information on the autocorrelation pattern of the data. A more effective way of combination should be based on quite different models, as theoretically it can be shown that a hybrid model will have lower generalization error if dissimilar models that disagree with each other strongly are combined.

THE MODEL

The hybrid model used in this study is relatively simple to understand and easy to implement in practice. We assume that a time series contains two basic components, a linear component L_t and a nonlinear component NL_t. The model can be written as:

$$Y_t = L_t + NL_t + a_t$$

where Y_t is the time series observation at time period t; L_t and NL_t are the linear and nonlinear structures of the time series, respectively, and a_t is the random error term.

The basic idea of this hybrid approach is to let ARIMA model the linear part and let ANN model the nonlinear part and then combine the results from both linear and nonlinear models. The model building process involves the following three steps. First, an ARIMA model is built based on the raw data to estimate the linear component. The residuals from the ARIMA model should contain some nonlinearities (since we believe that a real data set always contains more or less nonlinear relationships). Then we apply ANNs to the residuals to estimate the nonlinear component. Finally, we combine these two parts together to make a forecast.

Let the estimated component from the ARIMA model be L^e_t and the estimated nonlinear component from ANNs be NL^e_t, then the combined forecast Y^e_t will be:

$$Y^e_t = L^e_t + NL^e_t$$

DATA AND MODEL BUILDING

Data

Three monthly time series are used in this study to demonstrate the effectiveness of the hybrid approach. They are the US industrial production (from the Federal Reserve Board) for clothing (1947.1-2001.12), residential utilities (1954.1-2001.12), and auto products (1947.1-2001.12). Data are first seasonally adjusted by using US Census Bureau's X-12-ARIMA seasonal adjustment procedure. Figures 1(a) through (c) plot the deseasonalized data which will be treated as the raw data in this study. From Figure 1, it is clear that all data series exhibit some upward trend, but different patterns.

Due to the trend observed in the time series, it is often necessary to detrend the series first. For ARIMA modeling, differencing is often used to achieve data stationarity. For neural network training, we elect to use linear detrending method. That is, a linear regression model is fitted to the data and then the fitted data are subtracted from the original data to form the detrending series. The neural network results are then scaled back to their original scales for direct comparison purposes.

Figure 1: Monthly US Industrial Production Time Series

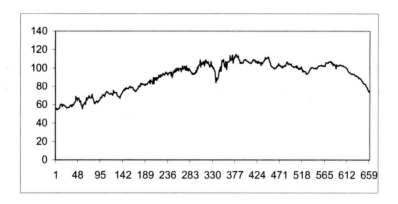

(a) Clothing

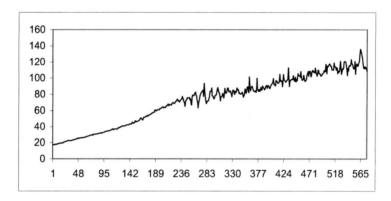

(b) Residential Utilities

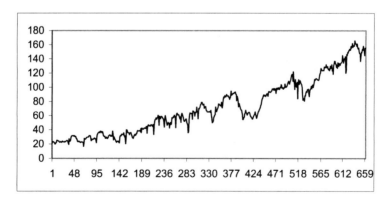

(C) Auto Products

For each data set, we reserve the last 12 months' data as the holdout sample for forecasting evaluation and the rest of the data (in-sample) are used for model selection and estimation. The holdout sample is not used in the model building process and hence it represents a set of true "unseen future" observations for testing the proposed model effectiveness as well as for model comparisons. In neural network modeling, the in-sample data are further divided into two portions of a training sample and a validation sample. The validation sample consists of the last 12-month observations while the training sample consists of all previous observations. The training sample is used to estimate the parameters for any specific model architecture. The validation set is then used to select the best model. For ARIMA modeling, all in-sample data are used to build the model and estimate model parameters. To be compatible, after neural network training and model selection, we combine the training and validation samples and reestimate the ANN model parameter with the best model architecture and then this estimated model is used for out-of-sample forecasting.

Model Building and Comparison

ARIMA model building follows the Box-Jenkins three-step iterative approach: model identification, parameter estimation, and model adequacy checking. As subjective judgment is often required in the model building process, it may be difficult to get the same result with different forecasters. To ease this problem, automatic ARIMA modeling tools have been developed and used in more and more practical situations. In this study, we use Forecast Pro's Expert Selection feature to conduct automatic ARIMA modeling. The capability of Forecast Pro has been documented in the recent forecasting competition (Goodrich, 2000).

Neural network model building is conducted via the standard cross-validation approach, i.e., the model parameters are estimated with the training data and then the validation sample is used to select the final model. With the training data we estimated many different neural network models in order to better capture the underlying behavior of the time series movement. In the experiment, the number of input nodes varies from one to six and the number of hidden nodes is chosen to vary from one to 10. Therefore, we consider 60 different models for each data set in the ANN model building process. The ANN architecture with the lowest mean squared error in the validation sample is chosen as the final model structure for out-of-sample forecasting.

The three-layer feedforward neural network is used in this study. We consider one-step-ahead forecasting and, hence, only one output node is employed. The logistic function is used as the transfer function for hidden nodes and the linear transfer function is used for the output node. Bias terms are employed in both hidden and output layers. A GRG2-based neural network training system (Subramanian & Hung 1993) is used in this study for all neural network trainings.

For each data set, we build three models: (1) an ARIMA model based on the whole in-sample data, (2) an ANN model using the cross-validation approach outlined above, and (3) the hybrid model. Three forecast error measures, the mean squared error (MSE), the mean absolute error (MAE), and the mean absolute percentage error (MAPE), are employed for model evaluation and model comparison.

RESULTS

We focus on the out-of-sample forecasting results. As mentioned earlier, for all three data sets, the last 12 observations in 2001 are reserved as the hold-out sample for model forecasting evaluation and comparison. As one-step-forecasting is exclusively considered here, each time a new observation is obtained, it will be used to make the next forecast. Both overall results and individual forecasts will be discussed here.

Table 1 lists three overall summary statistics in out-of-sample forecasting for the three data sets with the three methods. Several observations can be made here. First, the hybrid approach provides the best forecasting results for

Table 1: Summary Measures of Performance on Test

Data	Method	MSE	MAE	MAPE
Clothing	ARIMA	1.8920	1.1292	1.4637
	ANN	1.3242	1.0211	1.2979
	Hybrid	1.1847	0.9307	1.1953
Utility	ARIMA	17.1492	3.3896	2.9168
	ANN	14.8968	3.2978	2.8570
	Hybrid	13.7343	2.9894	2.5753
Auto	ARIMA	34.0911	4.9237	3.3215
	ANN	40.4236	5.3863	3.6328
	Hybrid	27.5191	4.0782	2.7550

all three data series judging by all three performance measures. The improvement of using the hybrid method over either pure ARIMA or pure ANN model can be considerable. For example, in the clothing series case, the decrease in MSE with the hybrid model over the ARIMA model is more than 37.4%, and over the ANN model, it is about 10.5%. Using MAE and MAPE, we find that the reductions in these measures with the hybrid model can be as high as about 18% compared to the ARIMA model and about 8% compared to the ANN model.

Second, neural network models may not be always better than linear ARIMA models for forecasting. Although for clothing and residential utility series, ANN models do provide better overall results than the ARIMA models, the ANN model is worse than the ARIMA model in the auto products case, judging by all three performance measures. This observation confirms the finding in the forecasting literature that no single forecasting method is the best for all situations. Therefore, the pre-selection of one type of model (linear or nonlinear) for a particular forecasting situation may not be appropriate.

Figures 2(a) through (c) show the point-to-point comparison between actual observations and the forecasts from the three models. In general, all three one-step forecasting models perform well in capturing the general pattern of the actual time series movement. In addition, these three models tend to behave similarly in terms of over- or under-forecasting in many out-of-sample periods. Although the hybrid model does not provide the best forecasts for all data points, it provides better forecasts than either ARIMA or ANN or both overall and in most of the individual points.

SUMMARY

This chapter demonstrates that by combining both linear and nonlinear models, forecasting performance can be significantly improved over each individual model used separately. The hybrid approach studied in this research overcomes the limitation of a pure linear or nonlinear modeling approach while at the same time takes advantage of their unique modeling capability to capture different patterns in the data. Moreover, the model is expected to be beneficial for practical applications as the model is easy to implement and the effort to experiment with a large number of forecasting models in order to select the "best" one can be reduced.

Future research may focus on the question: Under what condition is the hybrid model most appropriate or effective? Obviously, if a time series contains

Figure 2: Out-of-Sample Forecasting Comparison

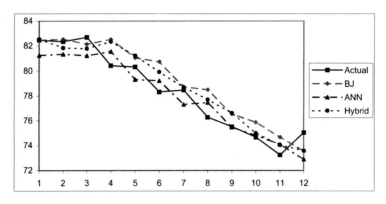

(a) Clothing

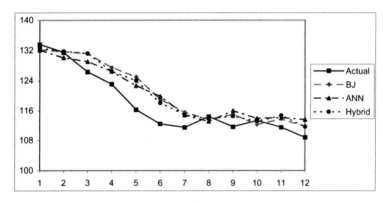

(b) Residential Utility

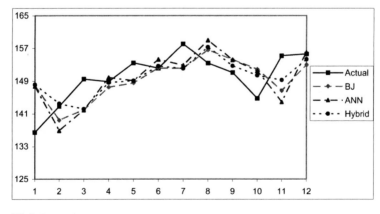

(C) Auto

only linear or nonlinear pattern or structure, the hybrid model will not be the best choice. In this regard, simulation study can be very useful since with simulated data, characteristics of the data generating process can be well controlled. In addition, note that in this study, we assume that the linear and nonlinear components are separable. A natural question is that what if the linear and nonlinear components are not separable? Is the hybrid model used in this study still effective? These questions should be addressed in the future research.

REFERENCES

Box, G. E. P. & Jenkins, G. M. (1976). *Time Series Analysis: Forecasting and Control*. San Francisco, CA: Holden-Day.

Clemen, R. (1989). Combining forecasts: A review and annotated bibliography with discussion. *International Journal of Forecasting, 5*, 559-608.

Donaldson, R. G. & Kamstra, M. (1996). Forecasting combining with neural networks. *Journal of Forecasting, 15*, 49-61.

Ginzburg, I. & Horn, D. (1994). Combined neural networks for time series analysis. *Advances in Neural Information Processing Systems, 6*, 224-231.

Goodrich, R. L. (2000). The Forecast Pro methodology. *International Journal of Forecasting, 16*, 533-535.

Khotanzad, A., Elragal, H., & Lu, T. L. (2000). Combination of artificial neural-network forecasters for prediction of natural gas consumption. *IEEE Transaction on Neural Networks, 11*(2), 464-473.

Luxhoj, J. T., Riis, J. O., & Stensballe, B. (1996). A hybrid econometric-neural network modeling approach for sales forecasting. *International Journal of Production Economics, 43*, 175-192.

Makridakis, S. & Hibon, M. (2000). The M3-Competition: Results, conclusions and implications. *International Journal of Forecasting, 16*, 451-476.

Makridakis, S., Anderson, A., Carbone, R., Fildes, R., Hibdon, M., Lewandowski, R., Newton, J., Parzen, E., & Winkler, R. (1982). The accuracy of extrapolation (time series) methods: Results of a forecasting competition. *Journal of Forecasting, 1*, 111-153.

Makridakis, S., Chatfield, C., Hibon, M., Lawrence, M., Mills, T., Ord, K., & Simmons, L. F. (1993). The M2-Competition: A real-time judgmentally based forecasting study. *International Journal of Forecasting, 9*, 5-22.

Mckenzie, E. (1984). General exponential smoothing and the equivalent ARMA process. *Journal of forecasting,* 3, 333-344.

Medeiros, M. C. & Veiga, A. (2000). A hybrid linear-neural model for time series forecasting. *IEEE Transaction on Neural Networks,* 11(6), 1402-1412.

Pelikan, E., de Groot, C., & Wurtz, D. (1992). Power consumption in West-Bohemia: Improved forecasts with decorrelating connectionist networks. *Neural Networks,* 2(6), 701-712.

Shi, S., Xu, L. D., & Liu, B. (1999). Improving the accuracy of nonlinear combined forecasting using neural networks. *Expert systems with applications,* 16, 49-54.

Subramanian, V. & Hung, M. S. (1993). A GRG2-based system for training neural networks: Design and computational experience. *ORSA Journal on Computing,* 5(4), 386-394.

Wedding, D. K. & Cios, K. J. (1996). Time series forecasting by combining RBF networks, certainty factors, and the Box-Jenkins model. *Neurocomoputing,* 10, 149-168.

Zhang, G., Patuwo, B. E., & Hu, M. Y. (1998). Forecasting with artificial neural networks: The state of the art. *International Journal of Forecasting,* 14, 35-62.

Zhang, G. P. (2003). Time series forecasting using a hybrid ARIMA and neural network model. *Neurocomputing,* 50, 159-175.

Zhang, G. P. & Berardi, V. (2001). Time series forecasting with neural network ensembles: An application for exchange rate prediction. *Journal of the Operational Research Society,* 52(6), 652-664.

Chapter XII

Methods for Multi-Step Time Series Forecasting with Neural Networks

Douglas M. Kline, University of North Carolina at Wilmington, USA

ABSTRACT

In this study, we examine two methods for Multi-Step forecasting with neural networks: the Joint Method and the Independent Method. A subset of the M-3 Competition quarterly data series is used for the study. The methods are compared to each other, to a neural network Iterative Method, and to a baseline de-trended de-seasonalized naïve forecast. The operating characteristics of the three methods are also examined. Our findings suggest that for longer forecast horizons the Joint Method performs better, while for short forecast horizons the Independent Method performs better. In addition, the Independent Method always performed at least as well as or better than the baseline naïve and neural network Iterative Methods.

INTRODUCTION

Artificial neural networks (ANNs) are a promising technique for time series forecasting. Forecasters using ANNs enjoy the benefits of the model-free nature of neural networks and the ability to model both linear and nonlinear time series. When using ANNs for multistep forecasting, there is a choice in methodology:

- *Joint Method:* use a single network to forecast all forecast horizons
- *Independent Method:* use a dedicated network to forecast each forecast horizon
- *Iterative Method:* use a single-step-ahead model to iteratively generate forecasts

The Independent method has the advantage that models are built specifically for each horizon being forecasted. In concept, each horizon is treated as a unique problem, independent of the other horizons being forecast. The resulting models can vary in number of lags included, linearity/nonlinearity of the chosen model, and the parameters estimated. The Joint Method has the advantage that estimated parameters can be *shared* across the forecasts. This may result in better parameter estimates based on increased degrees of freedom.

The issues to be considered when deciding between the Joint and Independent methods include the amount of data for model building, the forecast horizons for which forecasts are desired, and general methodologies behind the two methods.

This paper compares the Joint and Independent forecast methods for multistep forecasting with ANNs on a large set of real data series. The characteristics of each method are explored including the size and nature of models generated and performance with regard to forecast horizon, amount of data for model building, and model lag. We use relatively small data series compared to other studies, which may be more typical of a practitioner's experience. Our methodology is thoroughly described, including data preparation, network training, and experimental design.

We find that the Independent Method is superior for forecast horizons of one and two periods, while the Joint Method is better for forecast horizons of four periods. This is true for both large and small data sets. In general, the Independent Method significantly outperforms the Iterative method and the baseline Naïve Method. Also, the Joint Method consistently generates models with higher degrees of freedom for parameter estimation, which may explain its improved performance in longer forecast horizons.

BACKGROUND
Time Series Forecasting with Neural Networks

Among the many areas that feed-forward artificial neural networks have been applied to is the area of time series forecasting (Zhang et al. 1998a; Hill et al., 1996; Faraway & Chatfield, 1998; Tang et al., 1991; Tang & Fishwick, 1993; Adya & Collopy, 1998). Not only has this technique shown great promise under certain circumstances (Tang & Fishwick, 1993; Tang et al., 1991; Balkin & Ord, 1998; Zhang & Hu, 1998b), but it also has desirable properties as a time series forecasting tool, such as the ability to model arbitrary linear and nonlinear functions (Hornik, 1991; Hornik et al., 1989), few *a priori* assumptions (Cheng & Titterington, 1994), and the ability to model nonlinearities. See Zhang et al. (1998a) for a good review of neural networks used for forecasting.

Unfortunately, the flexibility of neural networks has resulted in substantial variations in applied methodology. This has led to inconsistent results (Tang & Fishwick, 1993; Hill et al., 1994), unrealistic expectations, and the tendency to treat neural networks as "black boxes." Several review papers (Hippert et al., 2001; Adya & Collopy, 1998; Maier & Dandy, 2000) have found substantial variations and lack of rigor in a majority of articles using neural networks for forecasting.

There are several characteristics of neural networks in the context of time series forecasting that make multistep forecasting an issue. Neural networks are nonlinear in nature, model-free, and tend to be parameter-heavy. We briefly discuss each of these characteristics below, with special consideration for how they affect the use of neural networks for time series forecasting.

Neural networks have the ability to model both linear and nonlinear time series (Zhang, 2001a; Zhang et al., 2001b). This ability is important because nonlinearities exist in real data series. For example, the M-3 Competition data set, one of the largest sets of real data series available, has nonlinearity in 25% of the series (Balkin, 2001). For some forecasting problems, such as exchange rate forecasting, linear models have not performed better than random walk (Zhang & Hu, 1998b; Hu et al., 1999). The challenge in using ANNs is that one cannot preclude the nonlinear involvement of a lag on the basis of a nonsignificant *linear* lag correlation. In other words, the wealth of knowledge and techniques available in the linear forecasting arena is not easily applied to nonlinear series.

Neural networks do not require the *a priori* determination of a functional model form. Neural networks have been theoretically shown to be universal approximators (under certain conditions, Hornik et al., 1989; Hornik, 1999). In traditional techniques, one would determine a functional form then estimate its parameters. Because neural networks approximate the function, both parameter estimation and function approximation are done simultaneously. The evaluation of multiple models becomes an exercise in determining the appropriate number of parameters (arc weights and node biases) to satisfactorily approximate the underlying function. This is more difficult than in traditional methods because the resulting parameters do not have the natural interpretations that exist in model-based forecasting.

Another challenge in using neural networks is that they tend to be parameter-heavy compared to traditional models. In many cases, a slight change to a neural network architecture can yield a large increase in the number of parameters in the model. It is, therefore, easy to inadvertently use so many parameters that the data is not sufficient to accurately estimate the parameters. At the low-parameter end, zero hidden nodes yield a linear model. At the high-parameter end, the number of parameters should create a reasonable ratio to the number of data points, allowing for adequate parameter estimation.

Multi-Step Methods

There are many methodological issues associated with the use of neural networks for time series forecasting. Researchers have studied model selection (Anders et al., 1999; Qi & Zhang, 2001), data sufficiency (Walczak, 2001), the effects of deseasonalization (Nelson et al., 1999), and many other topics (Zhang et al., 1998a). One issue that has had limited investigation is how to generate multiple-step-ahead forecasts.

Assume that a forecaster wishes to generate forecasts for multiple forecast horizons. For instance, one might wish to forecast sales in units for the next four quarters. As with other applications of neural networks, a central issue is development of a model with the appropriate number of parameters. In the following three sections we explicitly define three alternative methods for multistep forecasting. We do this to establish a common terminology and notation across the methods. In these descriptions, we use the term parameter to indicate an arc weight or node bias in the neural network. Terms that represent values from the time series are referred to as variables.

All of these methods have been used by researchers and practitioners in the past, so we are not suggesting a new method. However, past researchers' choice of method has been arbitrary, with no justification that the chosen method was appropriate.

Iterative Method

When posed with the issue of multistep forecasting, most researchers have resorted to using a single-step model, then iteratively using it to generate forecasts more than one step ahead (Zhang & Hu, 1998b; Hwarng, 2001; Hill et al., 1996; Balkin & Ord, 2000; Nelson et al., 1999). For example, assume a forecasting model with two lags:

$$y_{t+1} = f(x_t, x_{t-1}) \tag{1}$$

y_{t+1} being the estimate of x_{t+1}. To estimate two periods forward, the model becomes:

$$y_{t+2} = f(y_{t+1}, x_t) \tag{2}$$

To estimate three periods forward, the model becomes:

$$y_{t+3} = f(y_{t+2}, y_{t+1}) \tag{3}$$

This technique, which we refer to as the Iterative method, is a valid and intuitive way to handle multistep forecasting. It is commonly used for short forecast horizons in situations where the one-lag correlation is dominant over other lag correlations (DeLurgio, 1998). This method is used in traditional as well as neural network forecasting.

However, it has the well-known problem of propagating early errors into future forecasts. The errors from periods t+1 and t+2 continue to have an effect in later periods. For this reason, the technique has the potential to degenerate over longer forecast horizons due to error propagation. In other words, a poor forecast in an early period could have an adverse effect on later forecasts. The Iterative method is not the subject of this study, although we use it as a reference model.

Independent Method

A second option in multistep forecasting is to create independent models for each forecast horizon desired. In this situation, the models for generating forecasts for three steps ahead are:

$$\begin{aligned} y_{t+1} &= f(x_i \mid i = t) + e_{t+1} \\ y_{t+2} &= g(x_i \mid i = t) + e_{t+2} \\ y_{t+3} &= h(x_i \mid i = t) + e_{t+3} \end{aligned} \tag{4}$$

We term this the Independent method to indicate that each forecast model is developed independently of the others. This method has the advantage of not propagating errors forward and should, on average, perform better than the Iterative method as the forecast horizon increases.

There is also the appealing notion that each model is dedicated to forecasting its own forecast horizon. This is appealing because each forecast horizon may be a unique problem. With the Independent method, the models developed and ultimately chosen may differ substantially across the horizon to be forecasted — the differences can include their functional form, the lags included, and the estimated parameters.

Joint Method

A third option in multistep forecasting is to create a single model that simultaneously generates forecasts for all desired forecast horizons. In this method, the model for generating forecasts for three steps ahead is:

$$(y_{t+1}, y_{t+2}, y_{t+3}) = f(x_i \mid i = t) + e \tag{5}$$

The error term without a time index indicates that the parameter estimation is accomplished by pooling the error across the time periods. This is in contrast with equation 4 where the parameter estimation for each forecasted time period is only affected by the errors for that time period. The difference between equations 4 and 5 can also be observed by examining the parameters. In equation 5, the parameters are *shared* across forecast horizons. In equation 4, each forecast horizon's model parameters are estimated independently, while in equation 5, all of the model parameters are estimated using information from all forecast horizons.

A significant appeal of this method is that it offers another option in the attempt to match the number of parameters to the task at hand. For example, suppose a forecasting problem where four forecast horizons are desired has known nonlinearity and should use three lags (based on expert knowledge of the domain). Assume n is the number of data patterns in the fit set. Using the Independent method, we would need four networks, with each network having three input nodes, one hidden node, and a single output node. Each network would require six parameters, (InputNodes x HiddenNodes + HiddenNodes x OutputNodes + HiddenNodeBiases + OutputNodeBiases) = (3x1 + 1x1 +1+1) = 6, to produce each forecast. In cases where data is limited, there may not be enough data to accurately estimate the parameters of the models. The degrees of freedom for the parameter estimation of each network would be n-6, where n is the number of data points in the fit set.

Using the Joint Method, we would need a single network with three input nodes, one hidden node, and four output nodes. This network would have 12 parameters (3x1 + 1x4 + 1 + 4), but would forecast all four forecast horizons simultaneously. The degrees of freedom for the parameter estimation would be 3n-12. In most cases, 3n-12 > n-6 (when n > 3), meaning that the degree of freedom for the Joint Method is larger. One can see from this example that the parameter estimation using the Joint Method should be more accurate.

The disadvantage of this method is that adding a hidden node in the Joint Method adds many more parameters than in the Independent method. In the example above, an additional hidden node adds five parameters (number of inputs + 1 + 1) to the Independent method models, while it adds eight (number of inputs + number of outputs + 1) parameters to the Joint Method model. This can be even worse when more horizons are forecast. In general, the Joint Method usually has more degrees of freedom for parameter estimation. However, there is less ability to "tune" the parameters to the problem.

The main focus of this research is to compare the Independent and Joint Methods. We use the Iterative Method as a reference. We also use a Naïve Method that accounts for seasonality and trend as a reference method.

Related Research

Research involving ANNs is notorious for being inconsistent. Some articles conclude that ANNs significantly outperform traditional techniques, while some articles conclude exactly the opposite or find no difference at all. See Hippert et al. (2001), Adya and Collopy (1998), and Maier and Dandy (2000) for further comments on the variability of ANN methodology and suggestions for increasing the replicability of ANN studies. This section gives a brief overview of several papers closely related to the research in this study and discusses the differences in methodology.

Kang (forthcoming) studied the Independent vs. Iterative method on economic time series. This research did not use neural networks, rather an autoregressive model was used. They found that both methods were comparable, with one method outperforming another or vice versa on different series. They also found that, among other things, forecast origin, forecast horizon, and the time series affected the selection of a methodology.

Zhang et al. (1998a) refer to the Joint Method as the "direct" method (as compared to an iterative method). They summarize that results are mixed regarding a Joint Method vs. the Iterative Method, however, they hypothesize that the Joint Method should perform better in longer forecast horizons.

Hill et al. (1994) studied neural network forecasting on the M-competition data set, replicating previous research by others (Sharda & Patil, 1990; Foster et al., 1991). They concluded that the Joint Method performed much worse than the ANN Iterative method. They further found that the superiority of the ANN Iterative Method was more pronounced in longer forecast horizons. They found that the ANN Iterative Method performed about as well as traditional Iterative forecasting methods. They hypothesized that quarterly and monthly series may contain more nonlinearities than yearly series.

From the limited number of studies using the Joint Method, one can conclude that the Independent Method is favored among researchers. However, results from the studies that have directly compared the Joint versus Independent are mixed. We believe that the mixed results arise from the well-documented variations in neural network methodology (Hippert et al., 2001; Adya & Collopy, 1998; Maier & Dandy, 2000).

RESEARCH DESIGN

The primary focus of this study is the comparison of the Independent and the Joint Methods for producing multistep forecasts. Secondarily, we examine how these methods relate to deseasonalized and detrended naïve forecasts and the Iterative method described above.

We also examine several factors that may affect the choice of method for multistep forecasting. These factors include the amount of data available for model building, the forecast horizon, and the model lag (the time between the last data point used for model building and the data point being forecast).

Since methodology can vary substantially in ANN research we thoroughly discuss our methodology to aid in replicability. The data and its preparation are first discussed, followed by the ANN methodology. The choice of error measure and the overall experiment design is then discussed.

Data and Data Preparation

The data for this study consists of a subset of the 756 quarterly series from the M3 competition. The M3 competition data set is a large, well-studied data set and contains series of various lengths derived from various sources (Makridakis & Hibon, 2000). The M3 competition data also has series that exhibit both linear and nonlinear characteristics (Balkin, 2001).

The choice of quarterly data series was made since it provided a reasonable motivation for multistep forecasting; in practice, it is typical to wish to forecast the next four quarters. This choice also provided guidance in model building, since it is common to use the last four lags as the independent variables of a model.

The data was prepared by deseasonalizing, detrending, and normalizing, in that order. Nelson et al. (1999) found that deseasonalizing the data significantly aided the ANNs in their ability to make forecasts. Detrending was deemed necessary to fairly evaluate the neural network methods against the deseasonalized, detrended naïve forecast. Finally, it is common to normalize, since it aids in training (Zhang et al., 1998a).

We chose to use the earliest 80% of the data to build the models (in-sample) and the remaining 20% of the data to evaluate the models (holdout). All calculations in data preparation were performed on the in-sample data.

The quarterly seasonality indexes were calculated using a four-period centered moving average of the in-sample data, as in the classical multiplicative decomposition found in forecasting textbooks (DeLurgio, 1998). The deseasonalized data was produced by dividing each data point by the appropriate quarterly index, as in equation 6.

$$des_t = \frac{x_t}{Q_t} \tag{6}$$

The trend component was calculated on the deseasonalized in-sample data using a simple linear regression model using time index as the independent variable. The trend component was subtracted from the deseasonalized data points, as in equation 7. We chose to subtract the trend (as in an additive decomposition) rather than divide it out (as in a multiplicative decomposition) since we found that in certain situations, the trend component was near zero, which caused an ill-conditioned transformation.

$$\det_t = des_t - T_t \tag{7}$$

The deseasonalized, detrended data was then normalized by subtracting the in-sample mean and dividing by the in-sample standard deviation of the deseasonalized, detrended data, as in equation 8.

$$norm_t = \frac{\det_t - \mu_t}{\sigma_t} \qquad (8)$$

After the data preparation described above, the in-sample data has a mean of zero, standard deviation of one, and trend (slope) of zero. We next examined the data for outliers and significant changes from in-sample to holdout. We chose to remove these series, since they could potentially confound the results concerning which methodology to use.

Ultimately, we removed series where, in the deseasonalized, detrended, normalized data we found: (1) values above four in the in-sample or holdout data, (2) significant ($a = 0.01$) non-zero mean in the holdout data, (3) a trend of greater than 1 in the holdout data. We considered (1) to indicate outliers in either the in-sample or holdout, and (2) and (3) to indicate that there was a significant change in the generating process from in-sample to holdout.

The number of series removed was 607, leaving 149 series for the study. We were surprised that so many series were removed. In terms of outliers, one would not expect 607 series to contain outliers. However, the conditions (1) to (3) indicate a change in the nature of time series, rather than outliers in the time series. For instance, a time series can have an obvious change in trend without having any outliers in terms of standard deviations. Furthermore, detrending such a data series can exaggerate the change in the holdout set.

NN Methodology

In this study, we use feed-forward neural networks, consistent with the vast majority of research in this area (Zhang, Patuwo, & Hu, 2001b). We used Matlab v6 (Mathworks, Inc., 2001) as the environment, and the neural network toolbox Netlab (Nabney, 2001) to create and train the networks. Netlab closely follows the seminal work of Bishop (1995) in its implementation and uses the well-established algorithms of Matlab.

We use the "mlp" function of Netlab with linear output activation for every network (Nabney, 2001). This network has the following characteristics, all of which are consistent with Bishop (1995). All of the networks used at most a single hidden layer. The hidden layer nodes used the hyperbolic tangent activation function with bias. The output nodes of all networks used a linear function, with bias, which is appropriate since the outputs are not necessarily constrained. The linear output activation also indicates that the sum of the squared error (SSE) will be minimized in training because of the natural linkage of the linear output activation and SSE error function (Bishop, 1995). The networks were trained using the "netopt" function of Netlab with the "scg" option, indicating the use of a scaled conjugate gradient (SCG) method to minimize SSE.

The architectures studied are denoted by "AxBxC", where A is the number of inputs, B is the number of hidden nodes, and C is the number of outputs. The models with zero hidden nodes are purely linear, and have $A*C+C$ number of parameters. The models with hidden nodes are nonlinear, and have $A*B+B*C+B+C$ parameters.

Specifically, the Independent forecast method has architectures of the form AxBx1 for each forecast horizon. The Joint forecast method has architectures of the form AxBx4, which simultaneously forecasts four periods. The values of A in the architectures above vary from one to four, based on Hill et al. (1996) who found that four inputs worked the best for quarterly time series. The values of B vary from 0 to A. In other words, there are never more hidden nodes than input nodes, which is a common heuristic (Zhang et al., 2001a).

The network architectures examined were further restricted by a heuristic to ensure that the data was sufficient to estimate the number of parameters in the model. Specifically, the number of hidden nodes was limited to ensure that there were always at least three data points per parameter in the model.

All network architectures were trained 30 times starting from randomly selected values of arc weights and node biases. In situations where convergence of the scaled conjugate gradient (SCG) method was slow, training was stopped after 2,000 iterations. This was extremely rare, as the SCG method typically converges very quickly. We used the keep-the-best (KTB) heuristic based on SSE to retain the best network parameters of the 30 trained networks. Since the number of parameters is common among all 30 networks, any of the model selection criteria (such as AIC, BIC, GCV, etc.) would choose identically to KTB SSE. Using Matlab's "setseed" function, every architecture considered had its starting parameters randomly selected from the same stream of random numbers as a variance reduction technique.

For the Independent method, the following network architectures were considered: AxBxC, A in {1..4}, B in {0..A}, C = 1. For the Joint Method, the following network architectures were considered: AxBxC, A in {1..4}, B in {0..A}, C = 4. In some situations, the architectures were restricted by the heuristics described above. Note that in the Independent method, a separate network is developed for each forecast horizon. To chose among the network architectures, we use the generalized cross validation (GCV) (equation 9) metric with a value of c = 2.0 for model selection, as in Balkin and Ord (2000). Here, RSS is the square root of SSE, m is the number of parameters in the model, and T is the number of data points over which the SSE was calculated, i.e., the number of points in the in-sample. Many model selection metrics have been proposed, including the information criteria based AIC, BIC, and NIC (see Anders & Korn, 1999). Other researchers have found little difference in these criteria in practice (Qi & Zhang, 2001) and we have found GCV to perform well.

$$GCV = RSS \left(\frac{1}{\left(1 - \frac{mc}{T} \right)^2} \right) \tag{9}$$

Error Measure

A number of error statistics are used in evaluating forecasting performance. Some examples are the mean squared error (MSE), mean absolute deviation (MAD), and mean absolute percentage error (MAPE). The choice is especially pertinent when calculating statistics across multiple time series and across lead times. Tashman (2000) suggests using scale-independent error measures when calculating across multiple time series.

Scale and volatility of individual series can cause each series to contribute to the error measure differently. A data series with large values and abundant noise will most likely dominate over a data series with small values and little noise. Furthermore, a change in mean or variance over time can cause different forecast horizons within a single time series to contribute differently to the error measure.

We use the holdout sample absolute percentage error (APE) of the untransformed, original data series to evaluate the forecasting methods. To accomplish this, we first adjust our forecasts by applying, in reverse order, equations 6 through 8 to the network outputs. Then the APE is calculated from the original time series and our adjusted estimates. This is consistent with Hill et al. (1996), and recommended by Tashman (2000) in evaluations across time series.

Experiment Design

Our main experiment is summarized in equation 10. The dependent variable is the measure of absolute percentage error (APE) of the forecast. The method, M, takes on two values, Independent and Joint. The data series, S, takes on values one through 149, indicating which series is being forecasted. The horizon, H, takes on the values one through four, indicating the distance into the future of the forecast. The model lag, indicated by L, indicates the distance from the most recent data point used to estimate the model to the data point being estimated. This is an important variable, since the model is not recalibrated at each step forward. The values that the model lag takes on vary by series, depending upon how many data points are in the holdout sample.

$$APE = f(M,S,H,L) \tag{10}$$

In addition to the main study above, we will also examine how these methods compare to the Iterative and Naïve Baseline Methods. We will also provide statistics on the number of inputs used in the models and the number of parameters in the models.

We expect that, in general, the Independent Method will outperform the Joint Method, since each series and horizon being forecasted has a model that is developed specifically for that problem. We also expect that the horizon being forecast may influence which method, Joint or Independent, performs better. We expect this because, in general, a longer forecast horizon is harder to forecast and the Joint Method may benefit by its ability to better estimate model parameters. Finally, we expect that the amount of data available may also influence which method is better, since parameter estimation becomes more of an issue with small in-sample data sets.

RESULTS
Comparison of Joint and Independent Methods

Because the values of S, H, and L in equation 10 are common between the Independent and Joint Methods, it is possible to block on these variables and perform a paired t-test to evaluate the two methods' overall performance. As an example, for series $S = 5$, horizon $H = 3$, and model lag $L = 5$, we have an estimate, $y_I(S = 5, H = 3, L = 5)$, from the best Independent Model and an estimate, $y_J(S = 5, H = 3, L = 5)$, from the best Joint Model. From these values, we calculate the absolute percentage errors (APEs) for each, $APE_I(S = 5, H = 3, L = 5)$, $APE_J(S = 5, H = 3, L = 5)$. Since we can directly match the APEs on the values of S, H, and L, we take the difference, $d(S = 5, H = 3, L = 5) = APE_I(S = 5, H = 3, L = 5) - APE_J(S = 5, H = 3, L = 5)$ and perform tests on

Table 1: Paired t-Test on Independent APE – Joint APE

Mean	-0.25%
N	3886
std devn	0.0529
t-stat	**-2.9978**

this statistic. In general, this is a more powerful test than comparison of the mean APEs of the Joint and Independent methods. If there is no difference in the methods, we would expect that the mean of "d" would be zero. If the mean is significantly negative, then we would conclude that the Independent method, on average produces smaller APEs and would be preferred.

As shown in Table 1, the Joint Method has a significantly larger absolute percentage error on average. Note that the t-statistic is significant at the a = 0.05 level. Based on this information, a practitioner might choose to favor the Independent method over the Joint Method.

We hypothesized earlier that the Joint and Independent methods' performance might be affected by the amount of data available for model building and/or the forecast horizon. To examine this, we classified the data series as small if the in-sample contained less than 30 data points and large if the in-sample contained more than 30 data points.

Table 2 summarizes the paired differences of the Independent minus Joint Methods across horizon and size. The bolded t-statistics are significant at the a = 0.05 level. The t-statistics are given for reference and have not been adjusted to allow for multiple comparisons. Note that the t-statistics change sign and become significant as the horizon increases. For a multistep forecast of four periods, one should definitely choose the Joint Method over the Independent Method. More specifically, to achieve the best single-step forecast, use the Independent Method. However, to achieve the best 4-step-ahead forecast, use the Joint Method. So, in practice, one would create Independent models for horizons one through three, then a Joint model for horizon four.

Note that the t-statistics are larger for the Large data series. In part, this is caused by the larger number of observations (n) for the Large data series. This indicates that with more data, the choice of method is more significant. Also note, however, that the magnitudes of the means are larger for the Large data series. We conclude from this that choosing the appropriate method will have a greater effect when the data set is larger.

Table 2: Paired Differences by Horizon and Size: Independent APE – Joint APE

sizeclass		horizon 1	2	3	4	Total
Large	mean	-1.30%	-0.52%	0.33%	0.75%	-0.29%
	stddev	0.0757	0.0465	0.0619	0.0794	0.0672
	n	608	546	484	422	2060
	t-stat	**-4.2453**	**-2.5880**	1.1645	**1.9451**	**-1.9594**
Small	mean	-0.62%	-0.15%	-0.05%	0.20%	-0.22%
	stddev	0.0382	0.0256	0.0251	0.0220	0.0297
	n	587	500	413	326	1826
	t-stat	**-3.9079**	-1.3137	-0.4323	**1.6620**	**-3.0900**
Total	mean	-0.97%	-0.34%	0.15%	0.51%	-0.25%
	stddev	0.0603	0.0380	0.0486	0.0614	0.0530
	n	1195	1046	897	748	3886
	t-stat	**-5.5330**	**-2.9000**	0.9386	**2.2821**	**-2.9978**

Table 3 shows results similar to Table 2, except arranged by forecast horizon and model lag. As in Table 2, the bolded t-statistics are significant at the a = 0.05 level. The t-statistics are given for reference and have not been adjusted for multiple comparisons. There were instances of model lags of 11, 12, and 13 periods. They are not reported here to conserve space. In practice, one would recalibrate the model to avoid such long model lags.

Table 3: Paired Differences by Horizon and Model Lag: Independent APE – Joint APE

horizon		model lag										Total
		1	2	3	4	5	6	7	8	9	10	
1	mean	-1.83%	-0.87%	-0.72%	-0.70%	-0.49%	-0.71%	-0.88%	-1.10%	-1.77%	1.21%	-0.97%
	stddev	0.060	0.063	0.039	0.052	0.041	0.054	0.054	0.073	0.070	0.110	0.060
	n	149	149	149	149	149	118	116	104	60	17	1195
	tstat	-3.739	-1.681	-2.263	-1.630	-1.449	-1.419	-1.757	-1.529	-1.965	0.452	-5.533
2	mean		-0.96%	-0.49%	-0.14%	-0.18%	-0.39%	-0.03%	-0.11%	0.36%	-2.10%	-0.34%
	stddev		0.030	0.034	0.037	0.032	0.037	0.044	0.043	0.043	0.057	0.038
	n		149	149	149	149	118	116	104	60	17	1046
	tstat		-3.921	-1.760	-0.451	-0.678	-1.167	-0.073	-0.255	0.635	-1.519	-2.900
3	mean			0.06%	0.40%	0.11%	-0.19%	0.23%	-0.10%	0.45%	0.08%	0.15%
	stddev			0.055	0.069	0.026	0.035	0.049	0.051	0.028	0.024	0.049
	n			149	149	149	118	116	104	60	17	897
	tstat			0.136	0.707	0.520	-0.572	0.501	-0.195	1.258	0.146	0.939
4	mean				0.96%	1.04%	0.50%	-0.04%	0.59%	-0.56%	-0.74%	0.51%
	stddev				0.081	0.065	0.046	0.042	0.064	0.067	0.024	0.061
	n				149	149	118	116	104	60	17	748
	tstat				1.443	1.935	1.187	-0.107	0.941	-0.641	-1.257	2.282
Total	mean	-1.83%	-0.91%	-0.38%	0.13%	0.12%	-0.20%	-0.18%	-0.18%	-0.38%	-0.39%	-0.25%
	stddev	0.060	0.049	0.044	0.062	0.044	0.044	0.047	0.059	0.055	0.064	0.053
	n	149	298	447	596	596	472	464	416	240	68	3886
	tstat	-3.739	-3.204	-1.859	0.515	0.659	-0.970	-0.829	-0.618	-1.063	-0.498	-2.998

As before, the Joint Method seems to perform better at horizon = 4, while the Independent method performs better at horizon = 1. Note also, that the Independent method consistently forecasts better than the Joint Method across model lags when the horizon = 1. In larger model lags, with horizon above 1, there seems to be no difference between the methods.

*Table 4: Paired Differences by Horizon and Size: Independent APE –
Naive*

			horizon				
			1	2	3	4	Total
size	L	mean	-0.16%	-1.25%	-1.12%	-0.91%	-0.83%
		stddev	0.0391	0.0766	0.0991	0.1039	0.0809
		n	608	546	484	422	2,060
			-1.0309	**-3.7993**	**-2.4946**	**-1.7907**	**-4.6488**
	S	mean	-1.38%	-1.98%	-1.98%	-1.11%	-1.63%
		stddev	0.0798	0.0832	0.0816	0.0977	0.0846
		n	587	500	413	326	1,826
			-4.1962	**-5.3329**	**-4.9446**	**-2.0502**	**-8.2583**
	Total	mean	-0.76%	-1.60%	-1.52%	-0.99%	-1.21%
		stddev	0.0628	0.0799	0.0915	0.1012	0.0827
		n	1,195	1,046	897	748	3,886
			-4.1969	**-6.4730**	**-4.9752**	**-2.6882**	**-9.0972**

Comparison Against Naïve and Iterative Methods

As mentioned previously, ANN research varies widely, which has motivated some researchers to suggest that all ANN research compare results
against baseline methods (Hippert et al., 2001; Maier & Dandy, 2000). We
show in Table 4 some comparative statistics between the Independent method
and a baseline naïve forecast. Bolded t-statistic values are significant at a = 0.05
level and are not adjusted for multiple comparisons. The naïve forecast we use
is actually a seasonality- and trend-adjusted Naïve forecast. Overall, the
Independent method outperforms the naïve forecast about 1.21% on average
with a standard deviation of about 8.2%.

Another common method in forecasting is to iteratively use a one-step-
ahead forecast as described in this chapter. Table 5 gives comparative results
for the Iterative method vs. the Independent Method. (Note that horizon one
is not shown, since the forecasts are equal for the two methods at this forecast
horizon.) Bolded t-statistic values are significant at a = 0.05 level and are not
adjusted for multiple comparisons. In general, the Independent Method
performs as well as, or better than, the Iterative method.

Examination of Joint and Independent Methods

In this section, we investigate the characteristics of the Joint and Independent methods with regard to the models that were chosen by the two methods.
In situations where the forecasts are not significantly different, we are motivated
to choose models which are more parsimonious, i.e., have fewer parameters.

Table 5: Paired Differences by Horizon and Size: Independent APE –
Iterative

			horizon			
			2	3	4	Total
size	L	mean	-0.55%	-0.21%	-0.20%	-0.25%
		stddev	0.0585	0.0871	0.1004	0.0690
		n	546	484	422	2,060
		tstat	**-2.1792**	-0.5327	-0.4000	-1.6320
	S	mean	-0.18%	-0.55%	-0.34%	-0.23%
		stddev	0.0275	0.0331	0.0452	0.0287
		n	500	413	326	1,826
		tstat	-1.4286	**-3.3506**	-1.3599	**-3.4679**
	Total	mean	-0.37%	-0.37%	-0.26%	-0.24%
		stddev	0.0464	0.0678	0.0810	0.0540
		n	1,046	897	748	3,886
		tstat	**-2.5726**	-1.6133	-0.8729	**-2.7838**

We may also be interested in how frequently the methods choose linear vs. nonlinear models. In ANN terms, linear models correspond to network architectures with zero hidden nodes. Table 6 gives counts of the linear vs. nonlinear models chosen by the Independent method. In general, the Independent method chooses more linear than nonlinear models. Roughly 30% (179/ 596 = 0.300) of the models are nonlinear, which is fairly consistent with Balkin's (2001) assertion that about 25% of the M3 competition data series exhibit nonlinearity.

Table 7 shows the lags included in the chosen models for the Independent method. Clearly, simple models which include a small number of lags are chosen more frequently than other models.

Table 6: Counts of Linear vs. Nonlinear Models for the Independent
Method

		Model form		
		linear	nonlinear	total
horizon	1	74	75	149
	2	102	47	149
	3	117	32	149
	4	124	25	149
	Total	417	179	596

Table 7: Lags Included for Independent Models

		network inputs				
		1	2	3	4	Total
horizon	1	132	12	3	2	149
	2	122	15	8	4	149
	3	121	11	10	7	149
	4	130	8	3	8	149
	Total	505	46	24	21	596

The linear vs. nonlinear models for the Joint Method mirror Table 8, which shows the number of lags included in the chosen model. For the Joint Method, the chosen models were either of the form 1x0x4 or 2x1x4. There were only 13 series where the form of the chosen model was 2x1x4.

Finally, we are interested in how accurately the parameters of each model might be estimated, based on the degrees of freedom. The criteria used to choose between competing models typically factor in the number of parameters in the model, to favor parsimonious models. However, these criteria do not factor in the power of the model to estimate the parameters of the chosen model. In terms of parameter estimation, the degrees of freedom are calculated according to the formula:

$$df = \text{number of estimates} - \text{number of parameters} \qquad (11)$$

In equation 11, "number of estimates" is the number of outputs of the ANN model times the number of patterns used to train the model. Notice that the Joint Method typically has more parameters but, based on the degrees of freedom, it is likely that the parameters are more accurately estimated.

Table 8: Lags Included for Joint Models

		network inputs				
		1	2	3	4	Total
horizon	1	136	13	0	0	149
	2	136	13	0	0	149
	3	136	13	0	0	149
	4	136	13	0	0	149
	Total	544	52	0	0	596

Table 9: Average Parameters and Degrees of Freedom for Parameter Estimation for the Independent and Joint Methods

			Independent	Joint
horizon	1	avg params	2.7	4.6
		avg df	19.3	83.4
	2	avg params	2.2	4.6
		avg df	19.8	83.4
	3	avg params	2.0	4.6
		avg df	20.0	83.4
	4	avg params	1.8	4.6
		avg df	20.2	83.4
	Total	avg params	2.2	4.6
		avg df	19.8	83.4

DISCUSSION

In this chapter, we studied the Independent and Joint Methods for multistep forecasting using artificial neural networks on a set of 149 well-studied quarterly series. We also referenced these methods' performance against the well-known one-step-ahead Iterative method and a seasonality- and trend-adjusted naïve forecast. We expected the Independent method to perform best, in general, and that training sample size and forecast horizon might affect the choice of method.

Our recommendations are summarized in Table 10.

We found that for short forecast horizons, the Independent Method was superior, while for longer forecast horizons, the Joint Method was superior. This would indicate that, in general, the Joint Method should be used for forecasting four periods ahead. Based on the pattern in our t-tests, we expect that the Joint Method would also perform better than the Independent Method for five or more periods ahead. The benefit of using the appropriate method will vary with the size of the data series.

Table 10: Recommendations

Forecast Horizon	Method to Use
1	Independent
2	Independent
3	Independent or Joint
4	Joint

These results may seem counter-intuitive — if a method is best for a single step ahead, why would it not be better for four steps ahead? We believe that the answer lies in appropriately matching the model complexity with the problem complexity. A one-step-ahead forecast problem should be matched with a simpler forecast model, i.e., the Independent Method. Otherwise, we encounter poor generalization to the holdout. However, a simple model will not be able to represent more complex problems, such as forecasting four periods into the future. This would require a more complex model, such as the Joint Method.

Our results concerning the Joint Method are not consistent with the findings of Hill et al. (1994), who surmised from their research with the M-competition data that the Iterative method performed better than the Joint Method, especially in longer forecast horizons. We think the difference in our findings is due to the data preparation of the data series used in the findings. In this study, we took great pains to remove data series that might confound our results. It is well-known that very simple, short memory forecasters, such as naïve models, exponential smoothing, or one-step-ahead iterative method neural networks, perform quite well in situations where the mean and trend are shifting. Because the Joint Method produces more complex models than the Independent method, we expect that Joint models will be very poor forecasters when presented with holdout data not characteristic of the in-sample data they were trained on. Therefore, a study using data series with significant changes from in-sample to holdout might well conclude that the Independent Method is superior.

If the difference between our results and that of Hill et al. (1994) *were* due to shifts in the underlying data series, it would mean that recalibration of the Joint Method models is very important. In other words, the model lag may be more significant for the Joint Method than for the Independent or Iterative Methods.

We found that the Independent method always performed at least as well as or better than the naïve and iterative reference methods. This is counter to the findings of Kang (forthcoming). Kang's study used autoregressive models rather than neural network models, which may account for the different findings. Our findings support the use of neural networks for time series forecasting.

One should not conclude from this study that a single method is superior in all situations or for all time series. As shown by Wolpert and Macready (1997), a method that performs very well on one class of problems will perform poorly on other classes of problems. We suggest that all the methods be considered as the situation dictates. Ideally, many models are created using all methods and the best model is chosen by evaluating against a validation set.

However, in situations where this is not feasible, such as a small data set or limited computation time, our results give guidance for choosing an appropriate methodology.

This study shows clearly that the Joint Method for multistep forecasting is appropriate for certain problems. Practitioners should favor this method for multistep forecasting, especially when the forecast horizon is larger. While the superiority of the Joint Method cannot be predicted on a single problem, Joint models should be considered alongside Independent models. Joint models have the advantage of being simpler to implement in practice, since they require that only a single model be built for all forecast horizons. The Joint Method is likely to more accurately estimate the model parameters, based on the relative increase of degrees of freedom over the Independent method.

Another potential advantage of the Joint method may be the convenient skirting of the issue of which lags to include in a model. In traditional time series methodologies, linear lag correlations are calculated and only lags with significant correlations are included in the model. This is an appealing methodology, however, a lag that has a small linear correlation may be involved in a nonlinear manner with the other lags. Neural network practitioners either: (1) use linear correlations as estimates of a lag's importance to a model (as in Balkin & Ord, 2000) or (2) include all lags (typical to most research, Zhang et al., 1998a). By using the Joint Method, the question of whether a certain lag should be included in a certain forecast horizon model is obviated, since all included lags are used together to create all forecasts.

This study was limited to relatively well-mannered quarterly series from the M3 competition. The horizons being forecasted were limited to four steps ahead. Our results may not generalize to longer forecast horizons or to data series outside our set. We would like to see more applied studies where the Joint, Iterative, and Independent methods are used to generate competing models. We suggest that a study with simulated time series would also be very useful in studying the Independent vs. Joint Methods.

REFERENCES

Adya, M. & Collopy, F. (1998). How effective are neural networks at forecasting and prediction? A review and evaluation. *Journal of Forecasting*, 17, 481-495.

Anders, U. & Korn, O. (1999). Model selection in neural networks. *Neural Networks*, 12, 309-323.

Balkin, S. (2001). The value of nonlinear models in the M3-Competition. *International Journal of Forecasting*, 17, 545-546.

Balkin, S. & Ord, J. (2000). Automatic neural network modeling for univariate time series. *International Journal of Forecasting*, 16, 509-515.

Bishop, C. (1995). *Neural Networks for Pattern Recognition*. New York: Oxford University Press.

Chatfield, C. (1996). Model uncertainty and forecast accuracy. *Journal of Forecasting*, 15, 495-508.

Cheng, D. & Titterington, D. (1994). Neural Networks: A Review from a Statistical Perspective. *Statistical Science*, 47(2), 2-54.

DeLurgio, S. (1998). *Forecasting Principles and Applications*. New York: Irwin McGraw-Hill.

Faraway, J. & Chatfield, C. (1998). Time series forecasting with neural networks: A comparative study using the airline data. *Applied Statistics*, 47(2), 231-250.

Foster, B., Collopy, F., & Ungar, L. (1991). Neural network forecasting of short, noisy time series. *Presentation at ORSA TIMS National Meeting*, (May).

Hill, T., Leoroy, M., O'Connor, M., & Remus, W. (1994). Artificial neural network models for forecasting and decision making. *International Journal of Forecasting*, 10, 5-15.

Hill, T., O'Connor, M., & Remus, W. (1996). Neural network models for time series forecasts. *Management Science*, 42(7), 1082-1092.

Hippert, H., Pedreira, C., & Souza, R. (2001). Neural networks for short-term load forecasting: A review and evaluation. *IEEE Transactions on Power Systems*, 16(1), 44-55.

Hornik, K. (1991). Approximation capabilities of multilayer feedforward networks. *Neural Networks*, 4, 251-257.

Hornik, K., Stinchcombe, M., & White, H. (1989). Multilayer feedforward networks are universal approximators. *Neural Networks*, 2, 359-366.

Hu, M., Zhang, G., Jiang, C., & Patuwo, B. (1999). A cross-validation analysis of neural network out-of-sample performance in exchange rate forecasting. *Decision Sciences*, 30(1), 197-216.

Hwarng, H. (2001). Insights into neural-network forecasting of time series corresponding to ARMA (p,q) structures. *Omega: The International Journal of Management Science,* 29, 273-289.

Indro, D., Jiang, C., Patuwo, B., & Zhang, G. (1999). Predicting mutual fund performance using artificial neural networks. *Omega: The International Journal of Management Science,* 27, 373-380.

Kang, I. (2002). Multi-period forecasting using different models for different horizons: An application to US economic time series data. *International Journal of Forecasting*, forthcoming.

LeBaron, B. & Weigend, A. (1998). A bootstrap evaluation of the effect of data splitting on financial time series. *IEEE Transactions on Neural Networks*, 9, 213-220.

Maier, H. & Dandy, G. (2000). Neural networks for the prediction and forecasting of water resources variables: A review of modeling issues and applications. *Environmental Modeling and Software*, 15, 101-124.

Makridakis, S. & Hibon, M. (2000). The M3-Competition: Results, conclusions and implications. *International Journal of Forecasting*, 16, 451-476.

Mathworks, Inc. (2000). *Using Matlab*. Mathworks, Inc. Retrieved from the World Wide Web at: www.mathworks.com.

Nabney, I. (2001). *Netlab: Algorithms for Pattern Recognition*. Heidelberg, Germany: Springer-Verlag.

Nelson, M., Hill, T., Remus, W., & O'Connor, M. (1999). Time series forecasting using neural networks: Should the data be deseasonalized first? *Journal of Forecasting*, 18, 359-367.

Qi, M. & Zhang, G. (2001). An investigation of model selection criteria for neural network time series forecasting. *European Journal of Operational Research*, 132, 666-680.

Sharda, R. & Patil, R. (1990). Neural networks as forecasting experts: An empirical test. *Proceedings of the 1990 International Joint Conference on Neural Networks Meetings* (Vol. 2, pp. 491-494).

Tang, Z., & Fishwick, P. (1993). Feedforward neural nets as models for time series forecasting. *ORSA Journal on Computing*, 5(4), 374-385.

Tang, Z., de Almeida, C., & Fishwick, P. (1991). Time series forecasting using neural networks vs. Box-Jenkins methodology. *Simulation,* 57(5), 303-310.

Tashman, L. (2000). Out-of-sample tests of forecasting accuracy: an analysis and review. *International Journal of Forecasting*, 16, 437-450.

Walczak, S. (2001). An empirical analysis of data requirements for financial forecasting with neural networks. *Journal of Management Information Systems*, 17(4), 203-222.

Wolpert, D. S. & Macready, W. G. (1996). No free lunch theorems for optimization. *IEEE Transactions on Evolutionary Computation*, 1(1), 67-82.

Zhang, G. (2001a). An investigation of neural networks for linear time-series forecasting. *Computers & Operations Research*, 28, 1183-1202.

Zhang, G. & Hu, M. (1998b). Neural network forecasting of the British pound/US dollar exchange rate. *Omega: The International Journal of Management Science*, 26(4), 495-506.

Zhang, G., Patuwo, B., & Hu, M. (1998a). Forecasting with artificial neural networks: The state of the art. *International Journal of Forecasting*, 14, 35-62.

Zhang, G., Patuwo, B., & Hu, M. (2001b). A Simulation Study of Artificial Neural Networks for Nonlinear Time-Series Forecasting. *Computers & Operations Research*, 28, 381-396.

Chapter XIII

A Weighted Window Approach to Neural Network Time Series Forecasting

Bradley H. Morantz, Georgia State University, USA

Thomas Whalen, Georgia State University, USA

G. Peter Zhang, Georgia State University, USA

ABSTRACT

In this chapter, we propose a neural network based weighted window approach to time series forecasting. We compare the weighted window approach with two commonly used methods of rolling and moving windows in modeling time series. Seven economic data sets are used to compare the performance of these three data windowing methods on observed forecast errors. We find that the proposed approach can improve forecasting performance over traditional approaches.

INTRODUCTION

Forecasting is an important part of decision making. The success of decision making is dependent, to a large extent, on the quality of forecasts. There are two major approaches to quantitative forecasting. Causal Methods model the relationship between a set of predictor variables and the value of the criterion variable to be forecast. Time Series Methods, on the other hand, use past or lagged values of the same criterion variable as a surrogate for all the underlying causal factors and model the relationship between these past observations and the future value. Each approach has its advantages and disadvantages as discussed in Bowerman and O'Connell (1993). This chapter will focus on the time series forecasting methods.

A time series is a chronological sequence of observations taken at periodic points in time. Many models exist for the task of time series forecasting. Some of these models include:

- Naïve or random walk: use the most recent observation as forecast.
- Moving average: use the average of a fixed number of past data points as forecast.
- Exponential smoothing: a weighted moving average approach that weights more heavily the recent values than the past values.
- Autoregression (AR): a linear regression technique that estimates the relationship among observations in a time series.
- Autoregressive integrated moving average (ARIMA): a versatile linear system that models the relationship among time series observations and random shocks (Box & Jenkins, 1976).
- Bilinear: a simple nonlinear model (Granger & Anderson, 1978).
- Threshold autoregressive: a specialized nonlinear AR model (Tong & Lim, 1980).
- Autoregressive conditional heteroscedastic (ARCH): a parametric non-linear model for nonconstant conditional variance (Engle, 1982).
- Artificial neural networks (ANNs): adaptive models based upon biological neural systems capable of representing nonlinear relationships.

These models represent some of the most popularly used linear and nonlinear approaches to practical time series forecasting. The first five models are linear while the rest are nonlinear. It is important to note that most of these models are parametric in nature. That is, the model form is assumed before the model is built from data. Among other things, the assumed model form specifies how many lagged observations of the variables are used as inputs to the function which forecasts future values. Therefore, a good knowledge on both data set and the underlying data generating process is necessary for successful forecasting applications of these models.

Artificial neural networks (ANNs) are a relatively new approach that has received an increasing amount of attention among researchers and business practitioners in time series forecasting. ANNs represent a mathematical attempt to emulate part of the function of a biological neural network or brain. With its relatively large number of parameters utilized in building a model, the neural network model is capable of representing an input-output relationship of a nonlinear system and it is fairly immune to noise (Haykin, 1994). The nonparametric and data driving properties of ANNs have made them valuable for general forecasting applications. Much effort has been devoted to neural networks to improve the forecasting performance. Zhang et al. (1998) provide a survey of some advances in the field.

One of the major issues in neural network forecasting is how much data are necessary for neural networks to capture the dynamic nature of the underlying process in a time series. There are two facets to this issue:

(1) How many lagged observations should be used as inputs to the neural network (or, equivalently, how many input nodes should the neural network have)?

(2) How many past observations should be used in training the neural network? Each training pattern is the actual historical value plus a number of preceding values equal to the number of input nodes.

Although larger sample size, in the form of a longer time series, is usually recommended in model development, empirical results suggest that longer time series do not always yield models that provide the best forecasting performance. For example, Walczak (2001) investigates the issue of data requirements for neural networks in financial time series forecasting. He finds that using a smaller sample of time series or data close in time to the out-of-sample can produce more accurate neural networks.

Determining an appropriate sample size for model building is not necessarily an easy task, especially in time series modeling where a larger sample inevitably means using older data. Theoretically speaking, if the underlying data-generating process for a time series is stationary, more data should be helpful to reduce the effect of noise inherent in the data. However, if the process is not stationary or changing in structure or parameters over time, longer time series do not help and in fact can hurt the model's forecasting performance. In this situation, more recent observations should be more important in indicating the possible structural or parameter change in the data while older observations are not useful and even harmful to forecasting model building.

In this chapter, we propose a weighted window approach to identify an appropriate size of time series for ANN model building. In addition, we believe that even with an appropriate training sample, each observation in the time series does not necessarily play an equal role in modeling the underlying time series structure and in predicting the future. More specifically, we believe that more recent observations should be more important than older observations and, therefore, should receive higher weights. The idea is superficially similar to that in a weighted moving average method where past lagged observations are weighted according to their relative position in the time series history. However, the concept of a weighted moving average concerns the actual function used to make a specific forecast, while the concept of a weighted window concerns the process by which historical data are used to learn the parameters of the model.

The rest of the chapter is organized as follows. In the next section, we provide a description of two traditional approaches of rolling and moving windows to training sample size selection in building neural networks. Then, the detail of the proposed weighted window approach is given. The research methodology along with the empirical evidence on seven economic time series is discussed next. Finally, we give some concluding remarks.

ROLLING AND MOVING WINDOW APPROACHES

In neural network time series forecasting, almost all studies adopt a fixed window approach in building and evaluating neural network performance. That is, all available data are divided into a training sample, a validation sample, and a test sample. The model is estimated and developed using the first two samples and then the established model is evaluated with the last sample. The division of the data is usually quite arbitrary and the rule of thumb is to assign more data to the training sample and relatively less data to other samples. Once the data splitting is done, the size of each portion of the data is fixed in terms of model building, selection, and evaluation.

However, the above approach is effective only if the data characteristics in each portion are about the same or the underlying data generating process, as well as the parameters characterizing the process, do not change from sample to sample. If the data are not stationary, i.e., changing in characteristics over time, then the static model built from a fixed section of historical data will produce poorer forecasts over time. Even if the time series under study is relatively stationary, there still is a disadvantage of using the static model to evaluate recent or future forecasts because of the possible changes in noise level or model parameters. Therefore, as time goes by, it is often necessary and beneficial to include new observations to update the model or model parameters.

There are essentially two approaches in updating forecasting models over time: the rolling and moving window approaches. The rolling window approach uses all available data to train neural networks while the moving window approach uses a set of most recent observations to estimate the model. Each time a new observation is received, the rolling window approach adds one training example to its database, consisting of the new observation as the new criterion variable and the next most recent k observations (where k is the number of input nodes) as predictor variables. The moving window approach differs in that as it adds the new training example, it also drops the oldest observations from the training sample to update the model. Thus, with rolling window, the sample size increases over time, while with moving window, the sample size is fixed. Figures 1(a) and (b) show the ideas in rolling and moving approaches.

The rolling window has a constant starting point in training neural networks. The main advantage of using this approach is that with increasing sample size, model parameters can be estimated more accurately because larger sample sizes will usually have smaller error variance. However, as indicated earlier, the disadvantage of this approach is that it will not work well when the time series process is changing over time. On the other hand, the moving window approach has a changing starting point in the training sample and is better positioned to reflect changes occurred in the underlying process of a time series. The disadvantage of the moving window approach is that an appropriate sample size is not easy to determine and a fixed sample size is not necessarily effective for all subsequent or future model updating and forecasting. In addition, the relatively smaller sample size with a moving window may also limit the power to accurately estimate the model parameters.

The rolling and moving window approaches have been evaluated by Hu et al. (1999) in the context of foreign exchange rate forecasting. Their purpose was to evaluate the robustness of neural networks with respect to sampling variation. They found that neural networks are not very sensitive to the sampling

Figure 1: The Rolling and Moving Window Approaches

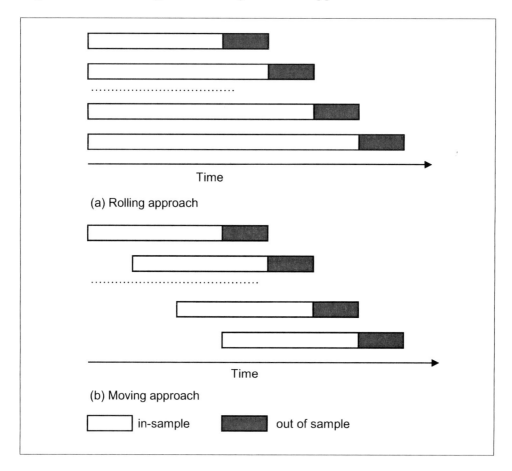

variation and both rolling and moving approaches perform about the same in out-of-sample forecasting. Because of the relatively stable condition for the specific exchange rate time series they studied, as well as the efficient market theory dominated for exchange rate movement, these results are not unexpected. In addition, their window size incremental was 12 months. That is, the model is updated not after every time period, but rather after observing 12 periods of data.

WEIGHTED WINDOW APPROACH

In this study, we propose a weighed window approach that is similar to the moving window idea discussed above. However, unlike in the moving window approach where past observations or prediction errors are treated equally, we consider a weighted objective function to train neural networks. That is, forecast errors are weighted differently with most recent errors receiving higher weight and older errors carrying less weight.

The parameters of the model are selected to minimize the weighted sum of squared deviations between the computed and actual forecast variable for the training examples in the window. For training examples in the most recent part of the window, the "core," the squared error is weighted 100%. For the remainder of the window, the squared error is weighted by a linear function that is equal to one for the oldest training example in the core and zero for the training example that is not in the window at all. In effect, the weights define a fuzzy set of recent data whose membership function follows a trapezoidal form whose core consists of the "completely recent" data and whose support consists of the entire window.

Different weighting schemes can be used to define weights for observations in a window of time series. A simple but natural choice is the linear weighting approach with which the size of weight decreases in a linear fashion from the most recent observation to the oldest observation in the window. Figure 2 shows a general linear weighting scheme that is defined by a support set and a core set. Outside the core, all observations have weights of less than one and within the core all observations receive the full weights of one. The core is defined as the most recent time interval and, thus, any older data will be discounted. On the other hand, support is the interval beyond which older data points will have zero weights. In other words, all observations that contribute to model building are at least as recent as the starting point of support. The importance of each data points in the support but outside the core attenuates in a linear descending pattern as shown in Figure 2. More specifically, we define weight for time period t as:

$$W_t = \begin{cases} 1 & \text{if } t \geq c \\ (t-s)/(c-s) & \text{if } s < t < c \\ 0 & \text{if } t < s \end{cases}$$

where s is the starting point of support and c is the starting point of core.

The weighted window approach does not modify the input data. Rather, our approach is to modify the objective function in training neural networks. Suppose we have N observations $y_1, y_2, \ldots, y_N$ in the training sample. Then using a network with k input nodes and one output node, we have $N - k$

Figure 2: The Weighting Scheme

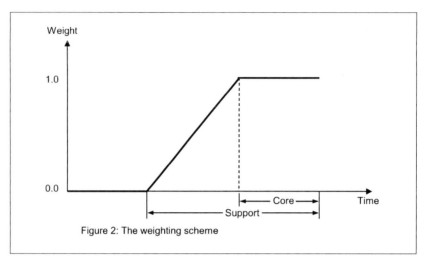

Figure 2: The weighting scheme

training patterns. The first training pattern is composed of $y_1, y_2, ..., y_k$ as the inputs and y_{k+1} as the target. The second training pattern contains $y_2, y_3, ..., y_{k+1}$ for the inputs and y_{k+2} for the target. Finally, the last training pattern is $y_{N-k}, y_{N-k+1}, ..., y_{N-1}$ for the inputs and y_N for the target. The training objective is to find the arc weights such that a weighted overall error measure, such as the weighted sum of squared errors (WSSE), is minimized. For this network structure, WSSE can be generally written as:

$$WSSE = \sum_{i=k+1}^{N} W_i (y_i - \hat{y}_i)^2$$

where $\hat{y}_i$ is the ANN forecast value for i^{th} observation.

METHODOLOGY

Data

Seven financial data sets were obtained from Economagic (http://www.economagic.com). All data sets were terminated at February 1, 2001, and in the case of daily data, we convert them to monthly by using the first recorded value in each month to maintain consistency and to allow the same point of prediction for all forecasts. These time series are:

(1) New one-family houses sold: 458 observations starting from January 1963.

(2) Federal funds rate: 560 observations starting from July 1954.

(3) One month CD rates (secondary market): 423 observations starting from December 1965.

(4) One month Eurodollar deposits: 362 observations starting from January 1971.

(5) US Treasury bill: 439 observations starting from September 1963.

(6) French Franc to US dollar exchange rate: 364 observations starting from January 1, 1971.

(7) German Mark to US dollar exchange rate: 364 observations starting from January 1971.

Each time series is split first by holding out the last 31 data points for final testing. The remaining data is then split by an 80/20 method. That is, the 80% of the earliest observations (training set) is used to estimate the parameters of neural network models and the remaining 20%, the validation set, is used to test these models in order to select the best model. The precise sizes of the training and validation sets are found by integer truncation.

Neural Network Model Building

The standard three layer feedforward neural network structure is exclusively used in this study. One output node is employed for one-step ahead forecasting. We use linear activation function for the output node and the sigmoid or logistic activation function for hidden nodes. Biases are used for both hidden and output nodes. The numbers of input and hidden nodes are usually not possible to determine in advance and, therefore, are selected via experimentation with the training and validation sample. This is the commonly used cross-validation approach. That is, parameters are estimated for each of candidate architectures using the training sample and then the final architecture is selected based on the validation sample.

For time series forecasting problems, the number of input nodes corresponds to the number of lagged observations used to determine the autocorrelation structure of a time series. This number was varied from two to nine in the experiment. On the other hand, we vary the number of hidden nodes from one to 10. For each ANN architecture experimented, the model parameters are estimated with the training sample while the best model is selected with the validation sample.

For moving and weighted window approaches, the architecture specification also includes the amount of observations used for training, which is also difficult to specify exactly in advance and is generally data dependent. To find the best size of the training window, we vary it from 50 to the highest integer multiple of 50 that was possible within the training set. The choice of 50 is somewhat arbitrary but follows the general recommendation in the time series forecasting literature that at least 50 observations are needed in order to build a successful forecasting model (Box & Jenkins, 1976).

For each moving window model, the amount of data in the support set that receives partial weights is also determined. In this study, we consider three levels of the size: 0, 50, and 100. The zero value means that all data points receive the same weight of one, which reflects the fact that a moving window is a special case of a weighted window. Otherwise, the oldest 50 or 100 observations in the support set are given fractional weights in proportion to their age. It is likely that some other models that incorporate WW might provide greater accuracy with different amounts of weighted data other than 50 or 100, but for parsimonious reasons this study was limited to these two values.

Error calculation for a given architecture was accomplished by doing a one-month-ahead forecast for each observation in the validation set. For an ANN model with k inputs, the last k months of the training set are input to the model to make a prediction for the first month of the validation sample. The prediction is compared to the actual and the error was computed. Then the last k training months and the first validation month are input to the same model (without reestimating the parameters) to make a prediction for the second month of the validation sample and calculate its error, and so on. This is done iteratively to evaluate the model for the entire validation period as well as the testing period.

In the model building phase, our goal is to find the most robust model that predicts well for the validation sample. Therefore, the best model is the one that gives the most accurate performance in the validation sample. The selected model is then used to examine the true out-of-sample forecasting performance in the testing sample that is not used in the model building phase.

Although there are many performance measures that can be use to judge the forecasting performance of neural networks, this study elects to choose the mean absolute percentage error (MAPE) as the overall performance measure because of its robustness and usefulness for model comparison across different time series.

Neural network training is the process of assimilating historical data and learning the input to output relationship. The process entails nonlinear optimization to estimate the model parameters. In this study, we use Generalized Reduced Gradient (GRG2) (Lasdon et al., 1978) to train the neural network models. GRG2 uses a generalized reduced gradient algorithm for general nonlinear optimization. As such, it is capable of solving a system of nonlinear optimization problems. Since a global optimum is not guaranteed in a nonlinear optimization training of a neural network, each network is trained 50 times with different initial random weights.

RESULTS

We focus on out-of-sample forecasting evaluation with three different methods. In this final testing phase, we have three sets of 31 error values for each data set, corresponding to three methods: rolling, moving and weighted window (WW). For direct comparison, we use absolute percentage error (APE) as the measure of forecasting error for each period in the hold-out sample and the mean absolute percentage error (MAPE) as the summary performance measure across all periods in the sample.

Table 1 gives the summary results of MAPE for all seven data sets across three different approaches. It shows that the neural network model based on the weighted window approach is the most accurate predictor for five of the seven data sets. These five data sets are: one month CD rate, Eurodollar deposit, federal fund rate, French Franc exchange rate and new one-family house sold. In some of these cases, the improvement of using WW approach over the rolling and moving approaches is substantial. For example, in the one-month CD rate forecasting case, the WW approach has more than 50% reduction in the overall error measured by MAPE over the rolling and moving approach. In forecasting new house sales, the WW approach reduces MAPE from rolling and moving approaches by approximately 45%. However, the WW approach is not as effective as rolling and moving approaches in two of the seven data sets: German Mark exchange rate and T-bill, although the difference between WW and rolling or moving is not considerable.

Table 1 shows the comparative results based on overall measure of MAPE. In order to examine differences among the three approaches in detail, we perform a separate ANOVA analysis for each data set. A complete blocking design with the blocking factor of time period in the test set is used for

Table 1: Summary Results of Out-of-Sample Forecasting

Data Set	Method		
	Rolling	Moving	Weighted Window
CD Rate	12.20	11.40	5.36
EuroDollar	4.98	5.25	4.13
Fed Fund	4.41	4.45	2.50
France Franc	3.26	3.29	2.78
German Mark	2.57	2.46	2.74
Houses	20.21	20.12	11.19
T Bill	5.04	5.27	6.18

the analysis to highlight the difference in modeling and evaluation approaches. See Neter et al. (1996) for details on block design. The 31 time periods are served as 31 levels of the blocking factor to better isolate the specific effects due to different approaches in neural network model updating. Table 2 summarizes the ANOVA results for all seven data sets. In the ANOVA tables, "Time" is the blocking factor while "Method" is the main factor to be investigated.

From Table 2, we find that the blocking effect is significant for all data sets, suggesting the usefulness of blocks in providing additional detection power of the model for the factor of main concern. In addition, the main factor "Method" is highly significant for three data sets. They are CD rate, federal fund, and house sale. For data sets of Euro Dollar deposit and France Franc exchange rate, there is no significant difference among the three approaches, although the weighted window approach outperforms the other two approaches judged by the average performance measure. Similarly, while the WW approach is worse than both rolling and moving approaches from the overall measure of MAPE, the difference is not significant.

To further identify the significant differences among the three approaches, we employ the Tukey's honestly significant test (HST) for three significant ANOVA data sets. At the 5% significance level, we find that in all three cases, there are significant differences existing between WW and moving and between WW and rolling. In addition, there is no significant difference between the rolling and the moving approach, which is in line with the finding in Hu et al. (1999). Therefore, one may conclude that employing a weighting scheme that emphasizes recent data can be very helpful for some economic time series.

Table 2: ANOVA Results

Data Set	Source of Variation	SS	df	F	P-value
CD rate	Time	5773.04	30	6.04	0.0000
	Method	867.19	2	13.6	0.0000
	Error	1912.97	60		
Eurodollar	Time	1813.91	30	4.05	0.0000
	Method	21.37	2	0.71	0.4952
	Error	901.71	60		
Federal fund	Time	897.85	30	8.99	0.0000
	Method	77.09	2	11.59	0.0000
	Error	199.55	60		
French Franc	Time	483.54	30	10.01	0.0000
	Method	4.91	2	1.53	0.2257
	Error	96.59	60		
German Mark	Time	233.95	30	14.67	0.0000
	Method	1.93	2	1.82	0.1716
	Error	31.89	60		
House sale	Time	5236.44	30	6.24	0.0000
	Method	1664.84	2	29.78	0.0000
	Error	1677.04	60		
T-bill	Time	2099.77	30	8.06	0.0000
	Method	13.57	2	0.78	0.4623
	Error	520.82	60		

SUMMARY AND CONCLUSION

In this chapter, we propose a neural network based weighted window approach in modeling and evaluating neural networks for time series forecasting. We believe that some time series in business, especially in economics and finance, may exhibit changing dynamics in the underlying data generating process. Therefore, the one-model-fit-all approach to building and evaluating the performance of a forecasting model is possibly not the best for this situation. By weighting the past observations differently and, more specifically, by having higher weights tied with more recent forecast errors, our weighted modeling approach is able to capture the dynamic nature of the process more quickly and, therefore, provide better forecasts for the near future.

Based on our empirical investigation, we find that the WW approach is fairly effective for economic time series forecasting. Of the seven data sets examined, we find that the WW approach is better than the traditional rolling or moving approach in five data sets from the perspective of overall prediction accuracy and it is significantly better than the rolling and moving approaches in three data sets. Although in two data sets, the WW approach is not as good as the rolling and moving judging from the overall MAPE measure, the differences are not significant.

Future research should address the question: under what condition is the proposed weighted window approach more effective? Theoretically, if the structure or parameters of the underlying process governing the time series changes over time, the weighted window approach should be more useful. However, it may be practically difficult to judge whether such situations have occurred. Practical approaches to identifying this changing environment are needed. Furthermore, in this study, we only consider a very simple way to assign weights, i.e., the linear weighting scheme. Better ways to assign weights should be developed that are tailored to different time series behaviors. Finally, the WW approach examined in this study may update the model too frequently with each and every new observation, which may cause the model to be unstable in terms of capturing the changing noises rather than the underlying pattern. Thus, the length and/or frequency to update model is an interesting research question to address.

REFERENCES

Bowerman, B. & O'Connell, R. (1993). *Forecasting and Time Series: An Applied Approach*. Pacific Grove, CA: Duxbury.

Box, G. & Jenkins, G. (1976). *Time Series Analysis: Forecasting and Control, 2nd edition*. San Francisco, CA: Holden-Day.

Engle, R. (1982). Autoregressive conditional heteroscedasticity with estimates of the variance of UK inflation. *Econometrica*, 50(4), 987-1008.

Granger, C. & Anderson, A. (1978). *An Introduction to Bilinear Time Series Models*. Gottingen: Vandenhoeck and Ruprecht.

Haykin, S. (1994). *Neural Networks: A Comprehensive Foundation*. New York: IEEE Press.

Hu, M. Y., Zhang, G. P., Jiang, C. X., & Patuwo, B. E. (1999). A cross-validation analysis of neural network out-of sample performance in exchange rate forecasting. *Decision Sciences*, 30(1), 197-216.

Lasdon, L., Waren, A., Jain, A., & Ratner, M. (1978). Design and testing of a generalized reduced gradient code for nonlinear programming. *ACM Transactions on Mathematical Software*, 4(1), 34-50.

Neter, J. Kutner, M. H., Nachtsheim, C. J., & Wasserman, W. (1996). *Applied Linear Statistical Models, 4th edition.* Chicago, IL: Irwin.

Tong, H. & Lim, K. (1980). Threshold autoregression, limit cycles and cyclical data. *Journal of Royal Statistical Society, B,* 42, 245-292.

Walczak, S. (2001). An empirical analysis of data requirements for financial forecasting with neural networks. *Journal of Management Information Systems*, 17(4), 203-222.

Zhang, G., Patuwo, B., & Hu, M. (1998). Forecasting with artificial neural networks: The state of the art. *International Journal of Forecasting*, 14, 35-62.

Chapter XIV

Assessment of Evaluation Methods for Prediction and Classifications of Consumer Risk in the Credit Industry

Satish Nargundkar, Georgia State University, USA

Jennifer Lewis Priestley, Georgia State University, USA

ABSTRACT

In this chapter, we examine and compare the most prevalent modeling techniques in the credit industry, Linear Discriminant Analysis, Logistic Analysis *and the emerging technique of* Neural Network modeling. K-S Tests *and* Classification Rates *are typically used in the industry to measure the success in predictive classification. We examine those two methods and a third,* ROC Curves, *to determine if the method of evaluation has an influence on the perceived performance of the modeling technique. We found that each modeling technique has its own strengths, and a determination of the "best" depends upon the evaluation method utilized and the costs associated with misclassification.*

INTRODUCTION

The popularity of consumer credit products represents both a risk and an opportunity for credit lenders. The credit industry has experienced decades of rapid growth as characterized by the ubiquity of consumer financial products such as credit cards, mortgages, home equity loans, auto loans and interest-only loans, etc. In 1980, there was $55.1 billion in outstanding unsecured revolving consumer credit in the US. In 2000, that number had risen to $633.2 billion. However, the number of bankruptcies filed per 1,000 US households increased from one to five over the same period[1].

In an effort to maximize the opportunity to attract, manage, and retain profitable customers and minimize the risks associated with potentially unprofitable ones, lenders have increasingly turned to modeling to facilitate a holistic approach to Customer Relationship Management (CRM). In the consumer credit industry, the general framework for CRM includes product planning, customer acquisition, customer management and collections and recovery (Figure 1). Prediction models have been used extensively to support each stage of this general CRM strategy.

For example, customer acquisition in credit lending is often accomplished through model-driven target marketing. Data on potential customers, which can be accessed from credit bureau files and a firm's own databases, is used to predict the likelihood of response to a solicitation. Risk models are also utilized to support customer acquisition efforts through the prediction of a potential customer's likelihood of default. Once customers are acquired, customer management strategies require careful analysis of behavior patterns. Behavioral models are developed using a customer's transaction history to predict which customers may default or attrite. Based upon some predicted value, firms can then efficiently allocate resources for customer incentive programs or credit line increases. Predictive accuracy in this stage of customer management is important because effectively retaining customers is significantly less expensive than acquiring new customers. Collections and recovery is a critical stage in a credit lender's CRM strategy, where lenders develop models to predict a delinquent customer's likelihood of repayment. Other models used by lenders to support the overall CRM strategy may involve bankruptcy prediction, fraud prediction and market segmentation.

Not surprisingly, the central concern of modeling applications in each stage of CRM is improving predictive accuracy. An improvement of even a fraction of a percent can translate into significant savings or increased revenue. As a result, many different modeling techniques have been developed, tested and

Figure 1: Stages of Customer Relationship Management in Credit Lending

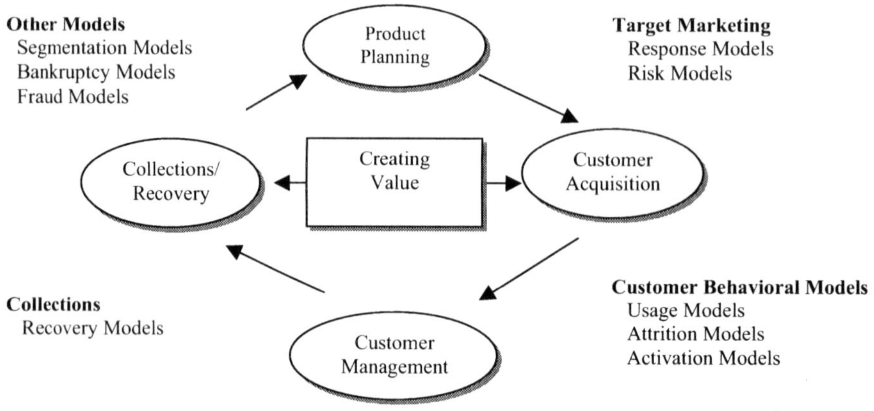

refined. These techniques include both statistical (e.g., Linear Discriminant Analysis, Logistic Analysis) and non-statistical (e.g., Decision Trees, k-Nearest Neighbor, Cluster Analysis, Neural Networks) techniques. Each technique utilizes different assumptions and may or may not achieve similar results with the same data. Because of the growing importance of accurate prediction models, an entire literature exists which is dedicated to the development and refinement of these models (Atiya, 2001; Richeson et al., 1994; Vellido et al., 1999). However, developing the model is really only half the problem.

Researchers and analysts allocate a great deal of effort to the development of prediction models to support decision-making. However, too often insufficient attention is allocated to the tools used to evaluate the model in question. The result is that accurate prediction models may be measured inappropriately based upon the information available regarding classification error rate and the context of application. In the end, poor decisions are made because an incorrect model was selected, using an inappropriate evaluation method.

This chapter addresses the dual issues of model development and evaluation. Specifically, we attempt to answer the questions, *"Does model development technique impact prediction accuracy?"* and *"How will model selection vary with the selected evaluation method?"* These questions will be addressed within the context of consumer risk prediction — a modeling application supporting the first stage of a credit lender's CRM strategy: customer acquisition. All stages of the CRM strategy need to be effectively managed to increase a lender's profitability. However, accurate prediction of a customer's likelihood of repayment at the point of acquisition is particularly important because regardless of the accuracy of the other "downstream" models, the lender may never achieve targeted risk/return objectives if incorrect decisions are made in the initial stage. Therefore, understanding how to develop and evaluate models that predict potential customers to be "good" or "bad" credit risks is critical to managing a successful CRM strategy.

The remainder of the chapter will be organized as follows. In the next section, we give a brief overview of three modeling techniques used for prediction in the credit industry. Since the dependent variable of concern is categorical (e.g., "good" credit risk versus "bad" credit risk), the issue is one of binary classification. We then discuss the conceptual differences among three common methods of model evaluation and rationales for when they should and should not be used. We illustrate model application and evaluation through an empirical example using the techniques and methods described in the chapter. Finally, we conclude with a discussion of our results and propose concepts for further research.

COMMON MODELING TECHNIQUES

As mentioned above, modeling techniques can be roughly segmented into two classes: statistical and non-statistical. The first technique we utilized for our empirical analysis, linear discriminant analysis (LDA), is one of the earliest formal modeling techniques. LDA has its origins in the discrimination methods suggested by Fisher (1936). Given its dependence on the assumptions of multivariate normality, independence of predictor variables, and linear separability, LDA has been criticized as having restricted applicability. However, the inequality of covariance matrices, as well as the non-normal nature of the data, which is common to credit applications, may not represent critical limitations of the technique (Reichert et al., 1983). Although it is one of the simpler modeling techniques, LDA continues to be widely used in practice.

The second technique we utilized for this paper, logistic regression analysis, is considered the most common technique of model development for initial credit decisions (Thomas et al., 2002). For the binary classification problem (i.e., prediction of "good" vs. "bad"), logit analysis takes a linear combination of the descriptor variables and transforms the result to lie between zero and one, to equate to a probability.

Whereas LDA and logistic analysis are statistical classification methods with lengthy histories, neural network-based classification is a non-statistical technique, which has developed as a result of improvements in desktop computing power. Although neural networks originated in attempts to model the processing functions of the human brain, the models currently in use have increasingly sacrificed neurological rigor for mathematical expediency (Vellido et al., 1999). Neural networks are utilized in a wide variety of fields and in a wide variety of applications, including the field of finance and specifically, the prediction of consumer risk. In their survey of neural network applications in business, Vellido et al. (1999) provide a comprehensive overview of empirical studies of the efficacy of neural networks in credit evaluation and decisioning. They highlight that neural networks do outperform "other" (both statistical and non-statistical) techniques, but not consistently. However, in Vellido et al. (1999), and many other papers which compare modeling techniques, significant discussion is dedicated to the individual techniques, and less discussion (if any) is dedicated to the tools used for model evaluation.

METHODS OF MODEL EVALUATION

As stated in the previous section, a central concern of modeling techniques is an improvement in predictive accuracy. In customer risk classification, even a small improvement in predictive accuracy can translate into significant savings. However, how can the analyst know if one model represents an improvement over a second model? The extent to which improvements are detected may change based upon the selection of the evaluation method. As a result, analysts who utilize prediction models for binary classification have a need to understand the circumstances under which each evaluation method is most appropriate.

In the context of predictive binary classification models, one of four outcomes is possible: (1) a true positive — e.g., a good credit risk is classified as "good", (2) a false positive — e.g., a bad credit risk is classified as "good", (3) a true negative — e.g., bad credit risk is classified as "bad", (4) a false negative — e.g., a good credit risk is classified as "bad." The N-class prediction models are significantly more complex and outside of the scope of this chapter. For an examination of the issues related to N-class prediction models, see Taylor and Hand (1999).

In principle, each of these outcomes would have some associated "loss" or "reward." In a credit lending context, a true positive "reward" might be a qualified person obtaining a needed mortgage with the bank reaping the economic benefit of making a correct decision. A false negative "loss" might be the same qualified person being turned down for a mortgage. In this instance, the bank has not only the opportunity cost of losing a good customer, but also the possible cost of increasing its competitor's business.

It is often assumed that the two types of incorrect classification — false positives and false negatives — incur the exact same loss (Hand, 2001). If this is truly the case, then a simple "global" classification rate could be used for model evaluation.

For example, suppose that a hypothetical classification model produced the following confusion matrix:

	True Good	True Bad	Total
Predicted Good	650	50	**700**
Predicted Bad	200	100	**300**
Total	**850**	**150**	**1000**

This model would have a global classification rate of 75% (650/1000 + 100/1000). This simple metric is reasonable if the costs associated with each error are known (or assumed) to be the same. If this were the case, the selection of a "better" model would be easy — the model with the highest classification rate would be selected. Even if the costs were not equal, but at least understood with some degree of certainty, the total loss associated with the selection of one model over another could still be easily evaluated based upon this confusion matrix. For example, the projected loss associated with use of a particular model can be represented by the loss function:

$$L = \pi_0 f_0 c_0 + \pi_1 f_1 c_1 \tag{1}$$

where π_i is the probability that an object comes from class i (the prior probability), f_i is the probability of misclassifying a class i object, and c_i is the cost associated with misclassifying an observation into that category and, for example, 0 indicates a "bad" credit risk and 1 indicates a "good" credit risk. Assessment of predictive accuracy would then be based upon the extent to which this function is minimized. West (2000) uses a similar cost function to evaluate the performance of several statistical and non-statistical modeling techniques, including five different neural network models. Although the author was able to select a "winning" model based upon reasonable cost assumptions, the "winning" model would differ as these assumptions changed.

A second issue when using a simple classification matrix for evaluation is the problem that can occur when evaluating models dealing with rare events. If the prior probability of an occurrence is very high, a model would achieve a strong prediction rate if all observations were simply classified into this class. However, when a particular observation has a low probability of occurrence (e.g., cancer, bankruptcy, tornadoes, etc.), it is far more difficult to assign these low probability observations into their correct class. The difficulty of accurate class assignments of rare events is not captured if the simple global classification is used as an evaluation method (Gim, 1995). Because of the issue of rare events and imperfect information, the simple classification rate should very rarely be used for model evaluation. However, as Berardi and Zhang (1999) indicated, a quick scan of papers which evaluate different modeling techniques will reveal that this is the most frequently utilized (albeit the weakest, due to the assumption of perfect information) method of model evaluation.

One of the most common methods of evaluating predictive binary classification models in practice is the Kolmogorov-Smirnov statistic or K-S test. The K-S test measures the distance between the distribution functions of the two classifications (e.g., good credit risks and bad credit risks). The score that generates the greatest separability between the functions is considered the threshold value for accepting or rejecting a credit application. The predictive model producing the greatest amount of separability between the two distributions would be considered the superior model. A graphical example of a K-S test can be seen in Figure 2. In this illustration, the greatest separability between the two distribution functions occurs at a score of approximately .7. Using this score, if all applicants who scored above .7 were accepted and all applicants scoring below .7 were rejected, then approximately 80% of all "good" applicants would be accepted, while only 35% of all "bad" applicants would be accepted. The measure of separability, or the K-S test result would be 45% (80% to 35%).

Hand (2002) criticizes the K-S test for many of the same reasons outlined for the simple global classification rate. Specifically, the K-S test assumes that the relative costs of the misclassification errors are equal. As a result, the K-S test does not incorporate relevant information regarding the performance of classification models (i.e., the misclassification rates and their respective costs). The measure of separability then becomes somewhat hollow.

In some instances, the researcher may not have any information regarding costs of error rates, such as the relative costs of one error type versus another. In almost every circumstance, one type of misclassification will be considered more serious than another. However, a determination of which error is the

Figure 2: K-S Test Illustration

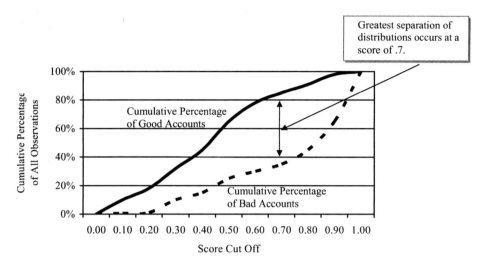

more serious is generally less well defined or may even be in the eye of the beholder. For example, turning to the field of medicine, which predictive mistake is "worse": the mistake of a false negative, where a diseased individual is told he is healthy and therefore may not seek a needed treatment, or the mistake of a false positive, where a healthy individual is told he has a disease that is not present and seeks unnecessary treatment and experiences unnecessary emotional distress? Alternatively, in a highly competitive business environment is it a "worse" mistake to turn away a potentially valuable customer to a competitor, or to accept a customer that does not meet financial expectations? The answer is not always straightforward and may vary with the perceptions of the evaluator. As a result, the cost function outlined above may not be applicable.

One method of evaluation, which enables a comprehensive analysis of *all* possible error severities, is the ROC curve. The "Receiver Operating Characteristics" curve was first applied to assess how well radar equipment in WWII distinguished random interference or "noise" from the signals that were truly indicative of enemy planes (Swets et al., 2000). ROC curves have since been used in fields ranging from electrical engineering and weather prediction to psychology and are used almost ubiquitously in the literature on medical testing to determine the effectiveness of medications. The ROC curve plots the sensitivity or "hits" (e.g., true positives) of a model on the vertical axis against 1-specificity or "false alarms" (e.g., false positives) on the horizontal axis. The result is a bowed curve rising from the 45 degree line to the upper left corner

— the sharper the bend and the closer to the upper left corner, the greater the accuracy of the model. The area under the ROC curve is a convenient way to compare different predictive binary classification models when the analyst or decision maker has no information regarding the costs or severity of classification errors. This measurement is equivalent to the Gini index (Thomas et al., 2002) and the Mann-Whitney-Wilcoxon test statistic for comparing two distributions (Hanley & McNeil, 1982, 1983) and is referred in the literature in many ways, including "AUC" (Area Under the Curve), the c-statistic, and "θ" (we will use the "θ" term for the remainder of this chapter to describe this area). For example, if observations were assigned to two classes at random, such that there was equal probability of assignment in either class, the ROC curve would follow a 45-degree line emanating from the origin. This would correspond to $\theta = .5$. A perfect binary classification, $\theta = 1$, would be represented by an ROC "curve" that followed the y-axis from the origin to the point $(0, 1)$ and then followed the top edge of the square (Figure 3).

The metric θ can be considered as an averaging of the misclassification rates over all possible choices of the various classification thresholds. In other words, θ is an average of the diagnostic performance of a particular model over all possible values for the relative misclassification severities (Hand, 2001). The interpretation of θ, where a "good" credit risk is scored as a 1 and a "bad" credit risk is scored as a 0, is the answer to the question — *Using this model, what is the probability that a truly "good" credit risk will be scored higher than a "bad" credit risk?* Formulaically, θ can be represented as:

$$\theta = \int F(p|0)dF(p|1)dp, \tag{2}$$

where $F(p|0)$ is the distribution of the probabilities of assignment in class 0 (classification of "bad" credit risk) and $F(p|1)$ is the distribution of the probabilities of assignment in class 1 (classification of "good" credit risk). The advantage of using the ROC is also its greatest limitation — the ROC incorporates results from *all* possible misclassification severities. As a result, ROC curves are highly appropriate in scenarios where no information is available regarding misclassification costs or where the perceptions of these costs may change based upon the evaluator. Alternatively, where some objective information is available regarding misclassification errors, then all possible scenarios are not relevant, making ROC curves a less appropriate evaluation method.

In this section and the previous section, we have outlined the issues and considerations related to both model development and model evaluation.

Figure 3: ROC Curve Illustration, θ = Area Under the Curve

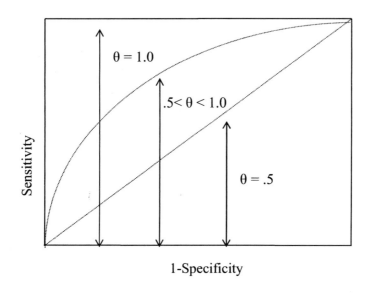

Based upon this discussion, we will utilize empirical analysis to address our two research questions:
1. Does model development technique impact prediction accuracy?
2. How will model selection vary with the selected evaluation method?

METHODOLOGY

A real world data set was used to test the predictive accuracy of three binary classification models, consisting of data on 14,042 applicants for car loans in the United States. The data represents applications made between June 1, 1998, and June 30, 1999. For each application, data on 65 variables were collected. These variables could be categorized into two general classes — data on the individual (e.g., other revolving account balances, whether they rent or own their residence, bankruptcies, etc.) and data on the transaction (e.g., miles on the vehicle, vehicle make, selling price, etc.). A complete list of all variables is included in Appendix A. From this data set, 9,442 individuals were considered to have been creditworthy applicants (i.e., "good") and 4,600 were considered to have been not creditworthy (i.e., "bad") on the basis of whether or not their accounts were charged off as of December 31, 1999. No confidential information regarding applicants' names, addresses, social security number, or any other data elements that would indicate identity was used in this analysis.

An examination of each variable relative to the binary dependent variable (creditworthiness) found that most of the relationships were non-linear. For example, the relationship between the number of auto trades, and an account's performance was not linear; the ratio of "good" performing accounts to "bad" performing accounts increased over some ranges of the variable and decreased over other ranges. This non-linearity would have a negative impact on the classification accuracy of the two traditional statistical models. Using a common credit industry practice, we transformed each variable, continuous and categorical, to multiple dummy variables for each original variable.

Prior to analysis, the data was divided into a modeling file, representing 80% of the data set, and a validation file, representing 20% of the data set. The LDA and logistic analysis models were developed using the SAS system (v. 8.2).

There are currently no established guiding principles to assist the analyst in developing a neural network model. Since many factors, including hidden layers, hidden nodes, and training methodology, can affect network performance, the best network is generally developed through experimentation — making it somewhat more art than science (Zhang et al., 1999).

With the basic MLP network model, the inputs into our classification networks were the same predictor variables utilized for the LDA and logistic regression models outlined above. Although non-linearity is not an issue with neural network models, using the dummy variable data versus the raw data eliminated issues related to scaling (we did run the same neural network models with the raw data, with no material improvement in classification accuracy). Because our developed networks were binary, we required only a single output node. The selection of the number of hidden nodes is effectively the "art" in neural network development. Although some heuristics have been proposed as the basis of determining the number of nodes a priori (e.g., n/2, n, n+1, 2n+1), none have been shown to perform consistently well (Zhang et al., 1999). To see the effects of hidden nodes on the performance of neural network models, we use 10 different levels of hidden nodes ranging from five to 50, in increments of five, allowing us to include the effects of both small and larger networks. Backpack® v. 4.0 was used for neural network model development.

We split our original model building file, which was used for the LDA and logistic model development, into a separate training file and a testing file, representing 60% and 20% of the total data file, respectively. Although the training file was slightly smaller for the neural network modeling method relative to the LDA and logistic procedures (8,425 versus 11,233 observations), the large size of the data set reduced the likelihood that the neural network technique was competitively disadvantaged. Because neural networks cannot guarantee a global solution, we attempted to minimize the likelihood of being trapped in a local solution through testing the network 100 times using epochs (e.g., the number of observations from the training set presented to the network before weights are updated) of size 12 with 200 epochs between tests. The same validation file used for the first two models was also applied to the validation of the neural networks.

RESULTS

The validation results for the different modeling techniques using the three model evaluation methods are summarized in Table 1. As expected, selection of a "winning" model is not straightforward; model selection will vary depending on the two main issues highlighted above — the costs of misclassification errors and the problem domain.

If the misclassification costs are known with some confidence to be equal, the global classification rate could be utilized as an appropriate evaluation method. Using this method, the logistic regression model outperforms the other models, with a global classification rate of 69.45%. Five of the 10 neural network models outperformed the traditional LDA technique, based upon this method of evaluation.

If costs are known with some degree of certainty, a "winning" model could be selected based upon the classification rates of "goods" and "bads." For example, if a false negative error (i.e., classifying a true good as bad) is considered to represent a greater misclassification cost than a false positive (i.e., classifying a true bad as good), then the neural network with 25 hidden nodes would represent the preferred model, outperforming both of the traditional statistical techniques. Alternatively, if a false positive error is considered to represent a greater misclassification cost, then the neural networks with 30 or 50 hidden nodes would be selected, again, outperforming the two statistical techniques.

Table 1: Comparison of Model Validation Results Using Multiple Methods of Evaluation

Modeling Technique	Classification Rate			Theta[4]	K-S Test
	Goods[1]	*Bads*[2]	*Overall*[3]		
Linear Discriminant Analysis	73.91%	43.40%	59.74%	**68.98%**	19%
Logistic Regression	70.54%	59.64%	**69.45%**	68.00%	24%
Neural Networks:					
5 Hidden Nodes	63.50%	56.50%	58.88%	63.59%	**38%**
10 Hidden Nodes	75.40%	44.50%	55.07%	64.46%	11%
15 Hidden Nodes	60.10%	62.10%	61.40%	65.89%	24%
20 Hidden Nodes	62.70%	59.00%	60.29%	65.27%	24%
25 Hidden Nodes	**76.60%**	41.90%	53.78%	63.55%	16%
30 Hidden Nodes	52.70%	**68.50%**	63.13%	65.74%	22%
35 Hidden Nodes	60.30%	59.00%	59.46%	63.30%	22%
40 Hidden Nodes	62.40%	58.30%	59.71%	64.47%	17%
45 Hidden Nodes	54.10%	65.20%	61.40%	64.50%	31%
50 Hidden Nodes	53.20%	**68.50%**	63.27%	65.15%	37%

1. The number of "good" applications correctly classified as "good."
2. The number of "bad" applications correctly classified as "bad."
3. The overall correct global classification rate.
4. The area under the ROC Curve.

If the analyst is most concerned with the models' ability to provide a separation between the scores of good applicants and bad applicants, the K-S test is the traditional method of model evaluation. Using this test, again, a neural network would be selected — the network with five hidden nodes.

The last method of evaluation assumes the least amount of available information. The θ measurement represents the integration of the area under the ROC curve and accounts for *all* possible iterations of relative severities of misclassification errors. In the context of the real world problem domain used to develop the eight models for this chapter, prediction of creditworthiness of applicants for auto loans, the decision makers would most likely have some information regarding misclassification costs, and therefore θ would probably not have represented the most appropriate model evaluation method. However, if the available data was used, for example, as a proxy to classify potential customers for a completely new product offering, where no preexisting cost data was available, and the respective misclassification costs were less understood, θ would represent a very appropriate method of evaluation. From this data set, if θ was chosen as the method of evaluation, the LDA model would have been selected, with a θ of 68.98. A decision maker would interpret θ for the logistic model as follows: *If I select a pair of good and bad observations at random, 69% of the time, the "good" observation will have a higher score than the "bad" observation.* A comparison of the ROC curves for the three models with the highest θ values is depicted in Figure 4.

DISCUSSION

Accurate predictive modeling represents a domain of interesting and important applications. The ability to correctly predict the risk associated with credit applicants or potential customers has tremendous consequences for the execution of effective CRM strategies in the credit industry. Researchers and analysts spend a great deal of time constructing prediction models, with the objective of minimizing the implicit and explicit costs of misclassification errors. Given this objective, and the benefits associated with even marginal improvements, both researchers and practitioners have emphasized the importance of modeling techniques. However, we believe that this emphasis has been somewhat misplaced, or at least misallocated. Our results, and the empirical results of others, have demonstrated that no predictive modeling technique can be considered superior in all circumstances. As a result, at least as much attention should be allocated to the selection of model evaluation method as is allocated to the selection of modeling technique.

In this chapter, we have explored three common evaluation methods—classification rate, the Kolmogorov-Smirnov statistic, and the ROC curve. Each of these evaluation methods can be used to assess model performance. However, the selection of which method to use is contingent upon the information available regarding misclassification costs and the problem domain. If the misclassification costs are considered to be equal, then a straight global classification rate can be utilized to assess the relative performance of competing models. If the costs are unequal, but known with certainty, then a simple cost function can be applied using the costs, the prior probabilities of assign-

Figure 4: ROC Curves for Selected Model Results

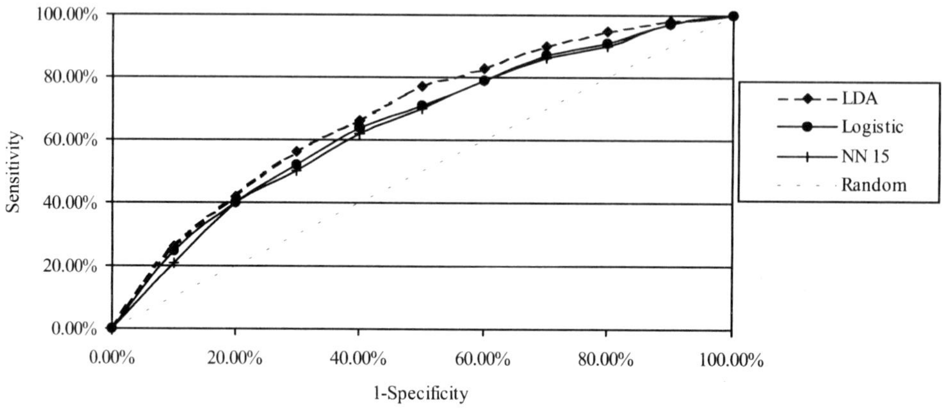

ment and the probabilities of misclassification. Using a similar logic, the K-S test can be used to evaluate models based upon the separation of each class's respective distribution function — in the context of predicting customer risk, the percentage of "good" applicants is maximized while the percentage of "bad" applicants is minimized, with no allowance for relative costs. Where no information is available, the ROC curve and the θ measurement represent the most appropriate evaluation method. Because this last method incorporates all possible iterations of misclassification error severities, many irrelevant ranges will be included in the calculation.

Adams and Hand (1999) have developed an alternative evaluation method, which may address some of the issues outlined above and provide researchers with another option for predictive model evaluation — the LC (loss comparison) index. Specifically, the LC index assumes only knowledge of the relative severities of the two costs. Using this simple, but realistic estimation, the LC index can be used to generate a value that aids the decision maker in determining the model which performs best within the established relevant range. However, the LC Index has had little empirical application or dedicated research attention to date. It represents an opportunity for further research, refinement and testing.

Clearly no model evaluation method represents a panacea for researchers, analysts or decision-makers. As a result, an understanding of the context of the data and the problem domain is critical for selection not just of a modeling technique, but also of a model evaluation method.

ENDNOTES

[1]   Federal Reserve System Report (2003). Retrieved on the World Wide Web: http://www.federalreserve.gov/rnd.htm.

REFERENCES

Adams, N. M. & Hand, D. J. (1999). Comparing classifiers when the misclassification costs are uncertain. *Pattern Recognition*, 32, 1139-1147.

Atiya, A. F. (2001). Bankruptcy prediction for credit risk using neural networks: A survey and new results. *IEEE Transactions on Neural Networks,* 12(4), 929-935.

Berardi, V. L. & Zhang, G. P. (1999). The effect of misclassification costs on neural network classifiers. *Decision Sciences, 30*(3), 659-682.

Fisher, R. A. (1936). The use of multiple measurement in taxonomic problems. *Ann. Eugenics,* 7, 179-188.

Gim, G. (1995). *Hybrid Systems for Robustness and Perspicuity: Symbolic Rule Induction   Combined with a Neural Net or a Statistical Model.* Unpublished Dissertation. Georgia State University, Atlanta, Georgia, USA.

Hand, D. J. (2001). Measuring diagnostic accuracy of statistical prediction rules. *Statistica Neerlandica,* 55(1), 3-16.

Hand, D. J. (2002). *Good practices in retail credit scorecard assessment.* Working Paper.

Hanley, J. A. & McNeil, B. J. (1982). The meaning and use of the area under a Receiver Operating Characteristics curve. *Radiology*, 143, 29-36.

Hanley, J. A. & McNeil, B. J. (1983). A method of comparing the areas under a Receiver Operating Characteristics curve. *Radiology,* 148, 839-843.

Kimball, R. (1996). Dealing with dirty data. *DBMS Magazine*, 9(10). Retrieved from the World Wide Web at: http://www.dbmsmag.com/9609d14.html.

Reichert, A. K., Cho, C. C., & Wagner, G. M. (1983). An examination of the conceptual issues involved in developing credit scoring models. *Journal of Business and Economic Statistics,* 1, 101-114.

Richeson, L., Zimmerman, R., & Barnett, K. (1994). Predicting consumer credit performance: Can neural networks outperform traditional statistical methods? *International Journal of Applied Expert Systems*, 2, 116-130.

Swets, J. A., Dawes, R. M., & Monahan, J. (2000). Better decisions through science. *Scientific American,* 283(4), 82-88.

Taylor, P. C. & Hand, D. J. (1999). Finding superclassifications with acceptable misclassification rates. *Journal of Applied Statistics, 26,* 579-590.

Thomas, L. C., Edelman, D. B., & Cook, J. N. (2002). *Credit Scoring and Its Applications.* Philadelphia, PA: Society for Industrial and Applied Mathematics.

Vellido, A., Lisboa, P. J. G., & Vaughan, J. (1999). Neural networks in business: A survey of applications (1992-1998). *Expert Systems with Applications,* 17, 51-70.

West, D. (2000). Neural network credit scoring models. *Computers and Operations Research,* 27, 1131-1152.

Zhang, G., Hu, M. Y., Patuwo, B. E., & Indro, D. C. (1999). Artificial neural networks in bankruptcy prediction: General framework and cross-validation analysis. *European Journal of Operational Research,* 116, 16-32.

APPENDIX A

Listing of Original Variables in Data Set

Variable Name   Variable Label

1. ACCTNO   Account Number
2. AGEOTD   Age of Oldest Trade
3. BKRETL   S&V Book Retail Value
4. BRBAL1   # of Open Bank Rev. Trades with Balances>$1000
5. CSORAT   Ratio of Currently Satisfactory Trades:Open Trades
6. HST03X   # of Trades Never 90DPD+
7. HST79X   # of Trades Ever Rated Bad Debt
8. MODLYR   Vehicle Model Year
9. OREVTR   # of Open Revolving Trades
10. ORVTB0   # of Open Revolving Trades With Balance >$0
11. REHSAT   # of Retail Trades Ever Rated Satisfactory
12. RVTRDS   # of Revolving Trades
13. T2924X   # of Trades Rated 30 DPD+ in the Last 24 Months
14. T3924X   # of Trades Rated 60 DPD+ in the Last 24 Months
15. T4924X   # of Trades Rated 90 DPD+ in the Last 24 Months
16. TIME29   Months Since Most Recent 30 DPD+ Rating
17. TIME39   Months Since Most Recent 60 DPD+ Rating
18. TIME49   Months Since Most Recent 90 DPD+ Rating
19. TROP24   # of Trades Opened in the Last 24 Months
20. CURR2X   # of Trades Currently Rated 30 DPD
21. CURR3X   # of Trades Currently Rated 60 DPD
22. CURRSAT   # of Trades Currently Rated Satisfactory
23. GOOD   Performance of Account
24. HIST2X   # of Trades Ever Rated 30 DPD
25. HIST3X   # of Trades Ever Rated 60 DPD
26. HIST4X   # of Trades Ever Rated 90 DPD
27. HSATRT   Ratio of Satisfactory Trades to Total Trades
28. HST03X   # of Trades Never 90 DPD+
29. HST79X   # of Trades Ever Rated Bad Debt
30. HSTSAT   # of Trades Ever Rated Satisfactory
31. MILEAG   Vehicle Mileage

32. OREVTR	# of Open Revolving Trades
33. ORVTB0	# of Open Revolving Trades With Balance >$0
34. PDAMNT	Amount Currently Past Due
35. RVOLDT	Age of Oldest Revolving Trade
36. STRT24	Sat. Trades: Total Trades in the Last 24 Months
37. TIME29	Months Since Most Recent 30 DPD+ Rating
38. TIME39	Months Since Most Recent 60 DPD+ Rating
39. TOTBAL	Total Balances
40. TRADES	# of Trades
41. AGEAVG	Average Age of Trades
42. AGENTD	Age of Newest Trade
43. AGEOTD	Age of Oldest Trade
44. AUHS2X	# of Auto Trades Ever Rated 30 DPD
45. AUHS3X	# of Auto Trades Ever Rated 60 DPD
46. AUHS4X	# of Auto Trades Ever Rated 90 DPD
47. AUHS8X	# of Auto Trades Ever Repoed
48. AUHSAT	# of Auto Trades Ever Satisfactory
49. AUOP12	# of Auto Trades Opened in the Last 12 Months
50. AUSTRT	Sat. Auto Trades: Total Auto Trades
51. AUTRDS	# of Auto Trades
52. AUUTIL	Ratio of Balance to HC for All Open Auto Trades
53. BRAMTP	Amt. Currently Past Due for Revolving Auto Trades
54. BRHS2X	# of Bank Revolving Trades Ever 30 DPD
55. BRHS3X	# of Bank Revolving Trades Ever 60 DPD
56. BRHS4X	# of Bank Revolving Trades Ever 90 DPD
57. BRHS5X	# of Bank Revolving Trades Ever 120+ DPD
58. BRNEWT	Age of Newest Bank Revolving Trade
59. BROLDT	Age of Oldest Bank Revolving Trade
60. BROPEN	# of Open Bank Revolving Trades
61. BRTRDS	# of Bank Revolving Trades
62. BRWRST	Worst Current Bank Revolving Trade Rating
63. CFTRDS	# of Financial Trades
64. CUR49X	# of Trades Currently Rated 90 DPD+
65. CURBAD	# of Trades Currently Rated Bad Debt

About the Authors

G. Peter Zhang is currently an Associate Professor of Operations Management and Decision Sciences at Georgia State University, USA. He received his B.S. and M.S. degrees in Mathematics and Statistics, respectively, from East China Normal University, Shanghai, China, and his Ph.D. in Operations Research/Operations Management from Kent State University, Kent, Ohio. His research interests include neural networks, time series forecasting, supply chain management, and statistical quality control. His work has appeared in *Computers & Industrial Engineering, Computers & Operations Research, Decision Sciences, European Journal of Operational Research, IIE Transactions, IEEE Transactions on Systems, Man, and Cybernetics, IEEE Transactions on Neural Networks, International Journal of Forecasting, International Journal of Production Economics, Journal of the Operational Research Society, Neurocomputing*, and others. He is on the editorial review board of *Production and Operations Management* journal. His profile has been published in Who's Who in the 21st Century and Who's Who in the World.

* * *

Pervaiz Alam is a Professor in the Accounting Department at Kent State University, USA. His research interest is in the areas of financial accounting, auditing, and decision support systems. He has recently published in the *Journal of Corporate Communications, Decision Sciences,* and *International Journal of Intelligent Systems in Accounting Finance & Management.*

David Booth earned his Ph.D. from the University of North Carolina at Chapel Hill. He currently holds the rank of Professor in the Department of Management & Information Systems at Kent State University, USA. His teaching and research interests include applied and robust statistics, artificial intelligence, wavelet analysis, quality control and operations management. His recent research has appeared in *Decision Sciences, Journal of Quality Technology, Technometrics, Journal of Chemical Information and Computer Science, Business Process Management Journal, Journal of Manufacturing Systems* and other similar journals.

Robert T. Chi is Professor of Information Systems at California State University, Long Beach, USA. He obtained his Ph.D. from the University of Texas at Austin and his M.S. from the University of Wisconsin at Madison. His teaching interests include decision support systems, data base management and system analysis, data communication, e-commerce, strategic information systems and Web development. He has received teaching awards at the University of Texas-Austin and has published more than 40 journal and conference articles in *Journal of Decision Support Systems, Annals of Operations Research, Journal of Operational Research Society, Journal of Management Information Systems, Journal of Electronic Commerce Research* and many others. He is the founder and Co- Editor of *Journal of Electronic Commerce Research.*

Scott Dellana is an Associate Professor and the Chair of the Decision Sciences Department at East Carolina University, USA. He received his Ph.D. in Engineering Management from the University of Missouri-Rolla. He is currently researching and writing papers in the areas of quality and artificial intelligence applications and has been published in a variety of journals. He has extensive industry experience in civil and aerospace engineering.

Ashutosh Dixit (Ph.D., Georgia Institute of Technology) is an Assistant Professor of Marketing at Terry College of Business, University of Georgia, Athens, Georgia, USA. He received a CIBER award to study in Japan and was an AMA-Sheth Doctoral consortium fellow. He was a runner-up, and his dissertation received an honorable mention, in the George Day Doctoral Dissertation Award Competition. He has won Terry Sanford Awards twice and the Coca-Cola Center for Marketing Award once for his research on the growth of discounters and on predatory pricing. His research interests include electronic commerce, pricing, and neural network modeling.

David Enke received his Ph.D. in Engineering Management from the University of Missouri - Rolla (UMR) in 1997. He was an assistant professor of System Science and Industrial Engineering at the State University of New York-Binghamton before returning to UMR as an Assistant Professor within the Engineering Management Department. His research interests involve the development of smart and intelligent systems, specifically using neural networks, knowledge-based systems, and data mining techniques in the areas of financial forecasting, financial engineering, investment, capital planning and budgeting, and electrical load and price forecasting.

Dorothy M. Fisher is Professor of Information Systems at California State University, Dominguez Hills, USA. She received an M.A. from Duke University and a Ph.D. from Kent State University. Dr. Fisher has had broad consulting experience with private firms as well as educational institutions. During the past 15 years, she has authored/co-authored more than 30 papers that appeared in *the Journal of Computer Information Systems, the Journal of Systems Management, the Journal of Applied Business Research, the Journal of Business Management,* and other academic and professional journals. Currently, she is the managing editor of the *Journal of Electronic Commerce Research*.

Michael Y. Hu is Professor of Marketing, Graduate School of Management, Kent State University, USA. He earned his M.S. and Ph.D. in Management Science/Marketing from the University of Minnesota. He has received the Distinguished Teaching Award from Kent State University and has published more than 100 articles in the areas of artificial neural networks, marketing research, and international business. His articles have appeared in the *Annals* *of Operations Research, European Journal of Operational Research, Decision Sciences, Journal of the Operational Research Society, Journal of Marketing Research, Marketing Letters, International Journal of Research in Marketing, Journal of International Business Studies, Financial Management, Financial Analyst Journal* and many others.

Ming S. Hung is Professor Emeritus of Operations Research at Kent State University, USA. His main areas of interests are neural networks and mathematical programming. His writings have appeared in *Operations Research, Management Science*, and *European Journal of Operational Research,* among others.

Melody Y. Kiang is Professor of Computer Information Systems at California State University, Long Beach, USA. She received her M.S. in MIS from the University of Wisconsin, Madison, and Ph.D. in MSIS from the University of Texas at Austin. Prior to join CSULB, she was associate professor at Arizona State University. Her research interests include the development and applications of artificial intelligence techniques to a variety of business problems. Her research has appeared in *Information Systems Research (ISR), Management Science, Journal of Management Information Systems, Decision Support Systems, IEEE Transactions on SMC, EJOR,* and other professional journals. She is an Associate Editor of *Decision Support Systems* and Co-Editor of *Journal of Electronic Commerce Research.*

Douglas M. Kline, Ph.D., is currently Associate Professor of Information Systems in the Department of Information Systems and Operations Management at the University of North Carolina at Wilmington, USA. His research interests include neural network theory, methodology, and applications, and information system design. His research has appeared in *Computers & Operations Research, OMEGA, IEEE Transactions on Systems, Man, and Cybernetics,* the *Journal of Business Strategies,* and others.

Rob Law is an Associate Professor of Information Technology at the School of Hotel & Tourism Management at The Hong Kong Polytechnic University. Prior to joining The Hong Kong Polytechnic University in 1995, he worked in the Saskatchewan Institute of Applied Science and Technology, University of Regina, and Bell Northern Research/Northern Telecom in Canada. Dr. Law actively serves the professional and research bodies in hospitality and tourism.

His research interests include hotel and tourism information technology, hospitality and tourism forecasting, and computer assisted hospitality education. His research papers have been published by the leading hospitality and tourism journals.

Kidong Lee earned his Ph.D. in Management Systems at Kent State University. He is currently Assistant Professor of Management Information Systems at the University of Incheon in South Korea. He has published in *Expert Systems with Applications*, *The Chemist* and other similar journals.

Leong-Kwan Li was born in Hong Kong. He was attracted to mathematics when he studied at the Chinese University of Hong Kong. There, he received his first degree and a M.Ph. degree. After teaching in a high school, he continued his study at the University of Southern California in Los Angeles. In addition to applied mathematics, he gained an M.S. degree in Electrical Engineering as well as his Ph.D. degree in Mathematics. His research interests are mainly in applicable applied mathematics including neural networks, numerical analysis, optimization, mathematical modeling and also financial mathematics.

Bradley H. Morantz is a Consultant to the Viral Immunology Center of the Georgia State University Department of Biology (USA), working on automated immunoassays. Dr. Morantz received his Ph.D. from the Decision Sciences Department of Georgia State University, with a minor in Computer Science. His M.S. is also in Decision Sciences. He has a B.S. in Computer Information Systems and Electrical Engineering, with additional course work in semiconductor devices and applied mathematics. His area of research is machine cognition utilizing hybrid artificial intelligence methods. He has been an invited speaker at various schools and universities as well as the IEEE.

Satish Nargundkar is an Assistant Professor in the Department of Management at Georgia State University, USA. He has published in the *Journal of Marketing Research,* the *Journal of Global Strategies*, and the *Journal of Managerial Issues,* and has co-authored chapters in research textbooks. He has assisted several large financial institutions with the development of credit scoring models and marketing and risk strategies. His research interests include data mining, CRM, corporate strategy, and pedagogical areas such as Web-based training. He is a member of the Decision Sciences Institute.

Wan-Kai Pang obtained his Ph.D. degree in Statistics from the University of Southampton (UK) in 2000. He has been working in the Department of Applied Mathematics at The Hong Kong Polytechnic University for almost 20 years as a lecturer in Statistics. His current research interests include computational statistics, Markov chain Monte Carlo methods, statistical reliability and Bayesian modeling.

Leonard J. Parsons is a Professor of Marketing Science in the Dupree College of Management at the Georgia Institute of Technology, USA. He has been a member of the Graduate Management Admission Council's Research and Test (GMAT) Development Committee, chair of the American Statistical Association's Section on Statistics in Marketing, and a member of the Advisory Board of the American Marketing Association's Marketing Research Special Interest Group among other activities. He has served as marketing departmental editor of *Management Science* and associate editor of *Decision Sciences*, and has been on the editorial boards of the *Journal of Marketing Research*, the *Journal of Marketing*, and the *Journal of Business Research*.

Ray Pine has been with the School of Hotel and Tourism Management at The Hong Kong Polytechnic University since 1987, including three years as Head. His Ph.D. in Technology Transfer in the Hotel Industry is from Bradford University in the UK, and he is a Fellow of the Hotel and Catering International Management Association. Professor Pine serves on the editorial boards of seven journals, is Asia regional editor for *International Journal of Contemporary Hospitality Management* and *Journal of Tourism and Hospitality Planning & Development*, and has authored or co-authored four books, eight book chapters and more than 50 pieces of refereed work.

Jennifer Lewis Priestley is a Doctoral Student in the Department of Management at Georgia State University (USA), studying Decision Sciences. She has written papers on model development and knowledge management. She holds an M.B.A. from The Pennsylvania State University. Her previous work included positions with MasterCard International, VISA EU, Andersen Consulting and AT&T. Her research and teaching interests include data mining, business analysis and knowledge management.

Murali Shanker is an Associate Professor in the Department of Management & Information Systems, College of Business, Kent State University, USA. He received his Ph.D. from the Department of Operations and Management

Science at the University of Minnesota. His current research is in developing task-allocation strategies for distributed simulation models, and in conducting statistical analysis of the behavior of neural networks as applied to classification and prediction problems. He has published in journals like *Annals of Operations Research, Decision Sciences, Journal of the Operational Research Society, INFORMS Journal on Computing*, and *IIE Transactions*, among others.

Suraphan Thawornwong received his Ph.D. in Engineering Management from the University of Missouri - Rolla in 2003, and his M.B.A. and M.S. in Industrial Engineering from the University of Missouri - Columbia in 1999 and 2000, respectively. He is currently a senior analyst at the Risk Management Unit of Thailand Securities Depository Co., Ltd., a subsidiary of the Stock Exchange of Thailand (SET). His research interests include applications of computational intelligence, particularly neural networks and genetic algorithms, for financial forecasting and business decision-making.

Marvin D. Troutt is a Professor in the Department of Management & Information Systems and in the Graduate School of Management at Kent State University, USA. He is an Associate Editor of *Decision Sciences* Journal and a *Fellow* of the Decision Sciences Institute. He received his Ph.D. in Mathematical Statistics from The University of Illinois at Chicago. His publications have appeared in *Decision Sciences, Management Science, Journal of the Operational Research Society, European Journal of Operational Research, Operations Research, Decision Support Systems, Naval Research Logistics, Statistics*, and others. His current research interests include the statistics of performance data and applications of optimization.

Steven Walczak is an Associate Professor of Information Systems in the Business School at the University of Colorado at Denver, USA. He received his Ph.D. in Artificial Intelligence from the University of Florida, his M.S. in Computer Science from the Johns Hopkins University, and his B.S. in Mathematics from the Pennsylvania State University. Dr. Walczak has worked in industry for more than six years solving complex programming problems and is currently in his 12th year as an academic. His research interests are in applications of artificial intelligence including neural networks to various business and medical problems, knowledge management, and developing intelligent agents for information retrieval and other tasks. Dr. Walczak is widely published, including articles in various *IEEE Transactions*, *Decision Support Systems*, and the *Journal of Management Information Systems*, among others.

David West is an Associate Professor in the Decision Sciences Department at East Carolina University, USA. He received his Ph.D. in Operations Management from the University of Rhode Island. He is currently researching and writing papers in the area of artificial intelligence applications and has been published in a variety of journals. He has extensive industry experience in chemical engineering.

Thomas Whalen holds a Ph.D. in Systems Science from Michigan State University, USA. Dr. Whalen's research focuses on the application of approximate reasoning to decision making under generalized uncertainty, especially in the fuzzy area between ignorance and risk. Whalen has published more than 100 papers in major conference proceedings and academic journals, including *Human Systems Management, International Journal of Man-Machine Studies, IEEE Technology and Society Magazine,* and *IEEE Transactions on Systems, Man and Cybernetics.* Whalen is a senior member of the Institute of Electrical and Electronics Engineers and a member of the board of directors of the North American Fuzzy Information Processing Society.

Wing-Tong Yu is an Assistant Professor in the Department of Business Studies at the Hong Kong Polytechnic University. He obtained his Ph.D. in Finance from the University of Southampton, UK. His research interests include banking and financial markets, application of mathematical techniques in the pricing of debt and derivative securities, and credit analysis.

Index

M

Malaysian stock market index 82
market dynamics 59
market response models 24
market segmentation 143
market share models 28
marketing mix models 24
mean absolute percentage error
    (MAPE) 34
memory by delay 106
memory by feedback 106
Mexican stock market index 82
model bias 8, 173
model development 268
model selection 173
model variance 8, 173
model-based planning and forecasting
    24
modes of communication 174
moving averages 204
moving window 58, 254
multi-layer feedforward networks 173
multi-step time series forecasting 226
multi-step-ahead forecasting 4
multilayer perceptron (MLP) 159
multinational companies 196
multinomial logit (MNL) model 34
multiplicative competitive interaction
    (MCI) model 32
multistep forecasting 227
multivariate regression forecasting
    models 126

N

naïve walk 252
neural network 103
neural network design 10
neural network model building 220
neural network models 81
neural networks 81, 172, 268
neurons 3
nonlinear modeling capability 2
nonlinear pattern 214
nonlinearity 27, 49
normalizing 234

O

one-step-ahead forecasting 11
organizing feature map 159
overfitting 8, 175

P

perceptron neural network (PN) 57
posterior probabilities 173
prediction model 8, 268
principal component analysis (PCA) 54
probabilistic neural network (PNN) 57

Q

quadratic discriminant analysis (QDA)
    159
quantitative tourism 125

R

random walk 81, 200, 252
random walk behavior 197
reasoning neural network (RN) 57
recurrent neural network (RNN) 5,
    57, 195
recursive training 58
rolling window 254
root mean square error (RMSE) 207

S

sales response models 28
sample size 9, 253
Schwarz information criterion (SIC) 13
security investment 48
self-organization process 146
self-organizing map (SOM) 142
self-organizing map neural network
    (SOM) 57
short term memory 105
short-term exchange rates 195
Singapore stock market index 82
situational consumer choice model 173
stock indices 50
stock market index 50
stock price analysis 48
stock return forecasting 48

New Releases from IRM Press

- **Visual Perception of Music Notation: On-Line and Off-Line Recognition**
  Susan Ella George
  ISBN: 1-931777-94-2; eISBN: 1-931777-95-0 / ©2004
- **3D Modeling and Animation: Synthesis and Analysis Techniques for the Human Body**
  Nikos Sarris & Michael G. Strintzis
  ISBN: 1-931777-98-5; eISBN: 1-931777-99-3 / ©2004
- **Innovations of Knowledge Management**
  Bonnie Montano
  ISBN: 1-59140-229-8; eISBN: 1-59140-230-1 / ©2004
- **e-Collaborations and Virtual Organizations**
  Michelle W. L. Fong
  ISBN: 1-59140-231-X; eISBN: 1-59140-232-8 / ©2004
- **Information Security and Ethics: Social and Organizational Issues**
  Marian Quigley
  ISBN: 1-59140-233-6; eISBN: 1-59140-234-4 / ©2004
- **Issues of Human Computer Interaction**
  Anabela Sarmento
  ISBN: 1-59140-235-2; eISBN: 1-59140-236-0 / ©2004
- **Instructional Technologies: Cognitive Aspects of Online Programs**
  Paul Darbyshire
  ISBN: 1-59140-237-9; eISBN: 1-59140-238-7 / ©2004
- **E-Commerce and M-Commerce Technologies**
  P. Candace Deans
  ISBN: 1-59140-239-5; eISBN: 1-59140-240-9 / ©2004

Excellent additions to your institution's library!
Recommend these titles to your Librarian!

To receive a copy of the IRM Press catalog, please contact
1/717-533-8845, fax 1/717-533-8661,
or visit the IRM Press Online Bookstore at: [http://www.irm-press.com]!

Note: All IRM Press books are also available as ebooks on netlibrary.com as well as other ebook sources. Contact Ms. Carrie Skovrinskie at [cskovrinskie@idea-group.com] to receive a complete list of sources where you can obtain ebook information or IRM Press titles.

Information Resources Management Journal (IRMJ)

An Official Publication of the Information Resources Management Association since 1988

Editor:
Mehdi Khosrow-Pour, D.B.A.
Information Resources Management
Association, USA

ISSN: 1040-1628; eISSN: 1533-7979
Subscription: Annual fee per volume (four issues): Individual
US $85; Institutional US $265

Mission

The *Information Resources Management Journal* (IRMJ) is a refereed, international publication featuring the latest research findings dealing with all aspects of information resources management, managerial and organizational applications, as well as implications of information technology organizations. It aims to be instrumental in the improvement and development of the theory and practice of information resources management, appealing to both practicing managers and academics. In addition, it educates organizations on how they can benefit from their information resources and all the tools needed to gather, process, disseminate and manage this valuable resource.

Coverage

IRMJ covers topics with a major emphasis on the managerial and organizational aspects of information resource and technology management. Some of the topics covered include: Executive information systems; Information technology security and ethics; Global information technology Management; Electronic commerce technologies and issues; Emerging technologies management; IT management in public organizations; Strategic IT management; Telecommunications and networking technologies; Database management technologies and issues; End user computing issues; Decision support & group decision support; Systems development and CASE; IT management research and practice; Multimedia computing technologies and issues; Object-oriented technologies and issues; Human and societal issues in IT management; IT education and training issues; Distance learning technologies and issues; Artificial intelligence & expert technologies; Information technology innovation & diffusion; and other issues relevant to IT management.

It's Easy to Order! Order online at www.idea-group.com!

Mon-Fri 8:30 am-5:00 pm (est) or fax 24 hours a day 717/533-8661

Idea Group Publishing

Hershey • London • Melbourne • Singapore • Beijing

An excellent addition to your library